HOW TO MARKET PROFESSIONAL DESIGN SERVICES

Other books by Gerre Jones
How to Prepare Professional Design Brochures
Public Relations for the Design Professional

HOW TO MARKET PROFESSIONAL DESIGN SERVICES

SECOND EDITION

GERRE JONES

McGRAW-HILL BOOK COMPANY

New York   St. Louis   San Francisco   Auckland
Bogotá   Hamburg   Johannesburg   London   Madrid   Mexico
Montreal   New Delhi   Panama   Paris   São Paulo
Singapore   Sydney   Tokyo   Toronto

Library of Congress Cataloging in Publication Data

Jones, Gerre L., date.
  How to market professional design services.

  Includes index.
  1. Architectural services marketing.
2. Engineering services marketing. I. Title.
NA1996.J66 1983   720′.68′8   82-7783
                                     AACR2

1 2 3 4 5 6 7 8 9 0   KPKP   8 9 8 7 6 5 4 3 2

ISBN 0-07-032802-1

The editors for this book were Joan Zseleczky and Martha Cameron, the designer was Richard Roth, and the production supervisor was Sally Fliess. It was set in Aster by Waldman Graphics.

Printed and bound by The Kingsport Press.

CONTENTS

PREFACE

An author's preface, by definition, is a statement to introduce the book that follows and to explain or comment on its scope, intention, or background. A preface is, from its Latin root, "a saying beforehand"— and is not meant to be an abstract, a summary, or a condensation of the book.

Prefaces, for a variety of reasons, do not enjoy a wide readership. I've long suspected that one of the reasons most people skip over prefaces is that they expect to find little of substance in them. Past experience may tell a reader that the preface probably is little more than a justification by the author of his or her research and literary efforts— and, as such, it tends to become a kind of ego trip for the writer.

Stripped of all its mystique and trappings, writing itself is an ego trip, of course. At some point in his or her life an individual decides that he or she has accumulated enough knowledge or wisdom about a given subject to justify spending from six to eighteen months in research, typing, and editing to produce a manuscript of from 400 to 600 double-spaced pages. Some part of a publisher's staff then devotes up to another year to turn the author's output into a finished book. At least one large tree is sacrificed for paper on which to print the book, and finally one of the thousands of this year's production of books takes its place on the publisher's list and on bookstore shelves.

The corporate-level crap game known as publishing produces few winners and a host of losers. This second edition of *How to Market Professional Design Services* is proof that the first edition was lucky enough to be one of the winners.

The first edition was written during 1972 and 1973, at the urging and with the encouragement of *Architectural Record*'s late senior editor, Bill Foxhall. It was published in December 1973, in an accident of marketing timing and general propitiousness that could never have been planned. Just as many design professionals recognized the onset of the 1973–1975 recession—and the concurrent need to get their marketing efforts organized—along came a book called *How to Market Professional Design Services*.

How to Market Professional Design Services and an earlier book by Weld Coxe, *Marketing Architectural and Engineering Services,* were the only contemporary books about a subject that was, owing to the economic downturn, catapulted into a position of extreme importance in the minds of progressive engineering and architectural practitioners.

Since those two books appeared, many other writers have contributed to the literature about this rather narrow marketing specialty. Some wrote from practical experience and were of help; others eschewed the practical approach, and their untested theories succeeded only in further muddying already murky waters. Ignoring the negative—and, at times, suspiciously derivative—contributions, design professionals may now choose from a veritable library of books, pamphlets, articles, home-study courses, cassettes, and newsletters about professional services marketing.

Including the manuscript for this book, I estimate my written output about the marketing of design services has been well over 1.5 million words since 1971. That total takes into account several other books, various magazine articles, a total of ten years of monthly newsletters, a home-study course, and lecture notes for probably two dozen different workshop series on marketing subjects.

With this gold mine of printed information now available from various sources for the taking, it was a shock of sorts to come across the following statement recently in the 1962 edition of the *Architect's Handbook of Professional Practice:* "Little that is useful can be written about how to go about securing a commission."[1]

The *Handbook,* first published by the American Institute of Architects in 1920, and revised from time to time, approached marketing (then referred to as "project development") in a cautious—even simplistic— fashion twenty years ago. The *Handbook* also had this helpful suggestion for obtaining work: "The first necessity, of course, is to learn about the project. To do this *one should associate with people who may become prospects.*" (Emphasis added.)

The original 1920 *Handbook* contained no mention of marketing; the current edition has two complete sections on the subject—B-8, "Marketing Architectural Services" and B-9, "The Architect's Communications." The preface to "Marketing Architectural Services" forthrightly and unequivocally states:

---

[1]*Architect's Handbook of Professional Practice.* Excerpted from Section 3.04, "Project Development," 1963, with permission of the American Institute of Architects, Washington, D.C.

An architectural office cannot expect to receive commissions on a continuing basis by waiting for the door to open or the telephone to ring. . . . The AIA actively supports the concept of marketing. . . . Many of the more successful firms in this country have had organized marketing programs for decades.[2]

So we've seen progress of a sort since the first copies of *How to Market Professional Design Services* became available almost ten years ago. And progress has come in the overall management of design firms, as well as in their marketing programs. Perhaps 25 percent of all firms now operate under a written marketing plan, with the total growing each year. A considerably smaller group of firms has achieved an understanding of the importance of developing a full-scale business plan, but some progress is also noted in that area.

That the 1970s were an era of change in many aspects of our business and personal lives, including the onset and growth of double-digit inflation, is evidenced by price changes for the first edition of *How to Market Professional Design Services*. On publication in December 1973 the retail price was $14.50. As of this writing, the list price is $27.50—an increase of $13 or almost 90 percent. When you consider that the price rise averages out to around 10 percent a year, you'll have to agree that McGraw-Hill's pricing policy fell somewhat behind the rate of inflation for the same period.

In the preface to the first edition I commented that *How to Market Professional Design Services* represented the distillation of twenty-five years of personal experience in promotion and marketing. Simple—if disconcerting—arithmetic tells me that the experience now adds up to about thirty-five years. I can only hope that each of those years added to my base of knowledge; that it has not been a classic case of one year of experience repeated thirty-five times.

Another statement from the ten-year-old preface: "No one has all of the answers nor productively utilizes a significant percentage of the known, proven ways to develop new business." It still is true that no one has all the answers, but a growing number of design firms are daily applying "a significant percentage of the known, proven ways of developing new business." (A couple of related points—*nor* was used incorrectly in the sentence just quoted, and in the intervening years I have joined the anti-"utilize" school of writing. The perfectly good three-letter word "use" is a better choice in the vast majority of cases.)

---

[2]Ibid. Excerpted from Section B-8 (1980), with permission of the American Institute of Architects, Washington, D.C.

A final quotation from the original preface:

This book, therefore, is partly history, partly philosophy, partly an exposition on how-to-do-it (based to some extent on how-others-did-it), and partly a look into the near future of the design profession. Since today's accomplishments are tomorrow's history, many readers of this book may be witting or unwitting contributors to its future editions, depending upon how well or how badly they put the principles outlined into effect in their own practices.

Many readers of the first edition did take the principles set out in it seriously; put them into practice and survived the 1973–1975 and other, lesser economic downturns. They built upon the basics, adding to their marketing expertise and knowledge at every opportunity. Their firms were able to weather the dangerous and confusing economic climate of the past several years as double-digit inflation joined record-high interest rates.

There can be no question about the contributions made to this edition by readers of the first one. Much of that readership also comprised clients for consulting services, participants in hundreds of marketing management workshops, and faithful subscribers to the newsletter, *Professional Marketing Report*. The professional relationships and friendships so established have added much to my knowledge of what works and doesn't work—along with what is good and what is bad—in marketing professional design services. I fully intend to continue to capitalize on this practical and productive form of my own continuing education for as long as I possibly can.

In a very real sense, almost any how-to book is a modernized form of the ancient navigational guide known to sixteenth- and seventeenth-century English-speaking ship's pilots as a rutter. If you were among the 8 million readers of James Clavell's *Shōgun*, you may recall that rutters figured rather prominently in the many plot twists of the 1200-page novel. The word "rutter" is from the French *routier*, which, in turn, derived from the Portuguese *roteiro* (literal meaning: route or road). Spanish pilots knew it as a *derrota;* Dutch pilots as a *leeskaart* (reading chart); Italians as a *portolano* (port book); and German pilots referred to it as a *Seebuch* (sea book).

Rutters covered in detail such critical items as coastal elevations, tidal movements, wind patterns, phases of the moon, general directions and courses between ports, port conditions (including how to enter and leave and where to anchor safely), availability of fresh-water stores, and laws and customs of the sea. Rutters, which often were passed down from father to son, usually became heavily annotated through use. Corrections and additions to the original information might fill all available margin space.

The rutter's cumulative accuracy and potential assistance at sea were obviously dependent upon the experience, powers of observation, and reportorial abilities of its pilot-author. And pilots could never be certain of another's rutter until they had made the voyage themselves. Failure of a ship to return to home port could be taken as a sign the rutter was less than accurate in some or all respects.

The above is by way of suggesting that you look upon this revised version of *How to Market Professional Design Services* as a kind of rutter for the marketing of design services. The author *has* been there; the information herein and its presentation represent his best efforts. But until and unless you test the ideas, processes, systems, and techniques discussed and illustrated in your own marketing efforts, you will never know how much of the offered guidance through rough waters, shoals, and unfriendly natives applies to your practice. As any good pilot of a ship under full sail, feel free to add your own observations and experiences to the text; annotate and amend its pages wherever appropriate.

I cannot, in conscience, sign off on this particular preface without extending some long overdue credits. Thanks go first to my wife Charlotte and my daughters Beverly Putnam and Wendy Jones, M.D., of whom I am inordinately—some say insufferably—proud, and who have all contributed in various ways to my writing efforts over the years. Next for belated recognition are a few of the many people in the McGraw-Hill organization who have offered encouragement and editing and production help for my books. I understand that McGraw-Hill policy frowns on my singling out for mention my chief editor and good friend Jeremy Robinson; sponsoring editor and equally good friend Joan Zseleczky; and editing supervisors and teachers Carolyn Nagy, Tobia Worth, and Martha Cameron—but they know who they are, and the extent of their individual and collective contributions over the years.

GERRE JONES

Chapter 1
A DECADE OF CHANGE— AND A FEW CONSTANTS

Oliver Witte, former editor of *Building Design & Construction*, is a frequent (and knowledgeable) writer about the business side of professional design practice. In an editorial for the February 1981 issue of the magazine, Witte discussed the p's and q's for successful operation of design firms in the 1980s:

Profitability
Promotion
Productivity
Personnel
Quality
Qualifications

Under "promotion" were these trenchant comments: "Like it or not, marketing has become survival for firms of all sizes. Firms will have to specialize because owners demand it. Targets must be selected carefully because stakes are high. Part of the problem: The average salary for a marketing director is $42,500 but he only stays 2 years."[1]

And his conclusion: "Commissions will be won or lost primarily on professionalism—quality and qualifications. You must prove you can solve the client's problems better than the competition. Without strong performance on those criteria, nothing else has meaning."[2]

Five important lessons are embodied in those brief quotations:

1. Technical and production staff productivity and the quality of their product are (and always have been) the basic assets of any service firm. Take away or significantly dilute either, and the firm is on the road to trouble.

2. It is not enough to "be good"; the fact must be communicated over and over to clients and prospects.

3. It is foolish for a design firm to attempt to be all things to all clients. Specialization, with its implied heavy experience record, is the rule of the day.

4. Good marketing people are not cheap. And unless they believe the importance of their efforts is recognized, they'll move on regardless of salary. (This may change during the 1980s, as principals learn how to identify the real producers. As of now, many in marketing—even some of the highest paid—do not belong there. It has been a seller's market for some time, and a shakeout is overdue.)

5. Selectivity as to which markets and projects to pursue is of key importance to design firms. Forget the shotgun approach; those are real marketing dollars, not buckshot, you spread over the landscape. Depend on adequate market research to tell you where to aim—and then use a rifle with telescopic sights.

Allusion was made in the preface to the many and significant changes in marketing and selling professional design services since the first edition of *How to Market Professional Design Services* was published. It is worth noting that in the almost ten years since the first edition, many women have become active in marketing and sales for design firms. I don't know that anyone or any organization has the figures, but my best estimate is that around a third of those now in marketing are women—and their number and influence are growing by the year. The probable reader characterizations in the introduction to the first edition held up remarkably well, and we reiterate.

Experience tells us that most readers of this book will fit generally into one of these four broad categories: architectural, engineering, and planning students; the principals of newly established design firms; educators in the design professions; and experienced executives of large, established firms. Individual readers may find themselves reflected in one or more of the following reader profiles.

I

You are in your last year of engineering school. Since you had the good luck to have a classmate whose father is a partner in a medium-sized consulting firm in St. Louis, you have three summers of practical experience to your credit.

Last summer your boss did some griping about a large airport job that went on the shelf without warning. You also observed that other members of the firm occasionally got up tight over losing a job to another firm.

Because of these and other indications from your summer job that a steady flow of clients is important to the professional, you've begun to wonder whether or not a couple of additional courses—call them Business Development I and

II—should not be part of your school's curriculum. Perhaps a few other practical courses might also be considered—Introduction to News Writing, for example, to assist the budding consultant in preparing understandable news stories about his jobs—and Basic Public Relations, for all of the unexpected problems which can arise in dealing with clients, professional committees, the press, zoning and planning commissions, and the public in general. Survey courses in accounting, psychology, personnel practices, and business administration should be equally helpful in preparing the professional-in-training for a business career—what E. M. Forster called "the world of anger and telegrams" and what the less imaginative call "the real world."

Unfortunately, these extra classes could easily result in the addition of at least another year of study to the six or seven years of college already required of architectural and engineering students. Since few would seriously espouse that solution at this time, it is our earnest hope that this book will serve as much more than a primer for most of these untaught but patently desirable subjects.

Beyond this book, seminars and lectures on marketing professional services are offered periodically by certain management-oriented organizations and associations. Some of these courses are excellent, many are mediocre, and a few are useless or worse. The design professional's occasional attendance at the better-organized sessions should be considered a valuable and practical addition to his continuing education program. They are tax deductible, of course, as is the cost of this book.

II

You earned your professional degree a few years ago, served your internship in a medium- to large-sized office, passed the registration examination on the second try, and recently opened your own office with two fellow practitioners who shared your concern about stifling your creative talent by working on one multimillion-dollar project after another in a large multidisciplinary office.

Practical fellows that you are, you signed a contract for a $200,000 school addition before going on your own, and all three of you have a house design or two in your pockets.

Work on the school addition is rolling right along; construction documents will be completed on schedule—and over coffee a few mornings ago, one of you hesitatingly suggested that you'd all better "look for some work." It was not until that moment that you recalled one of the advantages of working on those multimillion-dollar projects in that too-large, insensitive office—someone else had always been responsible for bringing in the work.

This is probably as good a time as any to explain that several terms will be used interchangeably throughout this book. Business development, client acquisition, professional services marketing, client development—they all mean the same thing: selling your firm and its abilities to potential clients. Euphemisms abound in the design and consulting professions—in all professions, for that matter—and the man (or men) in charge of sales in your office may go by the title of director of client relations, executive assistant for business development, director of communications, consultant, or even by no title at all. We'll have more to say on this point later; let's get back to our reader characterizations.

III

As chairman of the Department of Community Planning in the College of Design and Architecture in a Midwestern university, you have seen your share of bright, ambitious young men and women graduate into the profession. Some of them return to your office from time to time with news of themselves and other former students—and of their successes and disappointments. A few of the older men come back as visiting critics or to be interviewed by an architectural selection committee for one of the many new buildings going up on what has become a rather overbuilt campus. Of this latter group you know of a handful who have built up highly successful practices in the fifteen or twenty years since they left school. Some of your other graduates work for these men as draftsmen or spec writers or planners.

You have made it a part of your own continuing education to draw out the "winners" among your former students during these brief reunions. Some years ago you reached the conclusion that it required a peculiar and uneven combination of designer-businessman-perfectionist-professional-administrator-promoter-egotist-Renaissance Man to become a standout in the design profession. Certainly not all of the top men have aspired to become "big" in the sense that their primary goal is to create a firm of hundreds of specialists, technical people, and special services groups.

What you would really like to be able to do, after all these years, is to impart to your students, before they graduate into the "dear school of experience," something of what makes the successful designers tick. Perhaps this book will be a partial answer for you and some of your students.

IV

Unlike the readers already described, you have been in the profession long enough to have won some very large and significant commissions. Examples of your firm's work are to be found in thirty-eight of the fifty states and in a half-dozen foreign countries. You occupy a top slot in your firm's organization chart; you may well be a partner by this time.

You have seen offices come and go in the almost quarter-century of your professional career. Some, founded at the right time in the right place, took off like the proverbial skyrocket. A few years later they also fizzled out like the skyrocket—through bad or lackadaisical management, a refusal to grow with the times, the death of a key principal, hardening of the corporate arteries, or a combination of these and related front-office ailments.

Other offices, some owned by bright young men who started out with your firm, progressed steadily over the years to a position of professional eminence and financial stability.

You have not missed much in your own years on the board nor now behind an executive desk. You doubt that there will be much in this volume you have not already done or seen or heard about. Since your own experience has shown the inescapable correlation between learning and growth and on the possibility that you may find a few helpful ideas—or at least affirmation of and justification for your own philosophy about business development— you are willing to take a look at this book.

It is architects, planners, and engineers such as you to whom most of this book's less-experienced readers will look for advice and help over the rough spots of their professional lives. We trust that you will indeed discover something of value in the following pages. Your comments and suggestions will be welcomed.

REFERENCES

[1]Oliver Witte, "Match Management with Professionalism," *Building Design & Construction*, February 1981, p. 9.
[2]Ibid.

Chapter 2
PRINCIPLES AND PSYCHOLOGY OF MARKETING

Since honesty is unquestionably the best policy—in writing as in selling—I must tell you that we are not going to be able to cover the entire subject of marketing psychology in this one relatively brief chapter. And, while we may also slight a few of the principles of marketing, be aware that many (but not all) of the principles of product marketing have equal application to professional services marketing. Those readers who want to dig deeper into the matter may put together a reading list from the footnote citations and from other readily available sources.

Should there be any lingering doubts, marketing is *not* a science—and this is one of the reasons many design professionals, especially engineers, often have problems in relating to the process. Some marketing techniques work for no apparent reason, and other techniques that by all logic *should work—perhaps did* work on previous occasions—fail miserably at the most inopportune of times.

A true science is based on, among other things, the ability to obtain results which can be replicated by others at a different time in another place. Because of the complex human-chemistry aspects of marketing and selling, along with the many and varied elements of behavioral psychology involved, meaningful replication of results is difficult to achieve. But regardless of the state of inexactness of marketing, there are a number of generally accepted principles, procedures, and techniques that can be applied—usually with productive results.

There are—to lay out the cold, hard facts—no secret formulas or easy shortcuts to success in marketing. Successful marketing results, as with most worthwhile human endeavor, are not built on eight-hour workdays or five-day workweeks. Anyone who tells you otherwise is a fool or a charlatan—or has never been on the sales firing line.

The recipe for successful professional design services selling is based on about equal parts of persuasive communication and supreme confidence in the ability of your firm and yourself—leavened with a better-than-average understanding of human motivational factors.

We will only touch on the complex areas of human and mass psychology and their application to behavior modification and client manipulation, but all these things underlie and influence effective selling efforts.

DEFINITIONS

With the disclaimers out of the way, it might be helpful to begin with some definitions:

> *Marketing*, sometimes called "distribution," is the performance of business activities connected with the movement of goods and services from producers to consumers or other users. In addition to the analysis of these activities, marketing involves the comprehension of consumer circumstances and attitudes that determine the character of a major part of marketing activities; the business organizations that perform these activities; and relevant aspects of government regulation. In marketing, the ability to recognize early trends is fully as important as knowledge of the current state of affairs.[1]

> *Selling* . . . is the personal, oral presentation of products or services to prospective clients for the purpose of making sales. [In the United States] it has become a highly developed technique, based on psychological analysis and psychological application. . . . The well-schooled salesman of today bases his presentation on his understanding of the customer's buying motivations as related to the particular product and by subtle stimulation and manipulation of these motivations the customer is led to want to buy the product. . . . The salesman ideally does more than make the customer desire the product; he tries to win the customer's regard for the company which sells the product [and] tries to extend the confidence and regard of the customer to himself.[2]

Substitute "design professional" for "salesman" and "services" for "product," and the definition of selling becomes directly related to the marketing of professional design services. Some of the differences between marketing and selling are highlighted in this shorter definition: Marketing, unlike sales, is the art of planning now for what to sell, how to sell it, and whom to sell it to in the future (at least two to five years). Sales, on the other hand, focuses on today's markets with today's clients.

Other important differences between the two will be evident from a study of the simplified marketing process diagram (Figure 2-1) and the more complex marketing matrix in Figure 2-2. Marketing is the umbrella over the whole process; selling is one part of the process.

THE PROPER ROLE OF MARKETING

Since marketing is called upon to (1) create demand and (2) set up opportunities for sales, the overall marketing process must begin long before such traditional subactivities as promotion, advertising, and sales. A narrow and essentially outdated view of the marketing function holds that this is it for moving products or services produced and priced by others—the production-oriented marketing philosophy.

Effective marketing begins with identification of the end user or client—and ideally provides guidance for those in production, accounting, personnel, finance, and other major divisions of a firm. One writer calls marketing "the coordinating force of the 'total system' which is the business itself." Peter Drucker suggests that the most important function of management is to create customers.

A Modern Marketing Concept   The modern concept of marketing, as opposed to the narrower view outlined earlier, holds that a firm should concentrate on customer satisfaction—at a profit. In other words, try to sell what clients want instead of producing things or offering services and then trying to sell the product or service. (One of the nine deadly sins of marketing: Promote what you want to design rather than what the market wants to build.) Marketing oriented to client wants can be reduced to these three primary elements:

   1. It is customer- rather than production- or design-oriented.

Figure 2-1   *The marketing process in simplified form. Research input is of prime importance in good planning; the results of intelligence or information gathering should flow to both planning and promotion.*

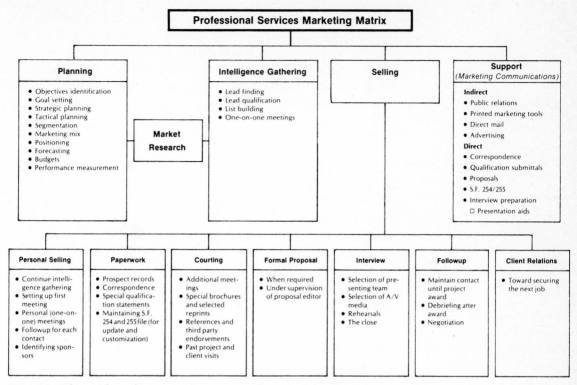

Figure 2-2 *The total marketing process as it applies to professional design services. The box at upper right labeled "Support (Marketing Communications)" essentially equates to the box labeled "Promotion" in Figure 2-1.*

2. It is an integrated, companywide effort.
3. It has the primary goal of profits rather than sales.

If you accept the concept of client-oriented marketing, it is possible that one or more of these internal changes must take place:

Changing management attitudes
Changing the firm's organization
Changing management methods and procedures

The last change, if deemed necessary, requires the person in charge of marketing to coordinate and integrate the total system, acting as a liaison between management and clients.

The Ford Motor Company's experience with two of its car models is a classic illustration of the point. The Edsel of some years ago was designed at management's behest—then a marketing plan was developed to sell it. But before the Mustang car was designed, extensive market research was done to determine customer needs and desires. The research results were matched against company objectives and resources, and only then was the Mustang designed and put into production. The marketing strategy for the Mustang flowed from the information developed by researchers. The Edsel, as we all know, was a production-oriented disaster; the Mustang was a resounding, customer-oriented success.

Where We've Come From   While it is not too difficult to trace the beginnings of organized professional design services marketing back to the mid-1960s (a very few practitioners understood and applied effective marketing techniques even before that time), some profess to see it just now appearing over the horizon. A promotional flyer for a workshop on marketing professional services held as recently as 1979 stated: "The formal marketing of professional services is a relatively new art for architects, engineers, developers, and contractors."[3] Any company that waited until 1979 to get its marketing program in place was in real trouble.

GOALS AND OBJECTIVES

You may be familiar with this quotation from an understandably anonymous marketing director: "Having lost sight of our objective, we redoubled our efforts." Unfortunately, a common problem among design firms is the lack of any real—or realistic—goals; with the concomitant, obvious lack of specific objectives for reaching the nonexistent marketing goals.

We return to the subject of goals and objectives in the next chapter, when we focus on key elements of the formal marketing plan, but at least a brief consideration of their role and importance is in order here.

Establishment of realistic annual goals is always a key consideration in charting a firm's future marketing activities. Implied is a serious, in-depth, self-examination for the purposes of:

1. Keeping plans and policies current and effective—to assure continuing, appropriate responses to changing conditions in the design profession and in client requirements.

2. Staying alert to the basic marketing fundamentals which apply to *all* firms regardless of size, location, or type of operation.

3. Answering the question, "What do we want our firm to be?" and the related, "What business are we in?" Unless and until you have definite and clear answers to those questions, your firm's marketing,

growth, and professional objectives will be difficult—if not impossible—to achieve. ("To be successful" or "to be profitable" are not acceptable responses at this point; precise, introspective answers are required.)

4. Helping to determine the desired image for the firm, a particularly relevant consideration for successful marketing programs. Planned or not, generated purposely or haphazardly obtained, you, your firm, and your staff will have an image. Once general agreement is reached about the image you want to project, internal and external objectives must be set up to lead to the establishment and projection of the desired image.

Goals are general and normally reflect the higher levels of company aspirations: "Where do we want to go with our firm?" Goals are usually set by senior management and are often arrived at through the "What if . . . ?" approach.

Objectives are more specific, established for most marketing activities so that goals can be achieved: "Where do we want to go with market A?" In other words, marketing objectives actually are time-phased subgoals for reaching the overall goals of the firm. Objectives should be

Results-oriented
Measurable
Realistic (attainable)
Specific (clear)
Acceptable to all departments, staff levels, and branch operations
Flexible
Consistent with each other
Challenging

Do not confuse goals and objectives with strategy and tactics. They are all related, as we'll see in Chapter 3, but there are important differences.

EFFECTIVE COMMUNICATIONS

Bound up in any discussion of marketing and its mix of selling, promotion, advertising, publicity, and public relations is the correlative requirement for effective communications. Communication, at its most basic level, is the process of transmitting thought from one mind to another. The communicator sometimes is referred to as the "source"; the act of communicating, the "signal"; and the one (or many) communicated with, the "recipient." The recipient or audience may be

An individual
A single audience of several hundred people
A noncohesive or cellular audience numbering in the millions

Examples of these three audience types would be (1) a conversation between wife and husband, (2) a talk about cost controls at an American Institute of Architects (AIA) regional conference, and (3) the total readership of a best-selling novel.

The whole of human activity may be viewed as a problem of communication. As all of us live in constant touch with our environment, any breakdown in sensory communication usually sends us rushing to a physician or a psychiatrist. Oddly enough, communication failures at the much more important intellectual level are often endured by otherwise intelligent people for long periods and usually with a kind of casual acceptance of the situation.

If we find we are having trouble seeing the image on the television set, we call a TV repair service or make an appointment to see an ophthalmologist—or both. But when we receive an unclear letter or brochure filled with obfuscated prose or read a newspaper item that is everything but informative, there is no panic, no rush to locate a specialist to translate or clarify—and certainly little, if any, hostility is visited upon the writer of the offending material. The public seemingly has a very low level of expectation for most communication.

Why, for example, write, "Kangaroos hop because they have big feet," when you can put it so much more splendiferously as "The macropodid tarsal structure allows effective ricochetal function by transfer of weight through the calcaneum. The fact that their phalangerid ancestors had already developed syndactyly and the use of digit IV as their main support digit thus predetermined the type of cursorial specialization possible in the macropodid hind limb"?

There are at least eight words in that sentence that average readers would have to look up in a dictionary before they could be reasonably certain of the meaning. Unfortunately for understanding (and communication), few of us read with a dictionary in reach, so such complex passages are seldom decoded.

The Communication Process   The communication process was illustrated many years ago by scientists at the Bell Laboratories in the form shown in Figure 2-3. The message to be communicated is encoded by the sender, sent through the appropriate channel, and decoded by the receiver. Through a reversal of the process (feedback), we determine whether or not the original message was decoded with the intended meaning by the receiver.

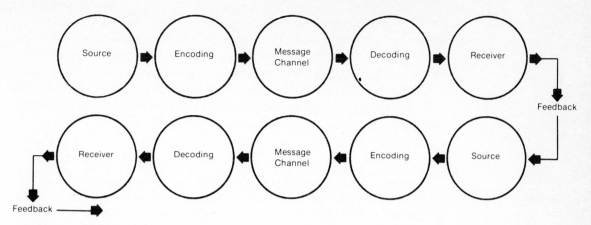

Figure 2-3 *The communication process.*

The process can be a tricky one, since meanings attached to various words and symbols may differ widely, depending upon the frames of reference and experience of the individuals or groups communicating. Figure 2-4 is another view of the communication process. If there is no overlap in the center—if sender and receiver have little or no common frames of reference and fields of experience—communication will be faulty or nonexistent.

In oral communication—conversation, personal selling, and the like—

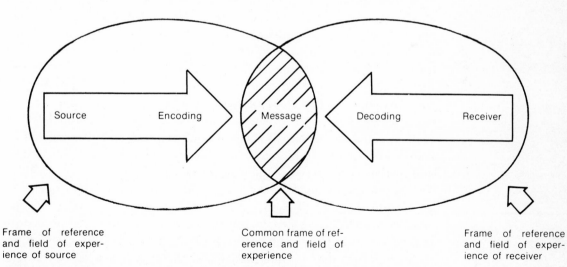

Frame of reference and field of experience of source

Common frame of reference and field of experience

Frame of reference and field of experience of receiver

Figure 2-4 *Another view of communication process. (Adapted from Wilbur L. Schramm and Donald F. Roberts, The Process and Effects of Mass Communication, rev. ed., University of Illinois Press, Champaign, 1971, p. 23.)*

we have the advantage of receiving immediate feedback. Spot judgments can be made as to how the message is being received and the remainder of the message can be adjusted as necessary. Written communication, though it lacks the immediate feedback factor, has a compensating advantage. Writers are able to organize their material fully and present it in a logical and persuasive sequence. There is no way to call back, edit, or rewrite an oral communication once it has been said.

In their excellent book, *Promotional Strategy*, Professors Engel, Wales, and Warshaw explain the communication process as beginning

> ... with some event which stimulates Mr. A to transfer his ideas or notions to Mr. B. He selects certain words which he then arranges in a pattern or sequence to be communicated to a recipient. The process of selecting and arranging the words is called "encoding." The encoded words are then transferred to Mr. B through some kind of signal, perhaps spoken or written language. When Mr. B receives the signal he searches for meaning (decoding) by comparing the signal against his accustomed thought patterns. Communication takes place when Mr. B encodes his reply and transfers it through signals to Mr. A.
>
> The message or signal is transmitted in the form of "symbols," which are nothing more than substitutes for the things they represent. A symbol acquires a more or less unique meaning through social consensus, and hopefully it will call forth the same response from both Mr. A and Mr. B when they are communicating.[4]

Suppose you are at a dinner party with a number of friends. The salad course has just been served, and a quick taste tells you that it needs salt. (The initial source-signal-recipient sequence involves only one individual—you—unless it can be argued that an inanimate object—the salad—may be a source.) You turn to the person on your left and say, "Please pass the salt." She answers, "Of course," reaches for the saltshaker, picks it up, and passes it to you. This familiar situation contains all the elements of any communication. The first step was the formulation of your idea; you wanted the salt. Words (symbols) were then selected (encoded) to convey your request and transmitted or transferred to your tablemate. She received and decoded your signal and responded by passing the saltcellar to you.

Formulation or encoding of ideas and their transmission normally are within the control of the speaker; but unless the ideas are formulated and transferred so as to get the desired response, the procedure is ineffective and communication fails. If, in the preceding example, your dinner companion had passed you the pepper instead of the salt, her decoding was faulty, and you would have had an obvious breakdown in communication.

SELL THE SIZZLE

Productive communications translate into persuasive selling when the sales message answers the primary question of every buyer, "What's in this for me?" Sell in terms of a prospective client's self-interest; sell benefits, not features.

"Don't sell the steak; sell the sizzle," advised the late Elmer Wheeler, salesman extraordinaire of the 1940s and 1950s and author of many commonsense books on the art of selling. Sizzle, he pointed out, appeals to the heart; steak appeals to the brain. Sizzle sells faster and better because the pocketbook is closer to the heart than the brain.[5] The gut level wins over intellect almost every time.

Another Wheelerism: "Always give the buyer a choice between something and something—never between something and nothing."[6] Related was his "Don't ask if—ask which," illustrated by a dentist asking, "Shall I fill that tooth now or wait until it hurts more?" and the doctor's inquiry, "Shall we go to the hospital now while you can still walk, or do you want to wait until the appendix bursts some night and you have to go in an ambulance?"[7]

The "which" question format is useful in setting up a meeting with prospects during or following a telephone cold call qualification (see Chapter 5). If the answer to your question, "How about getting together next Tuesday morning?" is negative, you've painted yourself into the proverbial corner—you have no fallback position. On the other hand, when you phrase it, "I'll be in your city next week. Which time is better for you, Tuesday morning at 10 o'clock or Friday afternoon at 4:30?" the prospect must now choose between alternatives; he or she doesn't have the luxury of opting for yes or no. (This particular wording of the question is called "forcing," from the world of magic. You know that few executives will voluntarily agree to a meeting just before quitting time on Friday, so you are forcing them to the Tuesday morning time. The technique has inherent dangers; it is not for beginners.)

When you use the either-or question format (Wheeler's recommended choice between something and something), prospects occasionally will answer that neither time is open on their schedule. Most marketers will rush in at that point to reassure the prospect, tell them that they understand—and add something like, "Don't worry, we'll try to work out a date later on." *Don't do that!*

When prospects tell you that their schedules are full, in response to your offer of two dates, they have failed you. You have done all you can be expected to do by first offering two possibilities—it is now up to the prospect to straighten the matter out to everyone's satisfaction. No response from you indicates that the next move is up to the prospect. Eventually (it may take ten to fifteen seconds of silence), the prospect will realize that you are waiting for him or her to suggest another time for the meeting—and will come up with an open date. At this point the game playing ends; you accept the suggested meeting date, thank the prospect, and close out the conversation.

Elmer Wheeler also observed, "We don't buy the product; we buy the product of the product." A slight revision makes his observation applicable to buyers of design services marketing: "We don't buy the service; we buy the product of the service."

¼-Inch-Drill School of Marketing   By now most of those involved in any way with sales and marketing surely are familiar with the ¼-inch-drill analogy to good marketing practice. (Technically, the product is a ¼-inch drill *bit*, rather than a ¼-inch drill. So low has precision and accuracy in language sunk!)

The point usually is made that X million ¼-inch drills were sold last year, and not one buyer had the slightest interest in becoming the proud owner of a ¼-inch drill. The universal buying motive was a desire for ¼-inch holes!

Salespeople who insist on trying to sell features instead of benefits— who stress the high grade of steel used in making the drill, the precision forming of the threads and shank, and the overall engineering design of the drill—will sell a few drills. But the salespeople who concentrate their pitch on the ease of use, low power requirements to operate the drill, and the cleanness of the holes made by the drill—the benefits— will sell many more.

Some marketers, aware of the importance of selling benefits rather than features of their service or product, plan presentations at an early stage by ruling a page into two columns. The left-hand column is for listing features—accurate estimating, strict observance of client budget restraints, meeting (or bettering) construction and occupancy schedules and deadlines of all types, significant experience with projects of the same type and scope, design awards won, geographic proximity of the office to the site, and the like.

Opposite each feature entry, in the right-hand column, the benefits to clients that result from each of the features are then listed. Most of the feature examples listed earlier translate into greater efficiency in progressing the job, but, more importantly, they relate to saving time and money for the client. Don't leave anything to chance in this exercise; explain how each of your firm's features translates into dollar savings, giving specific examples wherever possible.

The point here is to have a good supply of ready answers to the tacit but always implied question from clients: "What's in this for me?" After the list of features and benefits is completed and refined, salespeople can use it to remind themselves always to couple benefits with features in selling.

"Because" is the operative word in linking benefits and features in sales presentations. Begin with a benefit—"You will save money"—and immediately relate it to a feature: "*because* we have the most experienced estimating department in the state" or "*because* we've successfully designed ten projects very similar to yours in size and complexity in the last three years."

Sometimes it may seem more appropriate to begin a presentation with a feature. In such cases "so" is the magic linking word. "We send our entire design team to your city *so* all of you can fully share your requirements in the critical early stages." Or, "We use a computer to study space-frame roof designs *so* your building will have the safest solution."

Stressing benefits in presentations ensures that you will get the all-important minicommitments from prospects as the selling process moves along. Productive salespeople take prospects through a series of small but related commitments—always moving toward the close gradually rather than trying to rush into the big question—and the equally big answer—the prospect's final decision. Closing a sale is almost always a matter of degree, achieved through cautious, reasoned advances and occasionally marked by small retreats—but with all the seller's efforts and faculties trained on the final, formal close.

Since a final commitment may require anywhere from a month to several years to achieve, after the sales process gets underway, you should, in effect, close something on each call, that is, get agreements or an agreement from the prospect up to that point in the sales cycle.

Some refer to this technique as "incremental marketing." The process may be viewed as a series of minipresentations, with each designed to effect a specific change in the prospect's thinking. Get such minicommitments at the end of each selling increment or phrase. Figure 2-5 shows the process as a time-line diagram. The point is to make the final decision as easy as possible for a client. When you follow the strategy just outlined, the prospect will mentally have to move only from perhaps position L or M to Z (the close) rather than being forced to have to take the much longer decision trip from A to Z at one time.

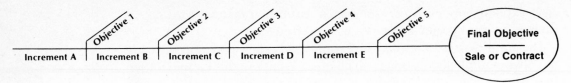

Figure 2-5 *The incremental marketing process, shown as a time-line diagram.*

Different Levels of Selling   Good salespeople, by necessity, operate on many levels. The commonsense level dictates that they learn the prospect's viewpoint and adapt to it. The vice president of marketing for a large, successful U.S. corporation expressed his ideas about the importance of relating to prospective clients: "I believe that all of the other qualities of a true salesman are of lesser importance. He can have enthusiasm, stamina, intelligence, personality, sincerity, and all of the other attributes of a salesman and still be a failure if he does not have the knack of finding the points of common interest. The important points are those which are of chief interest to the prospect—not to the salesman."

In my Marketing Management Workshops, I sometimes describe "jamjoint" sales techniques to illustrate one level of selling. As you will see, owing to the concentration on conditioning prospects, it is an effective—if not very professional—level of selling.

"Jam joints" are those small commercial enterprises to be found mostly along oceanside boardwalks in such places as Atlantic City. "Jamming" is also done in fairs, carnivals, and at other outdoor events which attract large numbers of people who are perfectly willing to pay out large sums of money for shoddy, cheap merchandise. A jam joint will sell a knife set, for example, for $45 that buyers must know they can buy at home for no more than $13.50. The operator of a jam joint is known, logically, as a "jammer," and clients are called, not so logically, "tips."

Jammers, who may count more wealthy high school dropouts in their number than any other business or profession, all have earned the street equivalent of at least one Ph.D. in human psychology and mass conditioning. They thoroughly understand that greed and pride of ownership are two of the most fundamental human motivators.

The small business operators, both men and women, known as jammers all use classic conditioning techniques to generate an impressive number of early positive responses from their tips (customers). This initial come-on (the less charitable might refer to it as the "con") is to (1) instill a positive response mode in the shortest possible time, (2) control the group's behavior by allowing no time for individuals to establish a negative mind set, and (3) quickly build trust and credibility in the jammer as an expert. Psychological experimenters have demonstrated that the communicator with the greatest credibility is the most persuasive communicator.

An account of a jammer whom I witnessed at work some years ago in Atlantic City will serve to illustrate most of these points. (In all honesty, I should state at the outset that Atlantic City has never been one of my favorite places to visit. Like many others in marketing, I have been forced to make annual treks there to meet with the physicians, teachers, dentists, bankers, and hospital administrators who apparently look upon an Atlantic City convention as something close to the ultimate lifetime experience. Making it the eastern branch of Las Vegas has not helped a bit, in my opinion.)

At any rate, I had arisen early and gone for a short stroll on the boardwalk, along which is located a strange mixture of very expensive shops and very shoddy jam joints.

As I returned to my hotel, I noticed a dozen or so people in front of one of the jam joints. Drawing closer, I could see that the jammer was painting some kind of sign on the front window of his shop. His concentration on the lettering seemed complete, but he really was using the glass reflection to count the tips collecting behind him on the boardwalk.

As I joined the watchers, he apparently felt the number of tips and the time were right. Turning around, smiling pleasantly, he seemed startled to see the group of intent bystanders. (Since there really is nothing to do in Atlantic City before breakfast, anything out of the ordinary is sufficient to attract most of those unfortunate enough to be up and about. He knew this.)

Recovering rapidly from his feigned initial surprise, he greeted his tips with a "Hello" as pleasant as his smile. And then the conditioning—the point of this narrative—began.

"How many of you are from out of town?"

"Are you having a good time?"

"How many of you watch TV?"

"How about that Johnny Carson—isn't he great?"

"How many of you gamble? Have you ever lost?"

"Who'd like to take home a nice gift?"

And so it went. With about ten brief questions, delivered in staccato fashion and all designed to encourage yes responses, the jammer conditioned the group to the point that any question he asked would be answered positively.

Let's analyze some of the jammer's manipulative queries:

"How many of you are from out of town?" Surely a safe yes answer in most resorts; perhaps safest of all in a place such as Atlantic City, where it is difficult to imagine any kind of voluntary permanent population exists.

"Are you having a good time?" To this observer, the jammer seemed to be on dangerous ground with such a question. On reflection, I decided he knew exactly what he was doing. Some people apparently do like Atlantic City, and the ones who were having a miserable time would not be likely to admit to a complete stranger that they'd spent a lot of time and money to get there—and they were hating every minute of it. A daring—but effective—line of questioning.

As to the TV viewership question, the deplorable statistics are available to anyone. Surely one of the safest yes questions around. Any viewers who will go to the trouble to stay awake long enough to watch Carson, who is not really controversial anyway, must like him.

Almost everyone considers himself or herself a gambler. There is little point in going to Atlantic City these days if you aren't one. And knowing full well that no casino is going to pay out anything like what it takes in, all gamblers will lose. Another safe yes question, with the added advantage of evoking an "we're all in this together" feeling.

"Who'd like to take home a nice gift?" Who wouldn't?

As soon as the jammer felt his conditioning had reached the optimum point, he glanced at his watch, mumbled something about it being coffee time, brightened as he looked back at the crowd, and, pointing out that he had not really planned to open this early, invited everyone inside to have some coffee on him—"and to take a look at some gifts for the folks back home." The word "gifts" was always stressed; there was never a mention of price. Jammers, as someone has pointed out, don't sell products—they sell the art of buying. And that is an important difference.

The successful jammer is a highly skilled and persuasive communicator, an adept manipulator of group norms who automatically uses most of the known effective techniques of persuasion. Jammers also benefit from selecting their audiences: tips who are away from home and office pressures and who are (mostly) having a good time and expecting a pleasant experience.

Many of the same jamming conditioning techniques are used by some door-to-door salespeople. Sellers of certain encyclopedias know that once the person in charge of a household begins to nod his or her head affirmatively, it is physiologically very difficult to switch over from the activating neck and shoulder muscles which move the head up and down to those muscles used to move the head from side to side—to signal a negative response. Accordingly, the preferred opening gambit is a series of quick questions designed to evoke the positive, up-and-down head movement.

To reiterate, the process just described is *not* at a professional level of selling, and no intelligent marketer would consider adopting it for design services marketing. But go back over the material once again; some of the techniques *can* be carefully adapted to professional services selling. And there are some other pretty good pointers—the part about success in selling depending to a great degree on selection of those whom you sell to, for instance.

More on the Selling Process   For those who prefer their selling principles reduced to lists, "Ten Ways to Get People to Respond to Your Sales Message" offers good advice in capsule form:

1. Find out what they want and need and show them how you can help them. (Henry Ford: "The way to a fortune is simple—find a public need and fill it.") And do it honestly, too! When a sales message is delivered the listener has one predominant thought in mind: "What's in it for me?"

2. Prepare a "Want and Need Questionnaire" to help determine the interests of a sales prospect. There is no sense in trying to sell your organization, product, or services if you have not found out the wants and needs of the person you are trying to convince. He just won't listen.

3. Prepare a list of all the products and/or services of your organization. Concentrate on all the unique benefits you offer. Then show how your products, services, and unique benefits will fulfill the wants and needs of the person to whom you are delivering the sales message.

4. Correlate the needs and wants of the prospect with the products, services, and unique benefits you offer. This will help you arrive at a Unique Marketing Proposition for your organization. If you offer what everyone else offers the prospect will not listen. If you offer something unique in terms of his interest he will start to listen.

5. Develop a unique selling idea or theme and communicate it through your salesmen, in sales letters, general brochures, product brochures, newsletters, direct mail, annual reports, packaging, advertising, billboards, point of purchase displays, exhibits, slide films or movies, or any other media.

6. Develop a unified graphic look around your selling theme, wherever it appears. It should be consistent and easily identifiable. Use all the principles of corporate identity to achieve this look—a look of quality that is distinctive and attention getting.

7. Be honest and straightforward in everything you do. People will stop listening if you are not. Especially in the 70s. [Most particularly in the 80s.] The younger generation and the older one, too, are going to be far more difficult to convince unless you are straight with them.

8. You must really care about the prospect—and show it in every way. The more care and interest you honestly show, the more effectively your message will come through.

9. Your message must be repeated again and again because people are

skeptical, even though you want to help them. The more you repeat your message, in different ways, the more it will be believed.

10. Demonstrate not only with graphics and words that you want to help a prospect but with concrete action. Show in as many concrete ways—case histories, etc.—as possible how a prospect will benefit if he responds to your message. If all things are equal between two companies—equal products, services, quality, and prices—the company that uses these ten principles will communicate much better than the one that does not.[8]

COMMUNICATIONS FAILURES

The further a communication is removed from its primary source, the weaker the strength and authority of the communication becomes. Communications passed through secondary sources invariably become changed, diluted, and obscure—losing their clarity, purpose, validity, *and* persuasiveness.

An old party game involved the relaying of a simple message through a line of participants on a one-to-one basis. After the message had made its way through a dozen or so players, any resemblance between what the last person heard and what the originator started through the line was purely coincidental.

A favorite stunt in first-year journalism classes, to demonstrate the fallibility of prime, rather than secondary, sources, is to have several strangers burst into the classroom and rush to the front while carrying on a loud argument among themselves, punctuated by dire threats. Suddenly, one of the protagonists pulls out a revolver and appears to shoot one of the others at point-blank range. The perpetrator and the others then rush from the room, followed by the shooting victim, who has been miraculously restored to life.

At this point the professor asks the stunned students to write down the essential details of what they have just witnessed—including the number of participants in the episode; their sex, race, dress; what type of weapon was used; how many shots were fired—the barest and most obvious of details. Anyone familiar with the confusion of eyewitnesses at a police lineup will have a pretty good idea of how badly the journalism students do in trying to describe the scene they saw only moments before. It is always a sad and discouraging commentary on human powers of observation—and a dramatic demonstration of failure in communications.

How can we guarantee against such failures in communications? Unfortunately, there is no pat answer. Semanticists and psychologists have long studied the question but have arrived at few conclusions and no real solutions. We do know that effective and persuasive communication appears to involve empathy, with the speaker and the audience placing themselves in each other's shoes. This is also called role taking, with at least three primary requirements for it to succeed:

1. Some commonality of background and experience.
2. Some indication (feedback) from the audience that the speaker's signal is being decoded; a smile, an affirmative reply, a frown, or even no response at all helps the speaker to determine whether or not the recipient is getting the message.
3. The speaker (sender) must have some knowledge of the audience's motivational influences at the time of transmission.

In summarizing this chapter, we might draw on Victor Hugo's *The History of a Crime*, wherein he wrote, "More powerful than armies is an idea whose time has come." Certainly the idea of a businesslike approach to marketing the services of professional design firms is one whose time has arrived; arrived some time ago, actually. Perhaps slightly more relevant to the principles and practices discussed here is a remark attributed to an executive of the American Telephone and Telegraph Company (AT&T): "Silence is still the best substitute for brains, though it is not yet an absolute replacement." Where persuasive communications are concerned, however, there is no known substitute for brains; silence usually sends the wrong message. But, to exercise an author's prerogative, we will close with the explanation of his business role by a partner in a New York brokerage firm: "I don't sell. People buy from me."

REFERENCES

[1] Reprinted with permission from volume 15 of *Collier's Encyclopedia*, p. 416. © 1971 Crowell-Collier Educational Corporation.

[2] Ibid., p. 422.

[3] "Marketing Professional Services," College of Business Administration, Oklahoma State University, Stillwater, Okla., February 15, 1979.

[4] James F. Engel, Hugh G. Wales, and Martin R. Warshaw, *Promotional Strategy*, Richard D. Irwin, Inc., Homewood, Ill., 1967, pp. 12–13.

[5] Elmer Wheeler, *How to Sell When Selling Is Tough*, Doubleday & Co., Inc., Garden City, N.Y., 1958, pp. 19–20.

[6] Ibid., p. 32.

[7] Ibid., pp. 32–33.

[8] Courtesy of Corporate Image Planners, Philadelphia, Pa.

Chapter 3
GETTING ORGANIZED

Think about the last time you shopped for a new car or a house—or almost any tangible item. If it was a new car, once you recovered from the shock of reading the bottom line of the price sticker, you began a visual and tactile inspection of the features that interested you most. Doors were opened and closed: if it was one of the new smaller models, you missed the satisfying "thunk" of closing doors on the much larger, gas-guzzling cars of the 1960s and 1970s. You probably looked under the hood. Even if you know nothing about engines, it's always nice to see a factory-fresh, sparkling-clean motor. No doubt you climbed into the driver's seat to spin the steering wheel, twiddle the dashboard controls, and check the decor and general comfort of the interior. Maybe you kicked a tire or two; certainly you looked in the trunk.

If you liked what you'd seen so far, it didn't require much urging from the salesperson to convince you to take a demonstrator car out for a test drive. During the demonstration ride all of your senses but one were on the alert as you appreciatively sniffed the new car smell, listened for alien motor noises and body squeaks, watched the speedometer climb as you shifted through the gears, and ran your hand over the genuine imitation plastic synthetic leather on the dashboard and door panels.

All this points up the primary difference between prospective customers for a product and prospective clients for a service. The difference is particularly important in selling design services since no one has yet figured out how to create a design services inventory. The end product of a design staff, a drafting department, and an estimating service cannot practically be stockpiled against future client demand. Moreover, the seller of any worthwhile service delivers it personally to the user; you can't buy a design for a 300-bed teaching hospital or a wastewater treatment plant in a supermarket or from a mail-order catalog. The most noticeable difference, perhaps, is in the manifest inability of buyers (clients) to compare the final product of one design firm's services against that of another so far as a specific project is concerned.

The purchaser of a product makes a buying commitment after production is completed and a sample is available for inspection and comparison with similar products. The product buyer may feel, smell, squeeze, kick, and heft the potential purchase in advance. Then the buyer orders "one like that" or "one like that, except in blue." The purchaser of a service, on the other hand, makes a commitment long before production begins based largely on intangible promises of the seller about past performance and staff capabilities, a much more difficult and demanding buying decision. The prospect's project rarely, if ever, will be exactly like any other project your firm has completed.

Stuart Riley and George Long, of the University of Lancaster's Department of Marketing, have classified the characteristics peculiar to professional services buying and selling under four headings and have applied the acronym HIPI to the whole. Their explanation of HIPI:

H = Heterogeneity: a service is not homogeneous.
I = Intangibility: you can't hold a service in your hands; you can't carry it away.
P = Perishability: your staff and overhead costs continue, work or no.
I = Inseparability: a client is always part of the deal. Production and consumption occur at the same time; storage of services against future demand is not possible.

These are only a few of the reasons that today's successful design firm must be run as a full-fledged business. The great majority of practitioners today understand the importance of organization throughout their offices, including, but certainly not limited to, maximum staff utilization, effective project control, enlightened personnel policies, sound financial operations, and productive marketing activities. Traditional operating procedures and the organizational style of corporate clients have finally made their way into the management approach of the architectural and engineering firms who serve them.

The initial planning effort by any business should be its long-range business plan—looking ahead from five to twenty-five years. Growing out of and supportive of the business plan is the marketing plan. Of my own knowledge many more design firms have developed and implemented a marketing plan than have true business plans—but the good news is that ten years ago practically no design firm had any kind of marketing plan.

In this chapter we'll concentrate on putting together a written marketing plan. The operative word here is "written." The difference is about the same as that between getting oral directions from someone about which roads to use in driving from New York to Seattle and having a detailed road map for the same route. Marketing plans that exist nowhere but in a principal's head are about as useful as a steamroller in a watch repair shop.

KNOW YOUR FIRM

At the beginning of the last chapter an attempt was made to define and differentiate between marketing and selling. Marketing has been defined in the recent past as "an early warning system," with sales standing ready to "zero in on specific targets."[1]

Theodore Levitt, professor of business administration at the Harvard Business School and a prolific, understandable writer on marketing subjects, offered this comment in the *Harvard Business Review:*

> Everybody by now knows that marketing and selling are not the same thing. Selling tries to get the customer to know what you have. Marketing tries to have what the customer will want—where, when, in what form, and at what price he wants. Goods and services should be created not because somebody thinks something will be useful, but rather because somebody thinks about the needs and wants of possible buyers and users—and thinks about them in enormous detail, with infinite attention to minutiae; the design of goods and services, their packaging, how they're distributed and sold, pricing, the training and management of those who sell them, their advertising and promotion, the product-line planning, and the auditing of results and of the competitive environment.[2]

The thrust of almost every modern attempt to define marketing in concrete terms is to the point of its being a deliberate, planned, and documented activity—fully committed to and adequately funded by top management. Successful marketing programs are largely attributable to the marketing plan on which they are based. Central to the effectiveness of any marketing plan is its reflection of the realities of both the firm it covers and the potential markets of that firm. In the short citation given earlier, Professor Levitt defined marketing and selling *and* set out most of the requirements for a good marketing plan.

Knowing your firm means knowing all you can about

1. Its principals (owners, partners, associates); your professional, technical, and administrative employees and their present and potential capabilities and specialties. Conversely, the internal investigation should also familiarize you with your staff's drawbacks, limitations, and deficiencies.

2. The general practice mix: what it traditionally consists of, and—of at least equal importance—what is missing from it and why.

3. Competitors: who and where they are, now and in the foreseeable future.

Only after a genuinely objective and introspective look has been taken at a firm as it now exists and operates—coupled with a thoughtful analysis of its goals for ten, fifteen, even twenty-five years from now—is one ready to embark upon an aggressive, productive, and professional program of business development. The short-range, scattershot, hit-or-miss approach to client development is never so productive in the long run as the reasoned, planned, and organized attack.

The principals may want to consider outside management and marketing consultants for all or part of this self-investigation. Many professional design firms do bring in consultants, with no particular relation to the size of the client firm. The sad history of many such studies, if we assume the consultant is competent, is that clients heed only the advice and recommendations they believed or wanted to hear in the first place—and ignore or denigrate the parts of the final report that run counter to preconceived ideas.

Regardless of whether the decision is to establish an in-house investigative task force or to hire a marketing consultant, the principals should be prepared mentally to accept and act upon most of the findings and suggestions for getting their professional houses in order.

The SWOT Team Diagnosis   Most of the important considerations for the initial environmental or situational analysis fall under one of these four headings:

Strengths
Weaknesses
Opportunities
Threats

Make up a quadrant diagram like that shown in Figure 3-1, labeling each quarter of the sheet as shown.

Strengths	Weaknesses
Opportunities	Threats

Figure 3-1 *Use a form like this for making the SWOT internal inventory of your firm.*

The initial letters of the four division headings give us "SWOT"—a kind of emergency marketing team for identifying both positive selling points (unique selling propositions) and incipient trouble spots before they become full-fledged disaster areas. Fill in the quadrants as they pertain to your firm.

Most marketers are pretty good at identifying strengths and opportunities of their organization, but they are less objective and forthcoming about the more negative weaknesses (constraints) and threats. Remember always to relate strengths to features, not to benefits.

Examples of strengths are these:

1. Good geographic coverage through sales offices in the five major cities in your marketing area.

2. On-staff experts in energy conservation applications—or in any "hot" new area in design services.

3. An experienced estimating department with a 95 percent accuracy rate.

4. Repeat business in the 70 to 80 percent range.

Examples of weaknesses follow:

1. High staff turnover at the associate and project manager levels.
2. A repeat client rate of less than 25 percent.
3. No staff experience in a growing project type.
4. No written marketing plan.

Examples of opportunities:

1. A new government funding program that enables you to recycle staff experience from other project types.

2. A newly won project in a distant growth market gives you the chance to open a branch office and market from it.

3. Your brother is elected governor of your state.

Examples of threats:

1. A contining increase in commercial interest rates.
2. High unemployment in your marketing area.
3. A sharp rise in lawsuits from clients.
4. Actions of your competitors.

This SWOT internal inventory should be a continuing process, to be updated at six- or twelve-month intervals. Some firms go through a similar exercise as an aid to developing strategy and tactics for individual presentations. Without complete honesty, thoroughness, and objectivity, the SWOT analysis may do more harm (by instilling a false sense of security) than good.

MARKET RESEARCH

So that they may be reasonably accurate in their business planning and forecasting, most marketers rely on a tool commonly known as "market research." One corporate planner suggests that intelligent forecasting is based on a hard look at those current circumstances that may have long-range effects. The planner is, of course, defining market research.

A more formal definition: Market research is a planned, organized effort to collect and analyze information for the purpose of making better marketing decisions. Specifically, according to researcher Randall Shores, market research "can identify new and emerging markets, show how to penetrate new markets, improve the delivery of A-E [architect-engineer] services to the client, and save the time, money, and effort of other members of the firm."[3]

The real purpose of information collecting and its subsequent analysis, that is, market research, is to reduce uncertainty about the consequences of a planning decision. In short, it is a marketing tool to assist and supplement executive judgment.

Whatever they may call it—or however they define it—sales and marketing people are always involved with some form of formal or informal market research; they couldn't operate otherwise. During periods of economic uncertainty, forecasting business trends is, at the same time, more important and much more difficult than in boom times. Market research and business forecasting go hand in hand; the usefulness of the latter depends heavily on the former.

Research Results   Some of the answers market research can give:

What kind of clients you've been getting
Where they came from
Why they came to your firm
What services your firm should promote
Where they should be promoted
To whom you should promote
What should be said in the promotion

The results of market research (both initial and continuing) should aid in arriving at answers to these three questions (among others):

1. What are the services we offer? (Directly related to the basic marketing question: What business are we in?)

2. Where is there an unsatisfied demand for the services we offer?

3. How can we cultivate and capitalize on this existing, identified demand?

To be effective *and* helpful, research efforts must be carefully planned, zealously controlled, and intelligently analyzed and correlated with previous research efforts. Too many principals and marketers confuse activity with accomplishment, panic with productivity, and razzle-dazzle with results.

Image studies (what clients, prospects, employees, and the general public think about a firm, its policies, and its work) are also considered market research. The most helpful image surveys—because they are the most objective—are conducted and evaluated by outside consulting firms.

Segmentation Through Market Gridding   A market segment is a client group with similar or related characteristics, with common needs and wants, and with similar responses to like motivations. A segment of a market can be expected to buy a service that appears to fulfill its common needs and wants. In a very real sense, clients automatically group themselves into natural market segments.

Segmentation criteria vary, but the process always begins with identification of a firm's strengths, weaknesses, opportunities, and threats (the SWOT analysis). After strengths are clearly defined, client needs must be identified. If segmentation is to work, identified firm strengths and isolated client needs must dovetail. Adding missing strengths and modifying perceived needs make one method of meshing the two for marketing purposes.

Segmentation enables marketers to focus their efforts logically and productively on targeted client groups. A potential target market often turns out to be a whole series of smaller, homogeneous markets. Each of these mini- or submarkets is a market segment.

Market grid development is an analytical approach to market segmentation. The market grid concept diagrams a market on the basis of relevant market characteristics, particularly the *need* areas. The diagram resembles a checkerboard, with each square in the overall grid representing a smaller market segment.

We'll use energy conservation studies to illustrate the concept of gridding. Figure 3-2 shows a gross market grid for such studies.

The gross grid in Figure 3-2 is set up for a design firm with an international practice. If your market area is less than national or international, the headings across the top might designate states, provinces, counties, or cities. Potential users of the service under analysis are listed

Potential user \ Region	Northeast	Southeast	Central	Northwest	Southwest	Foreign
Building and apartment owners						
Homeowners						
Corporations (including manufacturers)						
Government agencies						
Institutional (schools, hospitals, etc.)	✕					
Transportation (common carriers)						
All others						

Figure 3-2 *The gross market grid.*

down the left side of the grid. The more detailed this list, the greater help the grid will give in identifying all major market segments.

Each of the boxes in the gross grid should be further broken down into discrete grids. In Figure 3-3 we can analyze in detail the market for energy conservation studies for institutional clients in the northeastern United States. Are there obvious omissions of user types on the discrete grid? How about housing and health care for the elderly? Any others?

Each of the boxes on the discrete grid will be filled in with estimates of the market size—in dollars and numbers of projects where possible—

Type \ Size	Large	Medium	Small
Elementary & high schools			
Colleges & universities			
Hospitals	5 projects average $80,000		
Clinics			
Others			

Figure 3-3 *A discrete market grid for energy conservation studies for institutional clients in the Northeast.*

along with brief notes about how best to reach prospects with your story. As you obtain the information for each of the squares in the discrete and gross grids, you are engaged in market research, of course. The grids are a form of work sheets for you to use in compiling pertinent information.

The objective of the gridding process is to find homogeneous groupings of prospects whose requirements can be covered with essentially the same marketing mix. Analyzing other potential services—sewage treatment facilities or planning or health care, for example—is accomplished through separate grid sets.

Market Life Cycle   Along with organizing the results of market research through gross and discrete grid development, many marketers attempt to locate specific design markets on the market life cycle curve. The four-stage market life cycle in Figure 3-4 is adapted from the writings of Theodore Levitt and others.

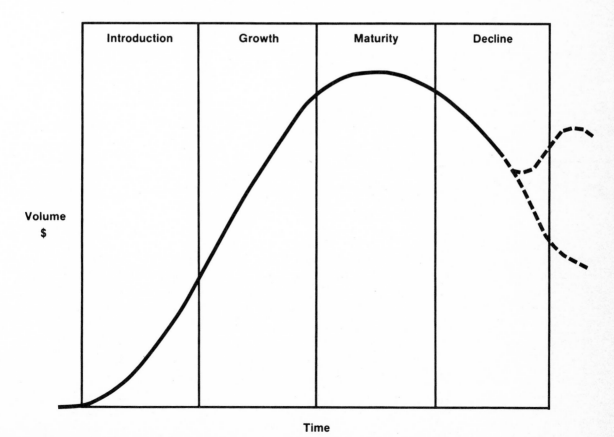

Figure 3-4   *The four-stage market life cycle.*

The vertical axis represents dollar volume; the horizontal axis shows time. The introductory stage of a market obviously starts at or near zero on the chart. The curve indicates recognition of a market rather than its actual beginning. Competition at this early stage is nonexistent to minimal.

The curve picks up rapidly as it goes into the growth phase. Competition naturally increases as the market becomes known and better defined. In the third (maturity) stage, supply catches up with demand, and pure competition results.

A decline sets in in the fourth and final sector. The life cycle curve begins to decay, and the situation becomes frantically competitive as established firms fight to hold their market share and newcomers try to pick up scraps of the fading project type. Few markets fade completely away. As the right side of Figure 3-4 shows, some external force or forces may cause the curve to recover to some degree, plateau again in a secondary maturity stage, and then drift into a decline once again.

It should be evident that the time to enter a market is as close to the beginning of the life cycle curve as possible. Good market research helps you identify new or recovering markets in their earliest stages. Once a market is well into the maturity stage, only those firms that discovered and entered the market early—and along the way built up an experienced staff and a reservoir of credibility—will continue to make money from it. If your market research is accurate, you should be able to avoid entering many markets on the down side of the curve.

Market Research Sources   The two basic sources for market research of all types are

> Primary sources
> Secondary sources

Secondary sources, because they are more plentiful and less expensive (much secondary material is free for the asking), will be our first line of inquiry. Secondary material is information and data already in existence and available from various sources. It has been searched, analyzed, and stored in some form by others for their own use. Most secondary source material has been published, but occasionally excellent unpublished material can be located.

Secondary material should always be investigated first, so that you will know what is already known. Use work from others when it relates to your needs. But there is an important point to keep in mind about all secondary source material; the information obviously was collected for the original user's particular interests and requirements. Only by chance and great good luck will it provide a complete solution for the needs of market researchers. Any holes left after all possible secondary material has been collected are filled in from primary sources.

Some of the sources of secondary information can be found in the departments and agencies of the federal government, which is the largest single—and the most overlooked—source of marketing information. Depending on your interests, these federal offices can be information gold mines:

Department of Commerce
Department of the Interior
Department of Agriculture
Department of the Treasury
Bureau of the Census
Federal Reserve Bank (also its ten individual branches scattered around the country)
Executive Office of the President
General Accounting Office
Congress (committee reports, the Library of Congress)
Government Printing Office

State governments have counterparts of many of the federal agencies, as well as such sources as state industrial directories, state magazines, and economic development commissions. City governments emulate state and federal administrative structures to some degree. Cities have economic development commissions and redevelopment commissions.

Trade, professional, and technical associations, along with industrial and business organizations, can be excellent sources of secondary research material. In addition to chambers of commerce at many levels, almost every industry and profession has at least one association. Many associations maintain market research departments of their own to serve their members. Material so collected normally is available to outsiders. One of the best lists of associations of all types is the *Encyclopedia of Associations,* published by the Gale Research Corporation, Book Tower, Detroit, MI 48226.

Commercial indexes (*Readers' Guide to Periodical Literature* and the indexes to articles in *The New York Times* and *The Wall Street Journal* are examples) and directories such as those published by Dun & Bradstreet and Moody's can direct you to productive sources of secondary source material.

Other secondary data sources include these:

1. Commercial research companies (Frost & Sullivan, Predicasts)
2. Banks—other than the Federal Reserve system. Many of the larger

banks issue annual forecasts (Citicorp, United California Bank, Bank of America)

3. Securities and Exchange Commission (various reports from publicly owned corporations)

4. Libraries—always a good place to begin information searches (private, public, and college and university libraries)

Once relevant secondary information is found, the researcher has two key considerations:

1. Does the information fit the researcher's needs—or can it be adjusted to fit?

2. Is the source a dependable one?

Primary Sources   Primary research, as was noted earlier, is to fill in any information gaps left after a researcher has drawn on all possible secondary sources. Primary information is originated for specific needs through such collection mechanisms as

Mail surveys, using questionnaires
Telephone surveys
Personal interviews
Panels

Since questionnaires for mail surveys must be heavily structured, they have the disadvantage of narrowly channeling respondents' answers. Telephone surveys usually are also pretty structured mechanisms, but they do allow for some elaboration on answers. Personal interviews are expensive and time-consuming and should provide the best information. Panels are used primarily for research into consumer products. Which method is used depends on a variety of factors, including the time available, budget, degree of reliability required, and the like.

To be strategically and tactically effective, market research collection should be a continuing process. Even a little information usually is preferable to total ignorance. Place little trust in those who do not want their decision making to be bothered or inhibited by facts.

THE MARKETING PLAN

In addition to serving as a guide to many present and near-future company activities, a good marketing plan can help a firm to find answers to these four questions:

1. Where are we now?
2. Where do we want to go?
3. How do we get there?
4. How do we know when we're there?

In formal marketing terms those four points are known as

The situational analysis
Goals and objectives
Programming and tasking
Performance measurement and analysis

Marketing plans can be short-range or long-range. Occasionally, the two forms are combined after a fashion, but the hybrid approach is not recommended for the long haul.

Short-range planning usually covers one year or less and deals with the more immediate concerns of a firm. Long-range planning, on the other hand, can cover from two to ten or even twenty years into the future. Most long-range plans do not exceed five years. In general, when a firm plots its prospective growth, objectives, and strategies over more than a five-year period, the result becomes more of a broad-gauged business plan than a functional marketing plan.

Because every business—especially a design firm—is different, there are no stock outlines for a marketing plan or a single, recommended plan for all companies to adopt. Certain elements are incorporated into many plans, as shown in Table 3-1.

Table 3-1   Marketing Plan Elements

Plan element	*Description*
1. Table of contents	A list of subjects covered in the plan
2. Introduction	Sets out the purposes and uses of the plan; contains pertinent definitions
3. Executive summary (also called management summary; executive digest)	Summaries of the main provisions of the plan. Similar in purpose to the executive summary of a formal proposal
4. Company's mission (or charter), scope, and goals	Sets out the nature of services offered; markets; firm profile; technical and staff capabilities; broad aims and objectives
5. Situational analysis	Explains facts and assumptions upon which the plan is based
Assumptions	Economic, environmental, political, social, technological, and competitive factors
Resources (of firm)	Personnel, talents, experience, capabilities

Table 3-1   Marketing Plan Elements (Continued)

Plan element	Description
Forecasts and potentials	Qualitative and quantitative information about the size of targeted markets (in dollars and job units); growth rates; client and prospect profiles; client desires, requirements, and attitudes
Market share	Company's share of potential total market (gross and discrete)
Sales history	Sales record over the past three to five years in traditional markets; current position versus objectives from previous plans (may include a market life-cycle curve chart)
Current and new opportunities	High-growth markets—old and new
6. Current marketing organization	Structure; lines of authority and responsibility
7. Objectives	Results to be produced (by meeting goals and quotas) to achieve the company's marketing objectives by the end of next year—and in future years
8. Strategies, policies, procedures	Outline of general courses of action (strategies) to reach objectives, along with an analysis of internal policies and procedures bearing on the marketing program
9. Marketing program (also called action program; action plan)	Sets out specific courses of action (tactics) for selling, promotion, market research, advertising, assigned marketing territories, and the like
10. Schedules and tasks	Who does what, where, when, how, and to whom (task assignment plus establishment of benchmarks for periodic appraisals of individual and collective marketing efforts)
11. Staffing plan	Availability and requirements, based on schedules and tasks set up in number 10
12. Budgets	Resources committed, costs, risk analysis
13. Controls	Explanation of procedures for monitoring, measuring, and controlling the progress of the plan and results from the marketing staff
14. Continuity	Procedures and policies to keep the marketing plan updated

The five most important elements of a marketing plan, giving a basic format or outline for the plan, are these:

Summary, with conclusions
Environmental (situational) analysis

Goals and objectives
Strategies and tactics
Recommended actions (the action plan)

Content of the summary is self-evident; it naturally is the last thing written.

The second basic element—the environmental or situational analysis—is a little more complicated. In marketing, you must deal with a series of internal and external conditions, usually referred to as "independent variables." These variables are classified according to whether they are subject to control or manipulation by the selling organization.

Marketing Mix (controllable variables)
  Product (service)
  Place (distribution)
  Promotion
  Price
Situational Factors (uncontrollable variables)
  Demand
  Competition
  Economic climate
  Technological developments
  Government regulations

Variables which can be controlled are known as the "marketing mix." Sometimes called the "four Ps"—product, place, promotion, and price—they must be combined strategically to enable a firm to satisfy and sell to each target group. The four Ps are coequal in most marketing mixes:

1. We develop a service (or a package of services) we believe will satisfy the needs of identified and targeted market segments.

2. We then select the best channels (place) for reaching target clients.

3. Promotion tells target clients about the availability of the services designed for them.

4. The price (design fee) is established on the basis of expected client reaction to the service offered.

The marketing mix, by definition, is controllable to a large degree. Situational factors, on the other hand, make up the uncontrollable, external conditions sellers must adapt to in formulating and implementing a marketing plan. Situational factors may comprise both threats and opportunities in the SWOT team analysis.

Goals and Objectives As you will recall, the importance and role of marketing goals and objectives were discussed in Chapter 2. Marketers occasionally become confused about the difference between *objectives* and *forecasts*. These definitions should help:

1. *Forecast:* A qualitative or quantitative estimate of what a marketer *expects* to occur in the future.

2. *Objective:* A qualitative target or measure of operations that a marketer *wants* to occur in the future. An objective meets these three criteria:

- Feasibility
- Acceptability
- Capability of being achieved through a firm's own efforts

Here are examples of specific objectives for several marketing concerns:

1. Sales Productivity
- Increase the *number* of industrial clients by X percent by December 31, 198—.
- Increase *penetration* of the health care facilities market by X percent by December 31, 198—.
- Attain sales performance goals for calls per marketer, expense per call, fee volume per project sold, and number of calls per day, by a given amount per week, per month, and per quarter.

2. Profitability
- Increase overall return on investment by X percent for FY 198—.
- Increase the profit rate for each office by X percent by December 31, 198—.

3. Market share
- Increase by X percent our market share of the industrial market by December 31, 198—.

4. Distribution
- Establish X new branch offices in specific geographic areas (list the areas) by December 31, 198—.

One large consulting firm listed seven "specific objectives for 1981" in its marketing plan:

1. Capitalize on hospital design capability.
2. Reestablish preeminence in the field of airport design.
3. Improve the firm's overall design image by augmenting design capabilities and actively seeking national media coverage of noteworthy projects.
4. Improve the system for pursuing project leads.
5. Develop active participation in local civic and cultural activities, to express concern for the community and to demonstrate our capability to design significant projects.

6. Improve techniques for preparing and presenting proposals.

7. Increase the percentage of repeat business.

How do you feel about that list of "specific" objectives? They are pretty general, aren't they? Number 4, for example, reads: "Improve the system for pursuing leads." That's hard to argue with as an objective, but it's too vague for an action plan or to serve as a basis for performance measurement. Tactically, how is the firm going to improve its system?

1. Through a new or improved record keeping system?

2. By training its marketers to make better cold calls?

3. By improving on information gathering techniques in early one-on-one visits?

4. Through production of new sales tools?

5. By developing a better callback and follow-up system?

6. By tasking each marketer with so many visits per week?

These questions and many others of equal specificity must be answered in a marketing plan.

Goals, as we saw in Chapter 2, are less specific than the objectives by which a firm reaches its goals. As someone has pointed out, goals have three primary attributes:

1. Goals should contain stretch for the individual. At the end of, say, ten years you should have acquired ten years of experience rather than one year of experience ten times over.

2. Goals should be attainable. If they are too easy, the sweet smell of success will be missing; if too difficult, frustration may be the only reward. Stretch and attainability are the Siamese twins of success.

3. Goals should be measurable; otherwise, you have no way of knowing when you've hit the target. When goals can be measured in both quantitative and qualitative terms, the results attained should be clear to all.

The Action Plan   Much of the material gathered thus far for other sections of the marketing plan will come into focus as the action plan is worked out. Some of the information asked for in the following paragraphs may not be readily available—or is not available at all—from your firm's records. You may decide that certain record systems should be modified or expanded to make it easier to draw up future marketing plans.

Unless you have developed an alternative approach you like better, use this formula to begin the plan workup:

$$ABC - Y = D$$

A = percent of average annual carry-over billings (backlog) for your firm plus 1. If the average carry-over is 18 percent, A is 1.18.

B = the total amount of billings, in dollars, serviced by your company this year.

C = the annual desired percentage rate of growth for your firm, plus 1. (Just to cover inflation, the growth rate should be at least 12 percent. For minimal growth, the figure for C might be 1.15.)

Y = the unserviced, unbilled fees under contract for this year which will be carried over to the next year or years.

D = new billings (the gross fee goal) required for next year if your firm is to grow at the rate shown in C.

Finding A   Table 3-2 shows how to arrive at the figure to substitute for A in the formula:

Table 3-2   Calculating *A* in the Formula *ABC − Y = D*

Year	Carry-over	Total gross billings
3 years ago	$185,000	$ 990,000
2 years ago	200,000	1,100,000
Last year	220,000	1,250,000
	$605,000	$3,340,000

$$\frac{605,000}{3,340,000} = .18 = 18 \text{ percent average carry-over}$$

In this example, A will be be 1.18.

Finding B   The figure for B will come from your accounting or finance department. If you are preparing the marketing plan for next year in October or November of the current year, use the firm's past billing history to help you estimate the probable fee income for the last two or three months of this year. For purposes of illustration use $1,500,000 for this year's billings.

Finding C   C, the desired growth rate, is a management decision based, it is to be hoped, on past performance and on a realistic view of current economic conditions in your marketing area. For the example we'll use a 20 percent rate, making C = 1.20.

Finding Y   Y is the same kind of figure as A: the unserviced, unbilled fees under contract that will be carried over to next year—possibly the next several years. But because records for this year are incomplete as you prepare a marketing plan for next year, Y must be partially estimated—and is set out separately for that reason. (The carry-over figures used for *A* presumably are based on firm records.) To illustrate the process we'll let $Y = \$225,000$.

The formula is worked out as follows:

$$ABC - Y = D$$

$A = 1.18$
$B = \$1,500,000$
$C = 1.20$
$Y = \$225,000$
$D = 1.18 \times \$1,500,000 \times 1.2 - \$225,000$
$\quad = 2,124,000 - 225,000$
$\quad = \$1,899,000$

Rounding off, $D = \$1,900,000$; an increase of about $400,000 (26.6 percent) in billings over this year must be attained to reach the goal of 20 percent growth, taking actual and expected backlog into account.

Example Number 2 works out the formula $ABC - Y = D$ for a larger firm of, say, around 200 people:

$A = 1.19$
$B = \$7,890,000$
$C = 1.22$ (a 22 percent desired growth rate)
$Y = \$1,578,000$
$D = 1.19 \times \$7,890,000 \times 1.22 - \$1,578,000$
$\quad = 11,454,702 - 1,578,000$
$\quad = \$9,876,702$

Rounding off, $D = \$9,877,000$, an increase of $1,987,000 (25.2 percent) more than this year's billings.

(This information, after further proving, should be passed along to personnel for that department's future planning. In the second example, if 200 people produced $7,890,000 in billings this year [approximately $40,000 in billings per employee], new staff will have to be added or production increased, or both. If there is no productivity increase, the additional billings goal of $1,987,000 could require up to fifty more people to service the work.)

It often assists planning—and makes the goals appear less formidable—to break up the answer to *D* into monthly and weekly goals. In the first example, monthly requirements are $158,000; weekly needs are $36,000. In the second example, the monthly quota is $823,000; weekly requirements are $190,000.

These figures do not include carry-over work since that is considered in the formula, but they do include the cost of marketing efforts to bring in repeat and referral work. Figure 3-5 shows the sources of a firm's billings. The diagram makes the point that, on the average, most of your marketing budget will be spent on getting some 25 percent of next year's billings (totally new work).

Solving $ABC - Y = D$ tells you what you need in fees next year. You must now do some more work to find out where the fees should come from. Compile figures for the three years before the current year, covering traditional project types for your company. This will enable you to determine the average fee per project and total billings per project type—both of which will be needed in the next computation.

The figures shown in Table 3-3 might represent the company in the second example.

Figure 3-6 illustrates a form that some firms have found helpful in compiling the necessary information.

Knowing that almost $2 million in new fees will be needed next year, you can now select project types to concentrate on to reach the $2 million goal. One more federal hospital (at a fee of $880,000) and one more commercial office building (at a fee of $1.1 million) will take care of the requirements—or two more industrial projects (at an average fee of $550,000), one small state hospital (at a fee of $600,000), and three more planning jobs (at an average fee of $125,000 each) will bring the firm up to the fee goal.

As you can see, this is essentially a judgmental exercise—based on the firm's past project history and your research into present and future markets. Keep in mind that this is a work-sheet approach for determining your dollar billing goals; it is not a form for the IRS or your accountant.

The marketing plan thus far has been based on the known past history of your firm plus market research input. Obviously, if your research

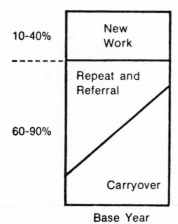

Figure 3-5 *Where the work comes from. New work averages 25 percent of total annual billings but requires most of the marketing budget to obtain.*

Table 3-3   Project and Fee Analysis

Project type	Number of projects	Average fee per project	Total billings per project type
		Last year	
I. Government			
A. Federal			
1. Office bldgs.	2	$ 975,000	$1,950,000
2. Hospitals	1	800,000	800,000
B. State			
1. Office bldgs.	1	750,000	750,000
II. Commercial			
A. Office/admin.	2	1,000,000	2,000,000
B. Industrial	4	500,000	2,000,000
C. Planning	3	130,000	390,000
		Total	$7,890,000

tells you that a specific project or client type is on the way out (is in the rapid decline section of the market life cycle), you'll adjust your thinking and the figures accordingly.

Nothing said thus far prohibits you from exploring new project or client types during the coming year (new in the market or new to your firm). One reason for doing market research is to pick up on new directions in markets. But new project types should be added to your list only *after* the historically safe project types have been listed and com-

	2 years ago		1 year ago		This year		Next year (est)	
	No. of Projects	$ Value	No. of Projects	$ Value	No. of Projects	$ Value	No. of Projects	$ Value
Market I								
A.								
B.								
C.								
Market II								
A.								
B.								
C.								
Market III								
A.								
B.								
C.								

Figure 3-6 *Use this form, adapted to your requirements, to help you determine traditional project types and fees for your firm.*

puted. Most marketers and principals prefer not to base marketing plans (and the future of their firm) on such "possibles." If projects from the new markets are obtained next year, they can be viewed as icing on the marketing cake.

The answer to $ABC - Y = D$ ($9,877,000 in the second example given earlier) should approximate the total of your computations in the recap and in your estimates of where the work will come from.

$7,890,000 (last year's billings)
+2,075,000 (from projects and projected billings)
$9,965,000

The goal for next year (D) is $9,877,000, so the estimated billings for new work to be brought in are close enough. If there is more than a 5 percent variance in the figures—especially on the low side—you need to go back and rework the sheet.

A Check on the Formula   Another approach to working out the marketing plan (and a check on the figures obtained from applying the $ABC - Y = D$ formula) comes at the subject from a different angle. The more ways you have to check the accuracy and practicality of a plan, the better. First, consider these marketing statistics and rules of thumb: Each full-time marketer should be responsible for between $1.5 and $2 million in annual billings ($25 to 40 million in construction costs). The $1.5 to 2 million includes both new business and generation of repeat and referral work. Our reference here is to an experienced, qualified marketer at or near the management level.

Several years ago, when I first set down the preceding numbers, many marketers and several principals questioned the individual billing quota. Another consultant, Robert Darling, independently arrived at a close approximation of the amount in his home-study course for the MGI Management Institute, *Successful Marketing of Architectural Services*.

Darling says that a "sales target for the full-time prospector should be established by taking his salary, plus fringes, plus direct expenses, multiplied by 20." He used an example of a $20,000-a-year marketing assistant (prospector):

(Salary + fringes + expenses) × 20 = sales target
($20,000 + $6000 + $4000) × 20 = $600,000 sales target

As we'll see in a few more pages, $20,000 doesn't buy an "experienced, qualified marketer," as stipulated in my equation. Substituting more realistic figures in Darling's sales target formula gives the following:

(Salary + fringes + expenses) × 20 = sales target
($50,000 + $15,000 + $20,000) × 20 = $1.7 million sales target

Darling also points out a necessary formula alteration to make it apply to part-time marketers—partners, associates, project managers, and the like. The modification: (Salary + fringes + expenses) × 20 × % of time factor = sales target.[4] In other words, the original equation is multiplied by 30 percent—if that is the percentage of time spent by a principal in marketing—to come up with a realistic sales goal for a higher-paid manager or owner.

1. Technical employees in most firms today should average $40,000 to $45,000 in annual billings. Some firms consistently hit from 15 to 25 percent higher than the guideline amounts.

2. One person working full time on cold-call qualification of prospects (primarily on the telephone) should average at least fifteen calls a day. (See Chapter 5, "How to Qualify Prospects.") That adds up to seventy-five calls per five-day week; 3750 calls per fifty-week year. If you use the conservative 50:5:1 ratio for guidance (fifty cold calls result in five presentations, from which you should get one job), the 3750 annual calls make the formula 3750:375:75. Seventy-five (2 percent) of the total number of cold calls should be converted into projects—and that is a very conservative conversion factor.

With dollar goals in hand, it is now time to task those in the firm who have marketing responsibilities. Figure 3-7 is a form to help you set up contact assignments for the action plan.

Unless you have in-house records to support a different win ratio, use the 50:5:1 proportion just discussed. The indicated win rate (20 percent) is about average. For example, if you want four dam projects next year, the 50:5:1 ratio tells you that 200 calls may be required. Individual assignments (so many calls per person) are listed on the tasking work sheet (Figure 3-7).

To finish out the work sheet and this section of the marketing plan, add up the number of calls to be made next year to get the work that will give the necessary billings as computed in *D*. A useful rule of thumb at this point is to estimate the time for each call at four hours. (See the bottom line of the tasking work sheet on the left side of the form.) If the work sheet shows a requirement for a total of 800 calls, you'll have an investment of 3200 hours in that segment of the marketing program. Modify any of these rules of thumb to reflect your own experience and records.

The four hours allotted to each call (or other type of contact) should easily cover all of the time required for research, follow-up (including additional calls on the same lead), proposal preparation, courting, and presentations. Remember that making the qualification cold call will take only a few minutes of the four-hour unit allotment. If a call takes

```
MARKETING PLAN WORKSHEET (Tasking for cold-call qualification assignments)


Number of      Calls required    Number of calls to be made    Person responsible     Number of
projects       per contract      per year          per week     for making calls       calls made

*1. _____   _____     _____   _____     _____   _____

                                                                _____   _____

2. _____    _____     _____   _____     _____   _____

                                                                _____   _____

3. _____    _____     _____   _____     _____   _____

                                                                _____   _____

4. _____    _____     _____   _____     _____   _____

                                                                _____   _____

5. _____    _____     _____   _____     _____   _____

                                                                _____   _____

6. _____    _____     _____   _____     _____   _____

                                                                _____   _____

        Total calls/year:    _____ x 4 hours/call =    _____  person/hours per year

                                                      x $_____  per hour chargeable rate

                                                      + $_____  annual base marketing budget

*These numbered entries refer to the project
 types listed on form in Figure 3-6.
```

Figure 3-7 *A marketing plan work sheet, for use in tasking cold-call qualification assignments.*

ten minutes to complete, three hours and fifty minutes remain from that call unit to apply forward to the relatively small number of contacts that will require more work in marketing and selling. (Business development, one marketing executive has observed, is an activity requiring one to deal routinely and constantly with negatives and failures; negatives in selection, when your firm is pared from the short list, and failures in that you must expect to land far less than half of the projects you pursue.) The 50:5:1 rule of thumb tells you that just one call in fifty leads to success; the other forty-nine calls aren't going anywhere. The fact that you don't know which of the fifty calls will be the one that leads to internal personal fame and corporate fortune is part of the challenge and most of the motivation. Try not to dwell on these more negative aspects of professional design services marketing.

To obtain your base marketing costs, multiply annual hours of work by individual hourly rates. It generally is considered improper to apply an overhead factor to these figures since you are dealing with overhead. Using the 3200 hours mentioned earlier as an example, times an average hourly rate of $30, gives a base marketing cost of $96,000. That figure, plus all other marketing costs for dues, brochures, audiovisual materials, public relations, and the like, can be related back to the dollar amount computed for D in the formula. A total marketing budget typically runs from 4 to 11 percent of gross billings.

Another marketing rule of thumb that may be helpful in checking your planning is this: marketing budgets average out to a 75:25 percent break between personnel costs and materials. If your marketing budget for next year is $100,000, with between $75,000 and $80,000 allocated to personnel costs and $20,000 to $25,000 for indirect costs, you are in the ball park.

The guidelines given thus far are based on the experience of several hundred design firms, augmented by the results of surveys conducted by various organizations over the past several years. A 1980 survey of design firms by Birnberg & Associates showed that the relationship of total staff to marketing staff averaged 55:1 (the median figure was 71:1). Another survey made the same year (for the Society for Marketing Professional Services) found the ratio of total staff to marketing staff to be 22:1.

Logic, without regard to the survey results cited, tells us that a firm with annual gross billings of approximately $1 million (and a $50,000 annual marketing budget) *may* be justified in adding a full-time marketing director. Based on yearly production of $40,000 per technical employee, a firm with thirty to thirty-five employees could consider hiring a marketing specialist.

My personal rule-of-thumb range for bringing in one or more full-time marketers calls for the firm to have a staff of between thirty-five and fifty. At that size the firm is large enough (has enough income) to support the cost of a marketer until he or she becomes productive—which could be as long as eighteen months from the time of hire. The other side of the coin is that the firm also has enough staff in all probability to handle the initial extra workload that will result from the marketer's activities; that is, new technical employees will not have to be added on a crash basis.

None of the preceding should be taken to mean that a firm having a staff of, say, thirty-five must have a full-time marketer—or that you cannot have one until you reach thirty-five people. I know of ten-person firms with full-time marketers and of 150-person firms without a full-time marketing staff.

Yet another approach holds that every hour devoted to selling design services should generate about twenty hours of billable work. A firm with thirty technical people working at 75 percent efficiency—thus assuming 2000 annual working hours—would require around 2250 hours of marketing support on an annual basis.

$$\frac{30 \times 2000 \times .75}{20} = 2250$$

This shows a requirement for 1.1 marketers for the firm with thirty technical employees, a further indication that a ratio of total staff to marketing staff of 35:1 for small- to medium-sized firms is about right. As a firm increases in size, the ratio may well hit the higher 55:1 proportion reported in the Birnberg study.

Performance Measurement In *Marketing Research: An Applied Approach,* the authors Thomas Kinnear and James Taylor make this cogent point:

> Modern marketing management requires a control mechanism to monitor the effectiveness of the marketing program and to detect changes in the situational factors. Control involves:
>
> 1. setting standards of performance in order to reach objectives.
> 2. measuring actual performance against these standards.
> 3. taking action to correct deviations in performance.[5]

In short, your marketing program must

Establish standards
Measure performance
Correct deviations from the plan

Some of the objective standards suitable for use in rating marketing effectiveness are

Number of cold calls made
Number of personal sales calls made
  ■ On prospects
  ■ On past clients
Amount of business brought in from past clients
Amount of business brought in from new clients
Proposals
  ■ How many RFPs (request for proposal) received
  ■ How many proposals written
  ■ Capture or win rate on submittals (numbers and dollars)
Accuracy of probability assignments to prospects

Number of formal presentations
- Designed and produced
- Appeared in, as MC or as contributor
- Win rate

Overall performance in meeting quotas for
- Leads found
- Contacts made (leads qualified)
- Proposals submitted
- Dollar volume of fees generated

Promotion return rate (the dollar value of projects won per marketing dollar invested)

Accuracy and timeliness of submitting required internal marketing reports

Attendance at scheduled marketing meetings

Oriented more to public relations and general promotional activities are these performance criteria:

General quality of marketing tools
- How many new ones produced

Effectiveness of advertisements (response to)

Public perception of firm's image
- Image improved, in status quo, or worse?

Number of news and feature articles written and placed

Number of design awards won

Number of trade shows and association meetings attended or exhibited at

These standards admittedly are more results-oriented than style-oriented. Some call the process managing to commitment; what it really means is that we shouldn't worry too much about how someone holds the bat, but should be much more concerned with how often he or she hits the ball.

We have dealt so far with monitoring those with a primary—or at least a major—marketing responsibility. Some of the same type of attention and emphasis on marketing results should be directed to the firm's nonmarketing staff. The regular employee review form should have at least one item related to the technical or production staff person's participation, effectiveness, and interest in business development activities. And it should be common knowledge internally that bonuses, promotions, raises, and other perks are dependent to some degree (the greater, the better) on how this rating item is scored by supervisors.

A performance evaluation sheet for marketers might take the general form of the one illustrated in Figure 3-8, which is based on several such rating forms now in use by design firms. Evaluating other staff members is a little more complex, for their general administrative, production, and technical skills must be fully considered as well. One firm covers overall performance by rating these eight points:

1. Effectiveness in carrying out assignments accurately and on schedule.
2. Technical knowledge.
3. Written and oral skills, especially in correspondence, report writing, and giving instructions.
4. Ability and judgment—as applied to problem recognition and resolution, decision making, and the like.
5. Business development activity, specifically, evidence of individual initiative in attracting new clients and in developing new projects among existing and past clients.
6. Client relations. Supervisors rate on the points of effectiveness, innovation, constructiveness, and responsiveness in dealing with clients.
7. Group development—the degree of success in individual counseling and advisory activities with his or her subordinate staff.
8. Participation in civic, professional, and social activities; covers the individual being evaluated and the degree to which he or she encourages participation by subordinates.

Items 3, 5, and 8 are specifically related to marketing activities; numbers 4 and 6 have some relationship to it.

Another firm's individual assessment form includes ratings of nonmarketing employees' personal and professional reputation outside the firm, their ability to identify prospects and new markets, and their record of securing new work. How such ratings are weighted in the overall evaluation is a key to the emphasis a firm wants placed on marketing. A few firms weight marketing activities as high as 40 percent of the total evaluation score.

THE MARKETING STAFF

One of the many principles of management tells us that, as a rule, 80 percent of key outputs are directly attributable to 20 percent of the key inputs. From that precept comes such management insights as these:

1. Twenty percent of a firm's staff is responsible for 80 percent of the firms's productivity.
2. Eighty percent of all internal resistance toward new systems comes from 20 percent of your employees.

```
Marketing Department Staff Evaluation


Marketing
Representative _____ Date _____

Evaluation Period _____

General Marketing Assignment _____

_____

_____



Special Assignments During Evaluation Period _____

_____

_____

_____



General Breakdown of Time Spent (as a percentage of time available)

                        This Period      Year to Date

    Sales Calls     _____

    Marketing       _____

    Billable Time   _____

    Other           _____

(See back of sheet for breakdown by activity units)



Comments and Overall Evaluation     (By: _____)

_____

_____

_____


Employee's Comments _____

_____

_____
```

Figure 3-8 *A form for evaluating marketing staff.*

This principle is no doubt about as mutable as most of those popularly supposed to govern management and marketing, but it can't hurt to try to select your marketing staff from the right 20 percent of your employees. (There, incidentally, is one of the true principles of the non-science, marketing. Hundreds, perhaps thousands, of marketing decisions are made every day on the simple basis of "if it can't hurt, it might help—so do it.")

In an effort to provide some guidance in what was essentially an uncharted professional area just a few years ago, a variety of job-person descriptions and definitions for marketing directors and coordinators have appeared in the last ten years. A fairly standard job description was presented by Weld Coxe at a University of Wisconsin marketing workshop in August 1977. The same material was used by Louis Marines in a Boston workshop sponsored by SMPS (Society for Marketing Professional Services) in 1980.

JOB DESCRIPTION: DIRECTOR OF MARKETING

General description: Under the general direction of the board, plans and coordinates all marketing activities of the firm. Respnsibilities involve developing and executing a marketing program which consists of establishing long-range marketing goals and near-term objectives; selecting target markets, building lists and screening leads; contacting and cultivating prospects and, in close coordination with the board, obtaining contracts for projects in the firm's design specialty.

Specific Duties:

1. Has major responsibilities for developing and executing a marketing plan which outlines all major aspects of a planned marketing effort including appropriate objectives, tasks, assignments of responsibility to individuals and budgets. The marketing plan is to be approved by the board. The remaining specific duties are to be performed within the framework of the marketing plan.

2. Determines what specific markets the firm will cultivate. This determination will be made after careful appraisal of the likely market opportunities for the firm in several possible markets that may be evaluated.

3. Determines volumetric objectives (for example, number of projects and fee volume) for the firm as a whole and for each selected target market.

4. Establishes performance objectives for each selected market. These objectives will include

   a. The number and fee volume of projects or commissions desired (in each target market).

   b. The number of interviews likely to be required to generate the desired number of commissions.

   c. The number of personal and telephone contacts likely to be required to generate the desired number of interviews.

   d. The number of organizations (for example, former and present clients, prospects, leads, and the like) to be contacted and cultivated.

   e. The number of days (per week, per month, and so on) to be spent by specific individuals in business development activities.

5. Operates directly or through designated marketing coordinator to develop lists of individuals, or projects, or of individuals and projects to be contacted.

6. Operates directly or through designated marketing coordinator to organize and screen leads and prospects to produce an efficient procedure for scheduling contacts.

7. Operates directly or through designated marketing coordinator to ensure that appropriate individuals are assigned, scheduled, and equipped to make the desired business development contacts.

8. Maintains a record and control system to alert appropriate individuals when contacts are to be made; the system is also to serve as a log for recording all marketing activities.

9. Maintains an activity review system for the marketing committee and the board as it may desire.

10. Maintains a control system to measure the performance of the marketing effort.

11. Develops strategies for cultivating prospects and obtaining work at the firm, specific target market, and individual prospect and project levels.

12. Makes direct contacts with leads, prospects, clients, influentials, and others; coordinates the activities of others who are also making contacts, presentations, holding interviews, and the like. This coordination activity will include providing others with materials and information needed to carry out the business development activities.

13. Takes primary responsibility for determining what materials and information are needed, coordinating the production of such materials and information. This will include graphic brochures, presentation materials, U.S. government Standard Forms 254 and 255, business development correspondence, and so on.

14. Takes primary responsibility for preparing proposals, coordinating such activities with appropriate management and project manager staff.

15. Plays a coordinating role in preparing content for interviews and presentations, including determining the appropriate participation by other specific personnel.

If it needs to be said, the ideal marketer of professional design services will be registered, with some experience in successful project design and administration. His or her degree in architecture or engineering will be supplemented with a business degree, preferably an M.B.A.

Marketing Staff Compensation   The amount you'll have to pay to bring a productive marketing director into your firm is subject to the usual job market vagaries and variables such as geographic location (of both the candidate and your office), specialties and major disciplines of your firm, the present condition of your marketing program, size of the firm (with concomitant requirements for annual fee and profit growth), and the like. These days it would be easier to tempt most marketers to move to Phoenix than to Detroit, for example, as well as to be able to offer a workable, in-place marketing plan rather than the opportunity to start at some form of marketing ground zero. It is a seller's market for those with a provable track record of selling success with other firms. Some marketing directors currently have annual incomes on a par with those who own the firm; a select few make more than the owners.

Dependable, applicable salary information is still somewhat difficult to locate. A 1980 study by SMPS and the *A/E Marketing Journal* offers limited guidance. Mean and median annual base salaries for eight marketing classifications were covered in the survey. Omitted were high and low ranges and the potentially significant effect of bonuses, profit sharing, stock options, and other fringe benefits such as company-provided automobiles, club memberships, educational benefits, and generous expense accounts. A summary of the 1980 results is presented in Table 3-4.[6]

Table 3-4   Summary of a 1980 Study of Marketing Salaries

Position	Mean	Median
Marketing principal	$46,119	$44,995
Marketing director	34,527	34,246
Public relations director	24,101	24,240
Marketing manager	27,620	25,600
Sales representative	26,533	27,002
Marketing coordinator	18,381	16,016
Administrative assistant	12,955	12,510
Graphics specialist	15,752	15,025

Average salaries for the three top positions by size of firm are shown in Table 3-5.[7]

Table 3-5   Average Salaries for Three Top Positions in Marketing

Size	Marketing principal	Marketing director	Marketing coordinator
1–25	$37,212	$25,125	$18,312
26–75	45,734	31,721	16,085
76–200	54,142	36,750	20,636
201–499	54,883	37,583	16,215
Over 500	50,000	39,000	23,000

We have, as you must realize, covered a lot of important ground in this chapter in an attempt to point you in most of the right directions for constructing and implementing an effective marketing plan. The next step is to develop productive lists of prospects, which is the subject of Chapter 4.

REFERENCES

[1]Rita Tatum, "Nationwide Survey Reveals Marketing's Total Effectiveness," *Building Design & Construction*, April 1976, p. 46.

[2]Theodore Levitt, "Marketing When Things Change," *Harvard Business Review*, November-December 1977, pp. 107–108. Reprinted by permission. Copyright © 1977 by the President and Fellows of Harvard College; all rights reserved.

[3]Randall Shores, "Market Research Methods," *A/E Marketing Journal*, March 1981, p. 3.

[4]Robert B. Darling, *Successful Marketing of Architectural Services*, MGI Management Institute, Inc., Larchmont, N.Y., 1978, Unit II, p. 3–11.

[5]Thomas C. Kinnear and James R. Taylor, *Marketing Research: An Applied Approach*, McGraw-Hill Book Company, New York, 1979, p. 11.

[6]*1980 Marketing Salary and Expense Survey*, the Society for Marketing Professional Services and *A/E Marketing Journal*, Washington, D.C., 1980, p. 5.

[7]Ibid.

Chapter 4
WHERE TO FIND PROSPECTS

"**E**thical purity, triply distilled, would restrain [the architect] from any more direct or semi-direct business chasing than is practiced by the family doctor. That would be exactly none at all, and so it was in the old days to a considerable degree."[1]

So wrote architect cum marketer Royal Barry Wills more than forty years ago. The term "business chasing" must have been a shocking one to his fellow practitioners in 1941; even today some professional dodoes have trouble with such terms as "marketing" and "selling." The euphemistic "business development" is still preferred in more firms than you would expect. Whatever name it goes by, selling *is* practiced in one form or another by every U.S. and Canadian design firm—and, increasingly, by design firms in Europe, in Australia, and in sundry other outposts of the free world. The primary differences among offices is in the degree, organization, and success of the chase.

PACAT SYSTEM

The bureaucratic-sounding acronym PACAT describes a base system for lead finding and intelligence gathering. The initial letters stand for participation, alertness, curiosity, awareness, and timing.

1. Active *participation* in community affairs.
2. *Alertness* to job leads from friends, family, and acquaintances in business, education, and government.
3. *Curiosity* to become *aware* of other disciplines and expertise beyond the normally assumed scope of knowledge; methods of construc-

tion financing, speculative building projects, and governmental participation in funding, to name a few.

4. *Timing* (the fourth and most critical dimension) as applied to everything we do.

Here is another method of outlining the client acquisition process:

Identification
Qualification
Investigation
Planning (strategy and tactics)
Pursuit
Close

PROSPECT IDENTIFICATION

Before marketers get into prospect sources, it is important for them to have a reasonable idea of what types of prospects they should be looking for. Some kind of internal breakdown of desirable prospects should be readily available to all of those with marketing responsibilities. If a firm has the capability, the list may be computerized.

Some firms, particularly those heavily into government projects, find the three-digit experience profile code in standard form 254 works well for this purpose. Ranging from "001—Acoustics; Noise Abatement" to "117—Zoning; Land Use Studies," the S.F. 254 code represents the best efforts of federal clients to cover the full gamut of project types.

Another standard building type of breakdown lists projects under six major divisions and eighteen subgroups. This less-detailed format may be more practical for smaller, single-discipline firms. (Note that most civil work in the following list would fall under the "other" subheadings.)

Commercial
   ■ Low-rise
   ■ High-rise
   ■ Industrial
Community
   ■ Planning and design, nongovernment
   ■ Urban design and redevelopment, including public housing
Federal government
   ■ Office and service
   ■ Hospitals-health
   ■ Defense and space
   ■ Other (not including housing)

State and local government
- Office and service
- Educational
- Hospitals-health
- Other (not including housing)

Institutional
- Educational, private
- Hospitals-health, private

Residential
- Private, single
- Low-rise (not including public housing)
- High-rise (not including public housing)

Finally, the classifications used for Dodge Construction Statistics should be detailed enough for practically any firm. The four major project types are

Residential
Nonhousekeeping residential
Nonresidential building
Nonbuilding structures-engineering construction

Under "residential," for example, are these subcategories:

One-family houses
Two-family houses
Apartment buildings; three or four housing units
Apartment buildings; five or more units; one to three stories
Apartment buildings; five or more units; four stories or more

The detailed categorization used by F. W. Dodge has the advantage of covering all types of engineering input, along with many specialized consultancies.

Selectivity   As this is written, the world's economic conditions are not the brightest. In some ways the times are comparable to those of the early 1970s, when the first edition of *How to Market Professional Design Services* was published. The most apparent difference is that many design firms have learned to market their services aggressively in the intervening decade. Competition for every project is greater—and, for truly significant projects, vying for position assumes major battle proportions. If you are to make the best use of your marketing budget, you must identify and capitalize on your real strengths. In two words—*be selective.*

Whereas proposals and formal presentations can rather easily be identified as high-cost stages of the marketing process, *any* pursuit of a job is a drain on the marketing budget. If a firm persists in what consultant David Travers calls "hopeless chases after the wrong jobs," hard times—even bankruptcy—lie ahead. In a 1975 article for the *AIA Journal*, Travers wrote:

> The inclination is to go after anything and everything, especially if you're a worried practitioner who is winding up drawings on the last job in the shop. The theory is: "Buy chances on enough lotteries, and you're bound to win one." Even the A/E juggernauts, who should know better, frequently base the decision on what work to pursue on something other than a hard appraisal of their chances to get the job and the costs of trying. A juicy commission on the horizon can cloud the judgment. For example, a Midwest firm with no hospital experience—not so much as an outpatient clinic to its credit—made a costly effort to get three large hospital projects, pitting itself against firms which had done thousands of beds. This is an instructive example of hope subduing reason.[2]

Resolve to put reason ahead of hope in your marketing efforts; know your real strengths (and weaknesses); identify the prospect- and project-types you have a real chance to get. With the thoughtful, objective self-qualification out of the way, we are ready to consider prospect qualification.

PROSPECT QUALIFICATION

Qualification, the second stage in the client acquisition process, deals with the important question: Is it a real job? In other words, is the project apt to go just so far down the line and then founder for one reason or another, or does it appear to stand a reasonable chance of being completed? Today's architects and engineers have little interest in designing vast projects—or even small ones—which do not go on to completion. Certainly, if the contract was properly negotiated, work done will be paid for up to the point the job goes on the shelf—but profits and reputations are not made from plans gathering dust in some corporation's storeroom or government warehouse.

Two prime indicators of the credibility of a prospective job are the status of its financing and the present status of its program development. If you skip ahead to the first paragraph of Chapter 5, which goes into painstaking detail about project qualification, you'll see that there really are only two questions to be answered in this early marketing stage:

1. Is it a job?
2. Is it a job for my firm?

Conscientious telephone prospect qualifiers could do worse than to type out and paste those two questions in a prominent place by their telephones.

PROSPECT MIX

Part of the success of any marketing program depends on the marketer's ability to maintain a continuous flow of leads into the marketing department. The prospect triangle (Figure 4-1) was developed to illustrate this point graphically.

At the top of the triangle, section A holds the hottest, most promising prospects: prospects with specific, identified jobs that your firm can do—all of whom have shown at least some interest in your firm. Many prospects in the A group will be past and lost clients—thus, the designation "Client Relations" for the handling of these leads. Prospects normally move out of section A through award of the project.

The second level, B, is composed of prospects the firm has reason to believe will have work coming up. The primary difference between A and B prospects is that the latter group probably has little, if any, direct knowledge of your firm or of your interest in being considered for a job. An example of a B prospect would be IBM (if you have not previously worked for the company). IBM-type corporations are continually building something somewhere. Because a marketing strategy must be developed to move B prospects into the A level, this segment is called "Stategic Marketing."

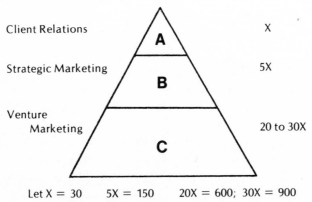

Let X = 30   5X = 150   20X = 600; 30X = 900

Figure 4-1 *The prospect triangle. X represents the number of hot prospects required to ensure steady work and continuing growth for your firm.*

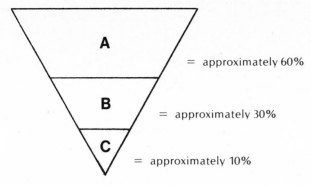

= approximately 60%

= approximately 30%

= approximately 10%

Figure 4-2 *Inverting the triangle gives some guidance for marketing budget allotments to cover each of the sections in the prospect triangle.*

Section C is a large, amorphous group of relatively unproven prospects. They might more properly be called "suspects" or "possibles." Fed from many sources, the leads in C may come from government and industry indexes, lists of hospital administrators, school superintendents, building owners, prison wardens—anything the prospect net might collect in its periodic sweeps that is not specific enough to go into section A or section B. Probably none of these prospects will be familiar with your firm. This is venture marketing in its truest sense. The importance of keeping section C full of leads—however nebulous or tenuous they may be at this point—should be evident.

Movement of prospects within the pyramid usually is upward following their entry as suspects and probables into section C. An occasional lead will go directly into B—or even into the A section.

Figure 4-2 shows the budget concentrations on each of the prospect triangle sections. As might be expected, the diagram takes an inverted pyramid form, with the largest share allotted to the relatively few prospects in section A. As guidance, perhaps 60 percent of the marketing budget will go to resolve the leads represented in A; around 30 percent, on the leads in B; and the remaining amount, for nurturing section C leads. The three-level prospect triangle concept may be helpful in assigning staff and budget to the most productive areas.

Another way of viewing the lead-finding process is shown in Figure 4-3. The linear model uses Categories 1, 2, and 3 rather than the lettered sections of the prospect triangle, with 1 corresponding to the triangle's section A, 2 to section B, and 3 to section C.

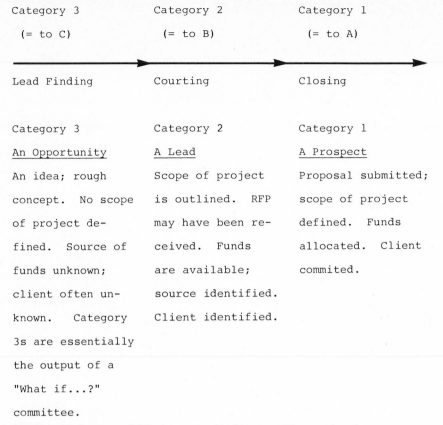

Figure 4-3 *A linear model for prospect development. The numbered categories correspond generally to the lettered divisions of the prospect triangle.*

PROSPECT SOURCES

In August 1977 the newsletter of the Society for Marketing Professional Services carried the results of a membership survey on lead sources. The question: "Apply percentages to show how you derive most of your new leads." The answers, averaged, were:

Personal prospecting and cold calls	45.51%
Tips, referrals	24.96
Clipping services, newspapers	14.74
Lead services (Dodge Reports, *CBD*, newsletter tip sheets, and the like)	13.79
Community service organizations (Lions, Rotary, Chamber of Commerce, YMCA, and the like)	9.06

Professional organizations (AIA, NSPE, ACEC, and the
like) 6.96
Other (most common: past clients) 21.49

This is the only such survey I know of, which is the primary reason for reprinting it. The results may or may not be valid today, but the percentages look about right.

In Marketing Management Workshops in past years, a sheet headed "Lead Generation" was distributed to participants. Lead sources were classified as either "live" or "printed."

The most obvious—and often the most neglected—live source of leads is clients—lost, past, and present. Lost clients are those you stayed with through selection interviews, losing out to another firm at the very end. The implications are that you did almost everything right to have been included on the final short list—and to abandon all hope at that stage is to write off a lot of marketing time and dollars.

Let lost clients know of your intention to keep trying with them. And make it clear that you now consider them to be part of your firm's marketing network; that you expect to hear about their future projects as well as job leads from their business and social contacts.

The same approach should be taken with past and present clients. Make it perfectly clear that you want and expect to do future work for them and explain your expectations concerning their activities on behalf of your prospect information-gathering efforts. Clients normally don't volunteer this kind of help, but most will respond positively when asked.

Another way past clients can be of significant help to your marketing program is by writing letters of endorsement when their job is finished. Once again, few clients volunteer to write such letters; it is up to the marketer or project manager to generate the endorsement at an appropriate time. Be ready with suggestions for the contents of the letter; better yet, have a sample of the kind of letter you want with you when the request is made. Some clients will ask you to write the letter for them on their stationery. That's acceptable—just be sure they sign it.

Nonclient live sources include

Your own staff
Bankers
Lawyers
Other consultants
Suppliers
Developers
Contractors

Newspaper business editors and reporters
Chamber of commerce
State and local development commissions
Politicians

Most of the nonclient live sources should give you no problem. Frequently ignored sources of much good information are newspaper editors and reporters, especially those who regularly cover business subjects. Don't make a pest of yourself, but don't hesitate to ask for brief meetings on a more or less regular basis, so they can keep you up to date about trends and any specific projects they know of (and can talk about without violating confidences).

Printed sources include

1. Commercial job-lead newsletters and other private lead sources.

2. *Commerce Business Daily* (the U.S. government's official lead tip publication).

3. State-issued publications on their own projects, such as the ones available from Florida and Maryland.

(It is important to keep in mind that leads from the preceding three sources are nonexclusive; all subscribers will have the lead information at about the same time.)

4. Newspapers. General: *New York Times, Washington Post,* local weeklies and dailies. Specialized: *Barron's, Wall Street Journal,* local business-oriented papers.

5. Clipping services. National (Luce, Burrelle's, Bacon's), regional, state, and local. Many firms have set up informal, in-house clipping services.

6. Corporate annual reports.

7. Noncommercial newsletters—free from banks, associations, government departments and agencies, and international lending agencies.

8. Magazines. General: *Time, Newsweek, Fortune.* Trades: *Architectural Record, Engineering News-Record, Building Design & Construction, AIA Journal, Consulting Engineer,* and the like.

9. Directories. Trade association listings; special publications such as the *Catalog of Federal Domestic Assistance.*

10. Press releases—from governmental, quasi-governmental, and international lending agencies (IADB, IMF, UNDP).

Commercial Job-Lead Publications Because all subscription rates seem to move inexorably upward, prices are not given for these publications. Rates for all of them have increased from 100 to several hundred percent since 1973 and the first edition of *How to Market Professional Design*

Services. If you are interested in learning more about any of the sources listed, write to the address given and ask for a review copy. Most publishers are happy to honor such requests; at the very least you will receive current promotional material with subscription costs.

All commercial lead services have one point in common: to find and qualify the leads they sell, someone must first pick up the telephone and call a prospect, inquire about potential building plans, and record the information in a usable format. If you still believe there is any more to successful lead finding and qualification than that, then the next chapter on prospect qualification should remove any remaining mysteries about the process.

Sales Prospector   This newsletter is published monthly in fourteen U.S. regional editions (sample regional coverage: New England states, Ohio River Valley; Texas, Oklahoma, and New Mexico) by Prospector Research Services, Inc., 751 Main Street, Waltham, MA 02254. A Canadian report also is available. According to a *Sales Prospector* promotion piece, the newsletter's sources include "permit applications, registry filings, news releases, press stories, and telephone conversations with local sources." Copies of the *Prospector* reviewed turned up relatively few listings before design consultants are hired. For architects and engineers, it is a better information source about the activities of their competitors than of substantive project leads.

Engineering News-Record   The "Pulse" section of *EN-R* carries bid calls, low bids, plans, and contracts. Few leads appear prior to hiring design consultants, but the section is worth following with some regularity. It is published weekly by McGraw-Hill, 1221 Avenue of the Americas, New York, NY 10020.

Weekly Construction Preview   (successor to the several job-lead newsletters from National Building News Service)   It is published by National Building News Service, Inc., Harrisville, NH 03450. The editor is Mark Wildman.

Million Dollar Project Planned List   It is a monthly job-listing service from Live Leads Corporation, 200 Madison Avenue, New York, NY 10016. Expensive. Projects of more than 50,000 square feet in size or $1 million in cost are listed in the planning stage and classified by state and building type. Aggregate construction value of the some 5000 projects covered on an annual basis now stands at around $32 billion. A companion lead service, the *Industrial Project Planned List*, features projects in industrial, manufacturing, warehousing, and engineering categories. The *Million Dollar Project Bid List*, also from Live Leads, is a monthly listing of projects in the bidding stage and, therefore, is of primary interest to suppliers and contractors.

The HSA Report   Published monthly, this newsletter concentrates on medical facility construction projects of at least $1 million in estimated construction costs. About a third of the jobs in most issues are in the stage before designer selection—and those are called out by asterisks to save search time. The same lead information is available to anyone who wants to contact continually the 3100 county and parish Health Systems Agencies in the United States. Short of that effort, if health facility design is of interest to your firm, the newsletter appears to be the easiest way to stay current. It comes from James & Douglas Publishers, Inc., P.O. Box 7375, Marietta, GA 30065.

Project Alert System   One of several marketing services offered by Tecton Media, Inc., *Project Alert* is available by state, select markets (health care, educational, industrial, commercial, and government), nine regions, or for any combination up to full national coverage. Subscribers are limited to a maximum of 100 firms per region. *Project Alert* interviewers annually call more than 20,000 major U.S. owners to ask about future construction plans, and this results in an average of 1000 leads a year for each region. At least half of the projects turned up are in the stage before designer selection. Subscribers receive weekly mailings of leads from their area or areas. (See Figure 4-4.) *Project Alert* is one of the few lead tip sources where costs have come down; annual cost for all regions (total U.S. coverage) in 1978 was $12,000. In 1981 the annual all-regions coverage was $6900. For information, contact Warren Friedman, President, Tecton Media, Inc., 350 Madison Avenue, New York, NY 10017. You might ask for a copy of Tecton Media's general capabilities brochure. Since corporate brochure design and production are another service offered by the firm, its promotional material is predictably first class.

Consulting Opportunities   A lead service, it is presently limited to A-E projects in Florida and can be obtained from Richard Pugh, P.O. Box 19814, Orlando, FL 32814.

Commerce Business Daily   Published five days a week by the U.S. Department of Commerce, it is available through the nearest Department of Commerce field office or from the Superintendent of Documents, U.S. Government Printing Office, Washington, DC 20402. It contains unclassified requests for bids and proposals, procurements reserved for small businesses, contractors seeking subcontract assistance, upcoming sales of government property, prime contracts awarded, research and development leads, current foreign government procurement offers, and nongovernmental export opportunities for American firms. All federal jobs are not listed in the *CBD;* see Chapter 12, "Selling to the Govern-

Tecton Media Incorporated   *Project Alert System®(PAS)®*   **New Business Lead**

350 Madison Ave., New York, N.Y. 10017 (212) 867-0820

Location   : (a)&(b)Chicago (c)Outway, Ill   Date: Feb. 25, 1977

Project (s) : (a)Manuf facil*-computr eqpt (b)Whse (new constr) (c)Whse (expan)

Value/Size : (a)$6-$8 mil; 240,000 sq ft; 2 story (b)Approx $2.75 mil; 150,000 sq ft; lo-rise (c)$1.6 mil; lo-rise

Owner   :
Castle Corporation   Line of Business: mfg computr prts/
549 Oldham St.-P.O. Box 3735   eqpt/data processr
Outway, IL 10498 Tel.: 821-453-0041

Contact   :
Ralph Simon, VP & Chief Engr.

Timetable : Begin Construction (a)Early '78   Completion (a)Mid-'79
                          (b)1979-80   (b)Late 1980
                          (c)Summer '77   (c)Nov '77

Status   : Architect: Selecting: Construction Manager:
                      (a)Apr '77   (a)&(b)Would use
                      (b)Spring '78   (c)Would not use
           Engineer:(c)w/in 60 days   Site:
                      (a)Sep '77   (a)&(b)Selected
                      (b)Spring '78
          Contractor:(c)w/in 60 days   Land:
                      (a)Early '78   (a)&(b)Acquired
                      (b)Fall '78
                      (c)w/in 60 days

Influencing Factors :

Comments   : Have in-house supervisory staff for programming & design.
              *Corporation plans 2 more manuf facils in Midwest over next 5 yrs; plans 1 renov of an existing plant.

<u>BUSINESS DEVELOPMENT RECORD</u>

<u>Follow-up</u>	<u>Principal</u>	<u>Action</u>	<u>Date</u>	<u>Comments</u>

® Service Mark of Tecton Media. Incorporated
c Tecton Media Incorporated 1975

Figure 4-4 *A sample lead sheet from Project Alert.*

ment," for some of the exceptions. Section R of the *Commerce Business Daily* carries most of the project announcements of interest to design firms.

From the State Capitals   Some three dozen newsletters on different subjects appear under the umbrella title *From the State Capitals*. Subscribers may take one, some, or all of the reports, which vary from weekly to monthly frequency. Of the most job-lead value to design firms are the reports about

Airport construction and financing
Highway financing and construction
Housing and redevelopment
Industrial development
Institutional building
Parks and recreation trends
Public health
School construction
Waste disposal and pollution control
Urban transit and bus transportation

Keyes Walworth took over publication of the *State Capitals* newsletters in 1981: Wakeman-Walworth, Inc., 396 Orange Street, New Haven, CT 06511.

The preceding services are only a sampling of the variety and coverage of printed lead sources for professional design firms—and is not intended to be a complete listing of all such services. Some, like *Consulting Opportunities*, cover a single state. A few others appear to be too specialized in their subject coverage to warrant listing here.

Some marketing consultants work to the specific requirements of a few clients. For example, David Rogier (Rogier Associates, 1111 E. 54th Street, Indianapolis, IN 46220) takes on exclusive lead search and generation assignments for individual client firms. By project or discipline type, Rogier's staff might contact 100 prospects on behalf of a design firm client. Similar in some respects to *Project Alert*, it differs chiefly in that any active leads uncovered will go only to the client that commissioned the Rogier survey.

Clipping Services   The long-established, major clipping services in the United States include

Luce Press Clippings
420 Lexington Avenue
New York, NY 10170

Burrelle's Press Clipping Service
75 E. Northfield Avenue
Livingston, NJ 07039

Bacon's Clipping Bureau
14 E. Jackson Boulevard
Chicago, IL 60604

There are many local clipping bureaus, serving metropolitan areas, single states, and multistate regions. Look under "Clipping Bureaus" in the Yellow Pages. (For whatever it's worth, when I was verifying addresses for the three clipping bureaus, the telephone operator at Bacon's was the only one who tried to market their services to me. She was pleasant [not pushy], offered to send me information, and quoted the current rates without being asked.)

The secret of successfully using news clippings as part of a firm's intelligence gathering is in the completeness of the instructions (specifications) the clipping service works from. Your original instructions are important, but they should be reviewed and amended as necessary, at least every six months. Clipping services can and do get off the track with individual clients. Their readers are not design professionals or technicians, so a tight set of specs is furnished as self-protection. Obviously, clipping services make a profit from producing clippings— whether or not the clippings are usable by their clients.

My instructions to clipping services are based on personal requirements at the time, but many of the specifications have general application. An important point: you must tell the service what to omit, as well as what you want to see.

Some U.S.-based firms will exempt clippings from Canadian publications because of the difficulties in going north of the border for work.

SAMPLE SPECIFICATIONS FOR A CLIPPING SERVICE

Area and Frequency of Issue. Clip daily papers only (no weeklies) in the following states: (Here you furnish a list of states. Your list could consist of all fifty states, three states, or one. Large firms might want to add Canada and all or part of Latin and South America. A really tight set of specifications will set minimum [and sometimes maximum] circulations for publications from which clippings are wanted, as "minimum 100,000 daily circulation.")

Subjects and Publications for Extra Attention. (Readers do a better job if you can give them key words or phrases to guide their search.) Under the category of trade and consumer publications, the following should receive extra attention:

Building and architecture
Business and financial

Churches
Engineering
Government
Hospitals and nursing
Medical and health
Remodeling and renovation
Schools and education

General. Within the preceding limitations as to frequency of publication, circulation minimums, geographic coverage, and special attention categories, mark and clip references to proposed construction, renovation, or additions to any building over (insert your minimum value figure here) in value and originating in the same city as the publication. Include municipal, county (parish), state (provincial), and federal projects.

Omissions. Spelling out the exclusions in a set of clipping specifications is just as important as explaining what you want clipped. For my own purposes these are the exclusions usually given:

1. Single family residence work (but do include multifamily dwellings and developments valued at more than $500,000).
2. Any project where it is reasonably clear from the contents of the clipping that the architect or engineer has been selected.
3. Any project illustrated by a rendering, model, or site plan, as indicative that the design firm already has been selected.
4. Items from the following publications: (Here you list newspapers, magazines, and newsletters regularly received and read in your office, or that you do not believe would be particularly helpful in your marketing efforts.)
5. Multiple clippings from wire service items and articles from multiple edition national newspapers and magazines. (Examples of the latter are *The Wall Street Journal* and *Time* magazine. An important project story might be picked up by one or both of the wire services and used by hundreds of their clients. You do not need 550 copies of the same story about a new office building in New York City or a proposed sewage treatment plant in Los Angeles.)

Corporate Annual Reports

Investor-owned companies must make periodic reports about the state of their financial health. The information to be found in the average corporate report goes far beyond the law's requirements—and some of the material is excellent intelligence for the marketing staffs of design firms.

Annual reports almost always open with a letter from the president or the chairperson of the board or from both to their stockholder publics. Even in the worst of times, these letters somehow seem to be cast in positive terms. Capital investments for the near and distant future, including buildings, are usually mentioned, with few, if any, details. Somewhere in the report proper, planned capital investments will almost always be discussed in greater detail. If the corporation was active during the preceding year in acquiring other companies, any planned improvements for the new subsidiaries often will be set out in the sections devoted to their future operations.

It requires but little practice and even less training to learn to spot these corporate-level portents of design work to come. The information is admittedly sketchy and incomplete at this point, but self-sufficient marketers can gather enough background intelligence from scanning an annual report to enable them to initiate a productive cold call to the corporate headquarters. From the cold call the marketer should obtain enough information about future work, including timing and scope, to enable him or her to develop a marketing strategy for the corporation. More on this aspect of intelligence gathering will be found in Chapter 5.

If you have been using corporate reports as information sources, you know that it is not difficult to get them. Some libraries have them, stockbrokers' offices are an obvious source, and you can always write to the public relations department of a company for a copy of the current report. Larger corporations maintain entire sections whose primary task is to get annual reports into the hands of the public. Still another source is the cooperative advertisements that appear in the financial publications each spring (*The Wall Street Journal*, *Barron's*, *Forbes*, and the like). Dozens of reports can be ordered by circling numbers on a coupon and sending it to a central office for servicing.

If, for example, you want to research paper manufacturers as a future market for your services, obtaining annual reports from a dozen or so of the leading paper companies would be an early, logical step in the process.

Noncommercial Lead Sources   In addition to corporate reports, there are a number of other information sources—mostly free—to draw on for both market trends and specific project leads. Federal Reserve banks furnish some of the best researched business information available. The Federal Reserve Bank of New York, 33 Liberty Street, New York, NY 10045, is a storehouse of free information about and for the business community. The bank's *Quarterly Report* is one publication to write for—others include the monthly review and the bank's annual report. And ask for a list of current pamphlets—at least one or two should be helpful.

All of the federal reserve banks have regular publications available to the public. If you are interested, write for information to any of these branches:

Bank and Public Information Center
Federal Reserve Bank of Boston
Boston, MA 02106

Publications Section, Research Department
Federal Reserve Bank of Chicago
Box 834
Chicago, IL 60690

Public Services Department
Federal Reserve Bank of Philadelphia
Philadelphia, PA 19105

Bank and Public Relations Department
Federal Reserve Bank of Richmond
Box 27662
Richmond, VA 23261

Research Department
Federal Reserve Bank of Dallas
Station K
Dallas, TX 75201

Office of Public Information
Federal Reserve Bank of Minneapolis
Minneapolis, MN 55480

Other Federal Reserve banks are in Cleveland, Atlanta, St. Louis, Kansas City, and San Francisco.

Individual private banks are also potential sources of good business information. These include the Morgan Guaranty Trust Company of New York (*World Financial Markets* and the *Morgan Guaranty Survey*), Citibank of New York (*Monthly Economic Letter*), First National Bank of Chicago (*World Report*), Chase Manhattan (*Business in Brief*), and the Harris Bank of Chicago (*Barometer of Business*). Some of these publications have a modest subscription fee. You might begin your search at home, asking your bank what it offers in the way of regular publications and what it can get for you (or suggest) from its correspondent banks.

It may come as a surprise to learn that American Express publishes regular economic analyses, as do practically all large financial institutions, and many of them are free on request.

For another view of general business news and trends, write to the American Institute of Certified Public Accountants, 1121 Avenue of the Americas, New York, NY 10036, for a list of the free periodicals published by member firms. You may decide that CPA (Certified Public Accountant) publications are less helpful than those issued by the larger banks, but look at a few of them first. Peat, Marwick, Mitchell and Company has a well-written quarterly, *World*.

Use of the remaining printed lead sources—magazines, directories, and news releases—should be self-explanatory. In the case of news releases, decide which corporations and government agencies you are most interested in; then send a letter to their public relations office, and ask to be put on their list to receive future news releases.

General References Marketers could quickly deplete their annual budgets by trying to have in-house copies of every publication they might find useful. Many of the important reference books will be found in local public, private, and university libraries. Here is a list of potentially helpful reference sources, to supplement or generate your own intelligence gathering efforts. After checking their current prices, you may decide to sacrifice a certain amount of convenience by using nearby library copies.

1. Corporate Sources
   - *Moody's Industrials*
   - *Thomas' Register of Manufacturers*
   - *Standard & Poor's Corporation Records*
   - *Standard & Poor's Register of Corporations, Directors and Executives*
   - *Dun & Bradstreet Reference Book*
   - *Dun & Bradstreet Middle Market Directory*
   - *Dun & Bradstreet Million Dollar Directory*
   - *Who's Who in Finance and Industry*
   - *Value Line Investment Survey*
   - *Directory of Corporations (Who Owns Whom)*
2. Banking
   - *Moody's Bank and Financial Manual*
   - *Polk's World Bank Directory*
3. Medical
   - *Directory of American Colleges of Hospital Administration*
   - *American Association of Medical Clinics Directory*
4. Education
   - *Patterson's Education Directory*
   - *American Universities and Colleges*
5. Political
   - *Congressional Directory*
   - *Who's Who in Government*
   - *U.S. Government Organization Manual*
   - *Congressional Staff Directory*
   - *Moody's Municipals and Governments*

- *The Municipal Yearbook*
- *Federal Telephone Directory*

6. Organizations
   - *National Trade & Professional Organizations of the United States*
   - *Encyclopedia of Associations*
   - *Profile (AIA Directory of Architectural Firms)*
7. Miscellaneous
   - *Moody's Transportation Manual*
   - *Moody's Public Utilities*
   - *Who's Who*—International, U.S., and Regional editions
   - *Directory of Directories*
   - *Directory of Special Libraries and Information Centers*

LEAD GENERATION

Some firms—and their number is growing—have set up internal committees charged with taking periodic overviews of present and future markets. While such groups go by different names, perhaps the "What if . . . ?" committee is the most descriptive. Related terms are spinning, branching, and linking. The think tank group are also called "Wild Blue Yonder" committees.

Why another committee? Simply to help the marketing staff of an architectural, engineering, or planning firm spot trends in project and client types ahead of the competition. The committee should also be able to pick up negative vibrations about markets that are giving signs of decreasing in importance (and fees) and those markets that are definitely on the way out.

Many aspects of the marketing process should be approached cold-bloodedly and logically. But flights of fancy, unadulterated fantasy, and unrestrained imagination also have their roles in a full-fledged, productive marketing program. The ideal "What if . . . ?" committee is composed of people from marketing, management, and the major design disciplines represented in a firm. Occasionally, representatives from other specialties and disciplines—economists, psychologists, bankers, developers, journalists, sociologists—are asked to sit in on a meeting.

Certain parallels exist between "What if . . . ?" committee meetings and the buzz sessions once so popular among corporate and association executives. While "What if . . . ?" committees are urged to forego inhibitions and to disregard most normal considerations of immediate practicality, that is, to let their minds soar unfettered into the wild blue yonder, the success of such sessions is predicated on considerable pre-meeting research and individual thinking by participants. The underlying questions in all "What if . . . ?" meetings are, "Where are the new markets, and how do we determine what they are?" Secondary considerations, to be answered later, are these: "Which of these identified, emerging markets can we logically pursue? When? And how?"

The type and degree of control exercised by the leader are important factors in the success of the session. The process might be further characterized as "managed serendipity." While that is an obvious contradiction in terms, if the atmosphere is conducive to the serendipitous approach, with the proper degree of direction or control of the situation, results should equal—even exceed—those obtained from a less structured session.

Timing of What if . . . ?" Meetings "What if . . . ?" meetings should be scheduled at three- to six-month intervals for maximum usefulness. Held more often than every three months, the sessions do not give participants time to charge their "free association" batteries. When they are separated by more than six months, there is a tendency to forget or drift away from the process. And, given the current pace of technologic change, some very promising prospects could be missed entirely if the think sessions occurred only on an annual basis.

Several of the consultants who serve as "facilitators" for various types of management planning meetings suggest that seven is the maximum number of people that can work together creatively in a "What if . . . ?" meeting. Other recommendations from the experts: the meeting room should be large enough, with good light and with easy access to writing pads and other materials that may be needed by committee members. A flip chart pad and easel are placed near the chairperson's seat. Telephone bells should be switched off; calls and messages, held until the meeting is over.

Only because *someone* must be in charge of any meeting or project is the word "chairperson" used earlier. "Discussion leader" may be a better term for the role. One member of the group is selected to act as a recorder. The recorder's primary task is to write all group-generated ideas on flip chart sheets. Notations should be as brief as possible. Some groups back up the flip chart notes by recording the session on tape.

As flip chart sheets are filled, they are numbered and torn off the pad, then taped to the walls in sequence. In this way all participants have a continuing, visual reminder of what has been discussed. Branching and linking of ideas are also aided and encouraged by the wall record.

Some "What if . . . ?" committee guidelines:

1. DO
   - Encourage every member of the group to participate.
   - Keep the pace fast.
   - Watch for signs of boredom; move rapidly to counteract them.
   - Encourage mental piggybacking to expand on an idea.
   - Maintain a high energy level.
   - Keep group members informed about where they are.
   - Use surprise.
   - Experiment.
   - Try humor, and encourage its use within the group as long as the discussion doesn't turn into a story-swapping session.
   - Record all ideas.
   - Emphasize quantity over quality at this stage.
   - Encourage participants to throw out their wildest, most improbable ideas. First thoughts are easier to tone down than to dream up.
2. DON'T
   - Criticize or evaluate; you are apt to slow or stop the free flow of ideas.
   - Compliment or question an individual; both tend to focus group attention on a single point.

Follow-up   As the emphasis in a "What if . . . ?" session is on free association and quantity, some forty to sixty or more ideas might result from one meeting. In a subsequent meeting, "What if . . . ?" ideas are subjected to a thorough evaluation and quality assessment. The sixty ideas might well be reduced to four or five deemed worthy of further research and development. And the firm should be well ahead of its competition with each newly identified building or client type (or significant variations in established building and client types). And that's the name of the "What if . . . ?" game.

Few, if any, of the potential marketing advantages will be realized if the firm does not have a plan for evaluating and following up on the committee's recommendations. The most promising ones must be worked into the overall marketing program.

A New York City design firm uses a variation of the "What if . . . ?" committee approach in its business development planning. The firm operates with eleven basic committees, each composed of partners, associates, and top-level technical staff. Every committee has continuing responsibility for watchdogging one building type—hospitals, office buildings, schools, government work, and so on. The groups are headed by senior partners experienced in the specialty involved.

The lesson to be drawn from all of this is that "What if . . . ?" committees, by whatever name they operate, can be an important force for aggressive marketing. The committee's usefulness and applicability are not limited to medium- and large-size firms. Successful design firms essentially create their own new markets, based on identified leads and logic and nourished by periodic think-tank ("What if . . . ?") sessions.

Organizational Activities The advantages of membership and active involvement by the principals of a firm in a variety of civic, business, religious, cultural, political, and professional organizations should be evident. In addition, the same kind of participation on the part of associates and other senior staff people should be encouraged.

If it hasn't been done recently, a good first step in assessing a firm's coverage of local, regional, and national organizations is to make an inventory of memberships currently held by all members of the staff. With the inventory in hand, obtain the remaining coverage desired through volunteers or assignment. Along with the organization checkup, an equitable policy for payment of dues and assessments should be implemented.

Two examples should illustrate the point about principal and staff participation in organization activities on a widespread, organized basis. The first is from an article in *ACEC Information*, the newsletter of the Association of Consulting Engineers of Canada (ACEC). The article, "Social Contacts in Business Development," was based on a 1977 survey of ACEC member firms to determine their activity level in various organizations.

> Consulting engineers from ACEC member firms have been: President of the Edmonton Eskimos, Governor of Eastern Canada and Caribbean District of Kiwanis International, President of the Winnipeg and other Chambers of Commerce, President of the Kingston General Hospital, President of the Royal Hamilton College of Music, President of the National Association of Underwater Instructors, Vice-Chairman of the Victoria Art Gallery, Chairman of the Board of Governors of the University of Victoria, Director of Via Rail Canada, Inc., and a whole lot more.
>
> They support church and synagogue, and are really involved with such organizations as the Boy Scouts, Red Cross, YM-YWCA, United Way, and such clubs as Rotary, Kiwanis, Kinsmen and the like.
>
> They are not too strong in the political arena, however, with only 14 listing involvement in politics and four having served as elected municipal officials. But 11 had served on school boards and another 17 on various other municipal boards.
>
> C-Es are golfers, curlers, tennis players and sailors—very often on the volunteer administrative side. A surprising number of them coach junior hockey and baseball teams.

They maintain close relations with universities and colleges, with 32 participating in academic matters as members of university and college boards and advisory committees.

As expected, they have a high involvement with professional associations such as provincial associations of professional engineers, the Engineering Institute of Canada and other bodies catering to specialized interests.[3]

The second example is a list of memberships held in professional, civic, and social organizations by a director of marketing for an A-E firm in Atlanta:

Professional
    Southern Industrial Relations Conference, Atlanta and Blue Ridge, N.C.;
        executive secretary.
    PERL. Inc., Atlanta; secretary and treasurer.
    Registered Professional Engineer, State of Georgia.
    American Institute of Industrial Engineers; senior member.
    American Institute of Architects; associate member.
    College Athletic Business Managers Association; member
    National Association of Basketball Coaches of the U.S.; allied member.
    National Association of Collegiate Directors of Athletics; associate member.
    Society for Marketing Professional Services; member.
Civic
    Scottish Rite Children's Hospital; advisory board member.
    Arthritis Foundation, Georgia Chapter; director.
    Georgia Tech Presbyterian Student center; chairman.
    Georgia Tech YMCA; trustee.
    Institute of International Education; S.E. board of directors.
    United Nations Association of the U.S.A.; vice president.
Social
    ANAK (Georgia Tech Leadership Honor Society)
    Atlanta Lawn Tennis Association
    Atlanta Tipoff Club; president.
    Athletic Hall of Fame, State of Georgia; life member.
    Braves 400 Club; director.
    Georgia Tech National Alumni Association; trustee.
    Naismith Basketball Hall of Fame; life member.
    National Football Foundation and Hall of Fame
    New York Athletic Club
    Pi Kappa Alpha Fraternity
    University of Tennessee Alumni Association

WASHINGTON REPRESENTATION

The percentage of government work in design firms at any given moment ranges all the way from near zero to practically 100 percent. Without question, federal, state, and local government projects have become almost the only game in many towns. This has caused a growing number of architectural and engineering firms to consider some type of visible, continuing representation in the nation's capital.

Many of the professional associations are headquartered there, and most try to give at least some guidance to members about how to find and land federal projects. The number of design firms with production offices in or near the District of Columbia has grown considerably over the last ten years.

There are a few reputable, independent Washington "reps" who represent several noncompeting design firms. These consultants, for a monthly retainer of from several hundred to several thousand dollars, offer varying degrees of experience, specialization, lead development, contacts, and influence.

Some Washington representatives provide a valid service; others somehow maintain personable staffs and plush offices on a combination of unkept promises, undelivered influence, hot air, and sheer gall. It is the latter group, of course, that design professionals must somehow avoid if they believe a representative in Washington will be helpful in landing federal work.

Washington lobbyists and representatives usually base their sales approach and fees on the premise that few lay people are qualified to find their way through the quagmire of red tape, bureaucratic indifference and ineptitude, and sundry other small- and large-scale obstacles on the Washington scene. While the premise is not necessarily false, the concomitant assumption that just any native is better equipped than the neophyte to serve as a guide to seats of influence and power is demonstrably dangerous.

Where a legitimate advisory and information service is provided regularly by letter, telex, and telephone, accompanied by personal consultation and assistance when clients visit Washington, D.C., few would quarrel with the idea that this is worth a reasonable retainer.

If you believe that Washington representation might be helpful to your firm, there are several ways to learn who the effective, professionally oriented representatives are. Staff members of professional societies headquartered there should be able to come up with the names of legitimate counseling firms. Your representatives in Congress (and their staff members) certainly know the Washington lobbyists—good and bad—and if your political fences are in reasonable order, you could get a few good leads from the Hill.

Other design professionals who already have Washington representation may be willing to provide the name of their agent. He or she may take on multiple, noncompeting firms.

What services should you expect from a Washington representative?

1. Regular calls on your behalf to the agencies and departments you specify, gathering information about appropriate upcoming projects and the status of those moving through the selection process. ("Appropriate" projects are those your firm has some experience with. Selectivity is just as important at the federal level as it is on your home grounds.)

2. Advice, through regular written or oral reports, about pending programs which could result in projects of interest to your firm.

3. For your own infrequent Washington visits, the rep should set up and confirm visits with prospects, current clients, your representative and senators, and anyone else you want or need to see. You should feel free to use the rep's office as a base of operations, for a message center, and in any other way that will help make your visit as productive as possible.

4. In emergencies the representative can deliver Standard Form (S.F.) 254s, S.F. 255s, general capability and special brochures, or any other promotional materials for you to a government office.

Basically, you should look on a rep as your primary early warning system for government projects of potential interest to your firm—and as your continuing, personal point of reference and contact in Washington. Whatever your expectations, get it all in writing at the outset.

Commission Agents   When shopping around for a Washington rep, you'll probably run across one or more of the commission agents in residence. These reps are a little more circumspect in their operations and sales pitch than was the case a few years ago, but the bottom line of their deal is that you'll pay them between 7 and 12 percent of your gross fee for their purported influence, contacts, and "handles" on upcoming projects.

In most cases these clout-for-a-fee consultants do provide a service of sorts for their money. They can advise on whom to contact in the agency for preinterview selling and on how to put together a S.F. 255 to show your firm in the best possible light. They may work with you on structuring and holding dry runs of your formal presentation. If you get the job, they can advise on negotiating techniques. Since there are other marketing consultants who offer similar advisory services on S.F. 255 preparation and presentation structure and production—for a much more reasonable fee—you'd be better off to check out one of them first.

The great majority of design firms will benefit far more from that approach than from the one-time, one-shot use of commission agents. If you need any more reasons to avoid the self-styled influence sellers, in recent months several firms have had contract awards voided—because they told the federal client no contingency-fee salespeople helped them win the job. It isn't illegal to use such agents; it *is* illegal to lie about their use to federal agencies. More information about commission agents will be found in Chapter 12, "Selling to the Government."

PROSPECT PROBABILITY RATING

At an early point in your selling efforts, it is important to back away from hot pursuit of the prospect and honestly analyze your real chances of getting the job. Selectivity is one of the many options marketers have; unless it is exercised and applied early and routinely, a firm's win or kill rate may become disastrously low.

Some firms have moved their prospect analysis (probability ratings) into the computer age by programming in-house equipment to apply key probability factors to practically every project uncovered by the marketing staff. Some of the factors considered in the computer analysis:

1. *Location of the project.* (Near an existing branch or project office? Transportation facilities available? Long- and short-range [strategic and tactical] marketing interest in the area?)

2. *Type of client represented.* (If public, what is the degree of political action to be dealt with? If private, what contacts and endorsements from past and present clients will help in the selling efforts? Applicable experience?)

3. *Size of project.* (By predetermined size guidelines, does the project measure up to the firm's standards? What is the probable fee? Can we make a profit on it? How much? Will we learn something by producing the job? What?)

4. *Competition.* (Whom are we apt to be competing against? What is our past win-loss record with each competitor?)

5. *Selling efforts.* (Do we have people particularly fitted to sell to this client? Who? Their qualifications?)

6. *Venture marketing considerations.* (Is this a client or project type important to our future growth? What future work might come from the prospect? What are the possibilities of the job's being wired? Other potential, related benefits?)

7. *Our own qualifications.* (Direct and related experience with the project type? Individual qualifications of potential design team? Their availability?)

Some marketers use a rating form similar to the one shown in Figure 4-5 to help in their prospect analysis. It is admittedly a subjective exercise, but so is a lot of what goes under the name of marketing.

```
PROSPECT RATING FORM


Prospect name _____        _____
                                                   Date
Contact _____
                                                        Rating
                                       Multiplier        Total

1.  Selling distance from office ____miles.      0.5    _____
    (0 miles = 10 pts.; 1500 miles = 0 pts.)

2.  Production distance from main office ___ mi.  0.5   _____
    (0 miles = 10 pts.; 2000 miles = 0 pts.)

3.  Degree of political involvement.             1.0    _____
    (City Hall = 0 pts.; none = 10 pts.)

4.  Size of fee.                                 3.0    _____
    ($50,000 fee = 0 pts.; $1 million = 5 pts.;
     over $3 million = 10 pts.)

5.  Timing.                                       3.0   _____
    (Intermediate or long range = 0 pts.;
     immediate = 10 pts.)

6.  Future potential with client.                2.0    _____
    (No future = 0 pts.; multiple structure or
     campus type = 10 pts.)

7.  Future potential in market.                  1.0    _____
    (No future = 0 pts.; expanding market = 10 pts.)

8.  Our firm's superiority.                      1.0    _____
    (Churches = 0 pts.; commercial, governmental,
     medical = 10 pts.)

9.  Competition.                                 2.0    _____
    (Superior = 0 pts.; inexperienced local = 10 pts.)



                        Total Possible Points            140



_____
Name of rater
```

Figure 4-5 *Rating form for use in noncomputer analyses of prospects and the probability of your firm's selection.*

Another approach to estimating prospect probability factors is shown in Figure 4-6. The form is from Unit I of the MGI Management Institute home-study course, *Successful Marketing of Architectural Services*.[4]

RECORD KEEPING

At the moment you decide, for all the right reasons, to pursue a prospective job, some type of prospect file should be set up. Complete and accurate documentation of client acquisition activities is fully as important as properly executed working drawings and specifications for any job you turn out of your office.

Record-keeping systems in use in design offices run the gamut from no real system at all ("pile it all in a basket, we'll get to it when we have time") to complex, computer-based programs. The latter stand ready to print out instantly, for each salesperson, a complete list of all

Go/No Go Factors			
Project _____ Prepared by _____ Date _____			

	Above Average 10 9 8 7	Average 6 5 4 3	Poor 2 1 0	Rating
Intelligence	Close client relationship	Generally good	Know nothing	
Qualification	Technically superior	Better than average	Questionable	
Location	Favorable	Not important	Unfavorable	
Time to prepare	Plenty	Enough	Not enough	
Cost to prepare vs. return	Favorable	Reasonable	Excessive	
Time to perform	Plenty	Enough	Questionable	
Competition	We have inside	Unknown	Wired for others	
Capability	Can meet all requirements	Understand problem and can perform	Questionable	
Price	Good profit potential	Competitive	Questionable	
Chance of success	50%	20 to 50%	Less than 20%	
			Total	

Approved by _____   Go __   No Go ___

Figure 4-6 *This form is also a guide to rating prospect probability factors.*

live prospects, along with contact names, previous work (if any) for the prospect, related experience, cost estimates, probability factors of landing the job, identified competitors, probable fees (and profits), and the degree to which marketing costs should be on a cost-effective basis.

Even the smallest and most junior firms need some type of record-keeping system for prospects. Admittedly, a much less complex system is indicated for the six to ten or so active prospects of a one- or two-person firm than is required for the hundreds—or thousands—of active prospects followed by large, multidisciplinary, multioffice firms.

Basic to any record-keeping system is the standard file folder. On the tab, as minimum guidance, goes the name of the prospect. As prospect folders accumulate, you may want to think about adding a few refinements: letter, number, and color keys on the tabs to indicate building type, location, size of the potential job, and the like. But first and foremost is the name of the prospect—Dade County Courts Building, IBM Office—Baltimore, or XYZ Warehouse—Akron. File the folders alphabetically by prospect name.

Every fact and scrap of paper that conceivably could be helpful in landing the prospect go into the folder—copies of correspondence, news clippings, copies of *Who's Who* listings, Dun & Bradstreet reports, memos to the file (on contacts, meetings, telephone calls, and the like), and, if the prospect is a publicly held corporation, copies of the company's last two or three annual reports. Among the first items to go into the file is the combined call report and qualification work sheet (see Figure 5-1).

A supplemental card reminder system is the last item in most business development record-keeping systems. Examples of a simple, useful, four-card file system are shown in Figures 4-7 through 4-10.

The system covers prospective, present, and past clients. The first card (Figure 4-7) is the Individual Prospect Card. This one is begun as soon as the new business call report work sheet is received. The prospect's name and the name of the one in your firm who will be the primary contact go on the lines in the upper right corner. The twelve lettered divisions along the top of the prospect card are for monthly follow-up reminders. On the example shown in Figure 4-7, the signal tab is on "F" for February.

Whenever a contact is made, the date of the contact and name of the person contacted are entered in appropriate columns. Space is also provided on the card for brief notes about the contact. Notations should be brief; a memo covering all important points of a meeting or other type of contact will go into the file folder for the prospect. Additional room is provided on the back of the card to continue contact notes if necessary. In the unlikely event that the prospect card becomes filled

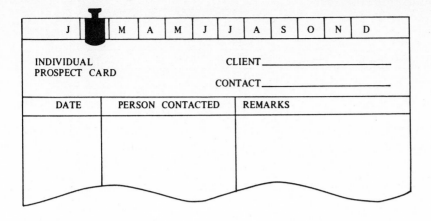

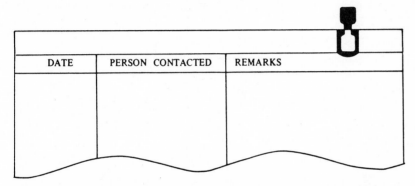

Figure 4-7 *Figures 4-7 through 4-10 illustrate a simple four-card filing system for recording prospect and client contacts. Figure 4-7 is the Individual Prospect Card.*

before the prospect is resolved, a second card can be stapled to the front of the full card.

If it is decided that monthly contacts with a particular prospect are desirable, then the colored signal tab is moved ahead a month at a time. From the prospect cards, following along the rows of tabs for the present month, the marketing department prepares and distributes contact lists for each marketer and principal on a regular schedule— perhaps on the first Tuesday of each month.

The Prospect Mastercard (Figure 4-8) consolidates information about prospects assigned to those in marketing. The marketer's name goes on the contact line at the top right-hand corner of the front of the card. Whenever an entry is made on the Individual Prospect Card, a companion notation is put on the mastercard. The person in charge of marketing,

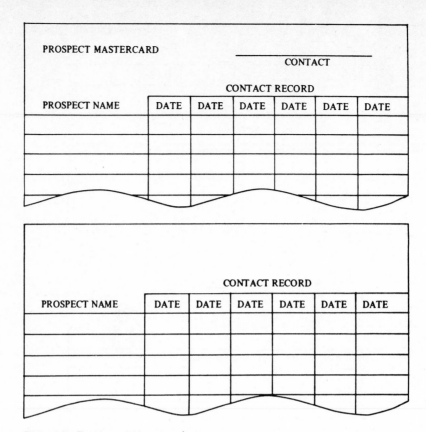

Figure 4-8 *Prospect Mastercard.*

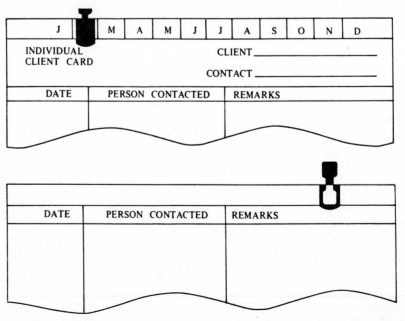

Figure 4-9 *Individual Client Card.*

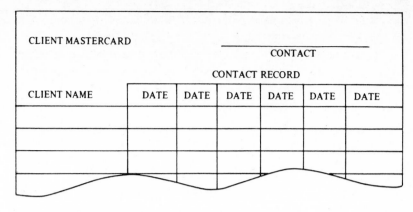

Figure 4-10 *Client Mastercard.*

through a quick review of the mastercards, can check on how many prospects are assigned to any one individual and whether or not he or she is overloaded in comparison to others in the firm with marketing assignments. Of even greater importance, a marketing director can tell from the mastercards if prospects are being followed up on a regular basis.

The third and fourth cards in the system (Figures 4–9 and 4–10) are similar to the two already described except they are for following up with past clients. As soon as the job is completed, an Individual Client Card is prepared in the business development office. As a rule, the partner-in-charge or the project manager on the job will be assigned as the continuing contact.

On almost every form used in a prospect records system, include space for the assigned contact person to jot down the next action required. Never leave the next step in marketing to chance.

A marketing form to supplement the card file system is shown in Figure 4-11. This simple listing of active prospects (essentially those from the A level of the Prospect Triangle) is useful as an internal information and reminder tool and also as an agenda for regular marketing meetings.

LOST-JOBS ANALYSIS

One measure of a marketing department's effectiveness is obtained through a thorough, objective analysis of jobs pursued unsuccessfully. Figure 4-12 shows the analysis format used by one A-E firm.

Over a period of time certain patterns should emerge from this study, especially if the lost client is inclined to be candid about why a firm was not selected. Most are. A firm may discover that it is consistently losing out on the final cut or that one firm always seems to win when the two offices are in contention. Another possible finding from call-backs is that one or more of your principals seem never to be able to bring home the job.

For the infrequently encountered prospect reluctant to provide details about why your firm was not selected (never ask prospects to justify their selections; rather ask them why you were "de-selected"), marketers are justified in pointing out that the client representative *owes* them such help in improving the firm's future presentations. The lost client may not know how much of an investment is required to go through formal presentations. Tell them—while explaining that your primary interest is in improving your *next* presentation to their selection committee.

Don't try to establish trends and patterns through lost-job analyses with insufficient information. It takes time to review the jobs lost, assuming that the necessary records are available to institute the study. For the findings to be significant, the survey should cover at least a three-year time span.

In summarizing the last two chapters, I would emphasize the obvious, but often ignored, point that there is no substitute for a planned, sensibly budgeted, and well-staffed marketing program. Scattershot, hit-and-miss, on-and-off marketing efforts are not only nonproductive—they eventually become counterproductive. Pursuing that particular point might tell you that no marketing program is better than a badly organized, sloppily executed one. But why take chances on the accuracy of that syllogism? Get organized, and stay that way through a continuing performance measurement system.

ACTIVE PROSPECTIVE CLIENTS			
Active Prospective Clients			Date
Project	Scope	Last Action Taken	Next Action Due

Figure 4-11 *Supplemental form for listing active prospects.*

Crendon, Mursford & Sicherhelli, Architects-Engineers

LOST JOBS SUMMARY

1 July 1981 through 31 December 1981

Date	Project	Contacts	Marketing Activities	Interview	Reasons for Loss
Jan. 81	Community Center Vardon, Neb.	Newspaper, mayor, 4 council members.	Letter of interest, brochure, 2 visits.	None	Shortlist had only local firms. Heavy pressure from local groups to use local firm.
Jan. 81	Headquarters American-National Insurance Co., Memphis	Local and HQ officials of Amer. Nat'l., including 2 board members.	Letter of interest, 2 visits, proposal.	CM&S 1 of 4 firms in first-stage interviews.	2 competitors had more experience in office bldg. design. CM&S inability to commit proj. mgr. at early date.
Feb. 81	Data Center Malmac AFB, Reno	Corps of Engineers, San Francisco, Malmac base engineer.	S.F. 255 in response to CBD announcement. 1 visit to Corps of Engineers office.	CM&S one of 10 firms interviewed by telephone.	We have too much Air Force work. Didn't learn of project until CBD notice--no time to really market our services

Figure 4-12 *Lost-jobs summary and analysis form.*

REFERENCES

[1]Royal Barry Wills, *This Business of Architecture*, Reinhold Publishing Corporation, New York, 1941.

[2]David Travers, "Marketing: A Method of Avoiding a Hopeless Chase After the Wrong Job," *AIA Journal*, January 1975, p. 24.

[3]"Social Contacts in Business Development," *ACEC Information*, May 1978, p. 6.

[4]Robert Darling, *Successful Marketing of Architectural Services*, MGI Management Institute, Larchmont, N.Y., 1980, Unit II, 4–9.

Chapter 5
HOW TO QUALIFY PROSPECTS

Now that you have some ideas about how and where to find prospect leads, we can logically progress to a discussion of how to qualify prospects quickly, through a low-cost, practically foolproof process. Effective prospect qualification, it must be understood, turns around the marketer's ability to get answers to these two questions:

1. Is it a job?
2. Is it a job for my firm?

The rapid, low-cost process involves the use of the telephone—making "cold calls" in other words. It is possible to qualify leads in other, more time-consuming ways, such as by personal visits or with letters, but our advice is to stick with the telephone.

WHAT TO EXPECT FROM COLD CALLS

Most design professionals are not too thrilled at the prospect of picking up their phone, calling a total stranger (and on an executive level at that), and asking a lot of searching questions about a project that usually is little more than a rumor—sometimes no more than a gut feeling that the company or government agency called *must* have *some* kind of building requirements *somewhere*. A certain amount of reluctance to involve oneself in such a situation is understandable, but a little reflection must tell you that that is a pretty fair definition of the average cold call.

Why do professionals resist and resent making cold qualification calls? For two primary reasons:

1. A fear of being rejected; of not being successful in the telephone information-gathering approach.

2. A dislike (intense in some cases) of selling design services on the telephone.

Both concerns are misplaced and are easily and quickly disposed of.

First, the purpose of a cold qualification call is to get information. And even the greenest, most bumbling caller will get at least some information. The prospect representative may tell you the project you are calling about is now under construction. That is information you didn't have before you called. The response may be more positive: "It's good you called today. We're just beginning to get a list of design firms together." *That's* information. The second kind of answer is naturally more helpful to your marketing efforts and interests, but you haven't failed in either case. Unless you deliberately condition yourself to fail before you dial (which doesn't make much sense), there is no way you can fail to get information from a cold call. You will not be rejected.

The second concern—selling by telephone—is even easier to handle. Nowhere in this chapter will you find a reference to selling design services by telephone.

There are several reasons for this, including the real difficulty many would have in trying to sell something as personal and professional as design on the phone. But the main reason *not* to "think sales" during a cold call is to avoid losing the person on the other end of the line. If your line of questioning, speaking rate, or nuances in voice or volume give any indication that this is a sales call, you are immediately equated with insurance, vacuum cleaner, and encyclopedia salespeople. You become an unwelcome intruder in the day's affairs, and you'll lose them.

It is much better to concentrate on having a friendly, interesting, stimulating, give-and-take conversation (which you control, of course) and let the fact that you and your operation sound pretty good sink in subliminally. A certain amount of low-key selling is implicit in any cold call, but it should never be thought of as the primary consideration.

Make a friend, not a sale; get information, not a project, with the first call.

ADVANTAGES AND LIMITATIONS OF THE TELEPHONE

The telephone can overcome the limitations of time and space. It's a triumph of human ingenuity, but on the telephone, with no visual contact, you must rely entirely on sound. The person you are talking to can't see the smile or frown on your face or the gestures you make to emphasize a point. Your speech must stand on its own. If your speech generally is good, your telephone speech generally is good, too. Bad speech sounds worse on the telephone, and good speech doesn't come across quite as well as it does in a face-to-face meeting.

Sounds are not reproduced in their full natural range over the telephone. Certain sound waves, especially in the highest and lowest ranges, are lost. What you actually hear is the middle part of the vocal range, with the extreme highs and lows missing. The mechanical larynx of the phone tends to flatten voices and dull personalities.

Other factors can contribute to the difficulty of hearing telephone speech—a bad connection, room or traffic noises, background conversation, a radio or TV set playing.

The imperfection of the human ear as a sound-receiving instrument further compounds the problem. So, although communication by telephone is a remarkable technological development, the instrument itself can be a barrier to understanding. The other person can't read your lips or facial expressions as an aid to understanding and interpreting your words, so your speech must be clear and distinct, preferably delivered a little more slowly than in ordinary conversation.

OVERCOMING THE TELEPHONE'S LIMITATIONS

Posture   Posture affects the clarity, intensity, and vitality of your voice. When your body slumps, your voice slumps as well. When you are sitting or standing erect, lung capacity increases, and your vocal organs receive an adequate supply of breath. Good posture makes for good voice quality and tone. In general, people find low tones more pleasing to the ear. High-pitched voices tend to sound strident and are especially irritating on the phone. You can lower the pitch of your voice to some degree by opening your mouth wider and moving your lips more as you speak.

If you are a busy person, you are probably tense, too, and that registers on the phone. Sit back and relax for a minute or so before you pick up the receiver.

Speaking with your mouth almost motionless, with very little movement of the jaws and lips (the Bogart speech syndrome), produces a higher-pitched voice because all of your speech muscles are tensed. That's what happens when people speak with a cigarette, a cigar, a pipe, or a pencil in their mouth. The more movement of the jaws and lips, the clearer and more distinct the words will be.

If you've never been on the other end of a conversation when the caller is eating, drinking, or chewing gum while he or she talks, the sounds have to be heard to be believed. And never cough or sneeze into the mouthpiece, unless your aim is to deafen (and alienate) the person on the other end of the line. Theoretically, such loud, unexpected noises could even cause caridac arrest in a person with a history of heart trouble.

Try gesturing as you speak, and don't be afraid to use facial expressions. The listener will be able to hear the extra movement and animation in your voice. "Smile as you dial," suggests one communication consultant. Smile as you talk, anyway.

Volume, Inflection, Articulation   Is your telephone voice too loud or too soft? Try this test. With the receiver held to one ear, cup a hand tightly over the other ear. Start talking. What you hear is very close to what the listener hears at the other end of the line.

As a general rule, hold the mouthpiece between a half-inch and an inch from your lips. Adjust the distance to compensate for more or less volume.

Use inflection to add color and shading to your telephone voice. It can hold the listener's attention as well as help to make what you say clearly understood. Work on your voice range; don't come over as a monotone. In their book *Talking Between the Lines*, Julius and Barbara Fast discuss unconscious messages transmitted in conversation. The Fasts point out that speech *signals* often supersede the actual words. Speech pauses are an example.

> How we pause between each word in a sentence and the length of these pauses send signals to the listener about the importance of what we're saying. The longer the pause, the deeper the feelings we communicate. But if the pause is too long, the depth of feeling registers as pomposity or even exaggeration. . . . But if the pause is too short, the listener may get an impression of coldness, even furtiveness.[1]

The Fasts also emphasize the importance of driving one's voice from as low in the chest cavity as possible. Chest resonators send the message that they are strong through use of low-pitched, forthright tones. Through-the-nose speakers, with their high, wispy voices, project weakness. (See the material under "Your Voice" in Chapter 10 for more detail on voice control.)

Most people can train their voices, lowering the origin in the chest by degrees. A tape recorder can be useful in such efforts. Be objective in listening to replays of your conversational voice. If you are unsatisfied with your resonation—and your voice tone doesn't project the image you want it to—you may want to get some professional voice coaching.

There is a little-known device for *temporarily* lowering your voice. Eating several ounces of bar chocolate serves to coat the vocal cords, effectively lowering a voice's register by several tones. Keep in mind that the effect is transitory; it would hardly do to have your voice suddenly soar from bass to tenor or soprano in the middle of a cold call.

In *How to Get More Business by Telephone,* Jack Schwartz has this to say about correct inflection:[2]

> Inflections reveal motive, hidden meaning, sarcasm, contempt, anger, indifference, interest, love, concern, respect, etc. Anticipation is denoted in an upward inflection. The voice naturally rises in inflection when one is interested, inquiring, seeking, anticipating. Voices fall at a "period," on arrival at a decision, completion. Therfore a too frequent use of the downward inflection gives the impression of self-importance, of "know-it-allness," of finality, or firm, dogmatic decision; if overdone it is particularly dangerous in telephone use, as it runs the risk of being considered "bossy," argumentative, and dictatorial. A mild use of it, however, is liked, as it registers decision and competence. A too generous use of inflection, up or down, gives a rather dizzy sense to the hearer; and a tone with little or no inflection is on the other hand monotonous and colorless.
>
> A trained voice ascends and descends the scale with a nice fitness and ease. A voice that stays at one key gets on the nerves of the hearer, quite as does one note struck constantly on the piano. A voice that runs up and down the scale at the right periods and without showing too giddy a temperament is best.

To check your articulation, read aloud the following list of sound-alike words to someone seated across the room:

ooze—use	bold—bolt
line—lion	had—hat
scold—sold	lose—loose
chill—Jill	oh—hoe
ear—hear	cold—coal

At least eight of the ten pairs should be heard correctly by the listener. Other articulation excercises are found in the children's verses about Peter Piper and his peck of pickled peppers, Theo Thistle, and the girl who sold seashells by the seashore.

Animation   *Inflection* is not strictly the same as *animation*. Dictionaries would define *inflection* as an alternation in the pitch or tone of voice; modulation. *Animation* would be defined as the quality of being animate: vitality, liveliness, spirit. Animation comes from a Latin word meaning "to fill with breath," literally, to breathe life into a telephone call, a personal interview, or a formal presentation.

Try this exercise to improve the animation in your voice. Write down the words "oh," "well," and "now." In the privacy of your office or home, pronounce each of the words into a tape recorder

As a question
In anger
In surprise
With enthusiasm
With pleasure
Undecidedly
Lightheartedly—with total lack of concern

Play the tape back, and listen to your first efforts. Try the words again, in a different order. You might want to add a few more words: "aha," "no," and "O.K."

Delivery Speed   Some human minds can take in as many as 600 spoken words a minute, but even fairly rapid public speakers seldom deliver more than 200 words a minute. The generally accepted statistics for retention are 20 percent for a spoken message, 30 percent for purely visual intake, and a combination of aural and visual messages is good for from 50 to 70 percent retention.

All of that means that a telephone conversation, under the best of circumstances, leaves something to be desired as a medium of communication, and a rapid-fire delivery is only asking for trouble. The telephone company recommends a rate of not more than 140 words per minute for relatively easy understanding.

Delivery speed in a face-to-face situation is a different matter. Recent psychological studies of the effects of time compression reinforce earlier research findings that rapid speakers are perceived as more knowledgeable, more trustworthy, and more persuasive. Time compression is a relatively new technology for speeding up speech in radio and television commercials without affecting voice pitch.

Time-compressed air ads, preserving broadcast quality at up to a 25 percent increase over normal delivery rates, have been shown to increase unaided and aided recall of a message by as much as 40 percent.

Some telephone consultants suggest that slowing your speech rate will increase credibility. Slight pauses—for effect—can help to emphasize a point while giving the person you're talking to time to digest what you just said.

Decreasing the volume of your voice also adds emphasis to what you're saying. A too-loud voice, on the other hand, may carry a negative message about your mood—angry, short-fused, overbearing, antagonistic, dictatorial, and the like.

Choice of Words   Simple, straightforward language is easier to understand on the telephone than complicated terms woven into long sentences. Avoid unnecessary technical jargon, inside terms, slang, and gobbledygook. Be careful of your grammar and sentence structure; all of these contribute to making you understood—or misunderstood.

Make a special effort to eliminate vocalized pauses—ers, ahs, ums, and the like. They are even more of a handicap to understanding on the phone than in a face-to-face conversation.

Spell hard-to-understand names and words. The telephone company requires its operators to learn a standard spelling key:

A as in Alice
B as in Bertha
C as in Charles

and so on to

X as in x-ray
Y as in young
Z as in zebra

Telephone operators also learn a special way of pronouncing numbers to make them easier to understand:

Three—with a trilled "r"
Four—two syllables
Five—two syllables

To get an accurate idea of how you sound to others on the telephone, arrange with a friend or business acquaintance to take a call from you. Hold a lengthy and complete conversation on any subject. Record it, play it back, and listen carefully. Prepare to be surprised; you are not likely to sound the way you *think* you sound.

PRECOLD-CALL PLANNING

In the last several pages we've concentrated on various telephone techniques—with hints and tips to help make *all* your telephone calls more effective. Now it is time to apply those techniques to making effective qualifying cold calls, but knowing that the telephone can be a productive means for reaching and qualifying a prospective client does not mean that you just pick it up and begin dialing. Unless the calls are planned in advance, you leave success to chance. The better and more thorough your planning, the more likely you are to exude confidence, be persuasive, and achieve your objectives. Sound planning *before* the call is almost a guarantee of success; no planning practically assures failure.

The major purpose of precall planning is to eliminate wasted time, both for you and the person you are calling. And the net result is to make more time available for concentrating your efforts where they will do the most good—with prospects who are more likely to be interested in your services.

For an effective call to qualify prospects or to set up appointments, the precall planning should be done in logical, organized steps. There are four key steps in this phase:

1. Establish criteria for qualifying prospects.
2. Develop a list of prospects.
3. Prepare an opening statement outline.
4. Prepare fact-finding questions.

There is little profit in spending time trying to sell your services to someone who has no use for them—or to someone for whom you have no interest in working. To flush out prime sales targets, you'll need to have some guidelines on who does and who does not constitute a valid prospect. The first step in precall planning, then, is to establish criteria for qualifying prospects.

Every firm will set up different standards. If you are selling computers, for example, you'd be wasting time going after companies with two employees and annual gross sales of $75,000. One A-E firm established these considerations as guidelines for deciding on which prospects to actively pursue:

1. Size of the potential fee
2. Whether the project could lead to larger projects—for the same or related clients
3. If it is in a field in which the firm desires recognition or more experience
4. If it is in a field where the firm has heavy experience—thus leading to lower design and production costs
5. The state of the economy at the moment
6. If it is a new client who may want to test the firm on a smaller or less significant job
7. Geographic location
8. The probable competition

Cost and size minimums also were set out by project types:

Athletic facility—$5.5 million
General hospital—100 beds
Research lab—$3 million
Clinic—fifteen doctors
Warehouse—$2 million

THE OPENING STATEMENT

Why worry about an opening statement? It helps bridge those critical first twenty to thirty seconds, which can make or break a cold call. An effective opening statement has three essential parts:

1. Identification of yourself (but no more than is absolutely necessary)
2. Establishment of early rapport to reduce any negative reactions to your call
3. Making an interest-creating comment or two to focus the prospect's attention on you and what you have to say

In preparing an opening statement, don't get carried away to the extent a marketing representative for a large engineering firm once did. He wrote out his entire opening statement, beginning with "Hello, my name is ———," and insisted on having it propped up in front of him for every qualification call. Most of the prospects he reached decided they were being called by either a recording or an idiot and hung up after about the third sentence. This former marketer now manages a McDonald's restaurant in Walla Walla, Washington, and is doing well in his new work.

So structure your opening remarks, but use common sense in the preplanning and keep the structure simple and flexible.

After you have identified yourself, the next step in an effective opening statement is to establish rapport. Occasionally, a telephone call—especially a cold call—will cause receivers to become defensive. They are then harder to get information from. A means of disarming the prospect is needed to reduce any unfavorable reaction he or she may have to the call. To overcome possible negative reactions and to condition the prospect to answer the questions to follow:

1. Make a friendly remark.
2. Mention something you and the prospect have in common.
3. Tactfully acknowledge he or she may be busy (but don't overdo this).
4. Say something to stimulate his or her pride.

Once you've put the prospect in a receptive mood, he or she will be much more likely to listen to the rest of what you have to say.

Finally, in the opening statement, make an interest-creating comment. It will help to focus the prospect's attention on your firm and its services. In planning such remarks, remember that what interests you may not interest the prospect—he or she probably has different points of view. You must mentally step into the prospect's shoes to come up with an adequate interest-creating comment.

Examples:

1. "We've just completed the same type of study for the town of Alton. How well do you know Mr. Brown in the city engineer's office there?"

2. "Our firm has worked on some of the largest treatment plants in the country—as well as having done a number of smaller projects."

3. "How long have you been with the XYZ Corporation?"

You can see from these examples, which may sound somewhat bland and innocuous out of context, that it is difficult to go very far into scripting a cold call. The main considerations are to feel (and be) comfortable (you can be completely at ease because you know where this conversation is going) and to be constantly alert to steer the call into any new areas that present themselves. *You must be in control of the call at all times.*

I consider part of the necessary control is to be involved from the beginning of a cold call. Accordingly, I place all calls myself. Something could occur or be said in any one of the several stages involved in reaching the right person in an organization. Anything out of the ordinary *could* be important later. You should not leave yourself open to unnecessary surprises at any point in a qualification call.

Related to the preceding comments is an interesting observation in Michael Korda's book *Power! How to Get It; How to Use It:*

> The person who receives a telephone call is always in an inferior position of power to the person who placed it. This explains why people with a sense of power do not like answering services or mechanical devices. People only have to phone and leave a message, and you become responsible for getting back to them.[3]

ADVICE FROM THE EXPERTS

Some communication consultants advise against beginning a cold call with personal or general questions—inquiries about the weather, local crop outlook, recent vacations, the answerer's health, and the like. This type of question is known in some circles as a "noninterrogative"; the feeling seems to be that such questions impede or shatter a smooth conversation flow. The same experts (most of whom, we suspect, have never made an actual cold call) will explain that people know strangers have no real interest in the state of their health or local weather conditions or where they spent their vacation.

Some of the best cold calls I've made, in terms of information obtained and friendships established during the calls, were opened with just such noninterrogatives. It is attitude, tone and volume of voice, and how the questions are asked that determine their contribution to establishing rapport. Since the goal is to set up the equivalent of an old friend relationship (in thirty seconds or less), greet the person who answers in about the same way you'd greet friends you haven't seen for a while. Most of us would inquire about their health, the family, the job, mutual acquaintances, and the like.

A PERSONAL EXPERIENCE

A few years ago I made a cold qualification call to one of the city departments in Omaha. That morning's paper carried a brief item about an 11-inch overnight rainfall in Omaha. You would not have to be a native of the area to know that floods must have followed the downpour.

The call was placed from Washington, D.C., and after about the tenth ring a distraught-sounding, out-of-breath woman answered. My mental computer selected this opening remark for me: "I didn't really expect anyone to answer there today. How in the world did you get to work?"

Because an observer timed it, I can tell you her answer took twenty-two minutes. The young woman had just come through the most traumatic experience of her life, and I was the first to ask how she had made it in to the office. Highly condensed, her reply described setting out from home with a neighbor in a rowboat, which soon grounded on a floating barn door. The rowboat began taking on water, so they transferred to a passing motorboat, which promptly hit a passing tree trunk. Making some high ground, the group was then picked up by a state police helicopter and carried to the downtown Omaha area. She made the last ten blocks to city hall in hip waders—and she *had* to tell someone about it!

When she finished, I told her that (1) it was quite a story, (2) she was a lucky person, (3) she was also a very dedicated employee, and (4) I needed some information about a city project I understood was under consideration. I got the information.

TWO KEYS TO SUCCESSFUL COLD CALLS

The last part of the four-part response to the Omaha city employee involves one of the most important points in prospect information gathering and qualification. People *want* to help. They seldom volunteer to help, but when they are asked—and allowed to perform—the response is invariably positive.

The underlying theme of at least the opening minutes of any cold call is that you need help, which the person called is in a position to supply. You must tacitly make it clear that you expect them to help.

The second factor, which also involves a basic human trait, is that people love to correct others. So at random points in a call allow the prospect to correct you; make a misstatement about something just discussed—then fall silent so the other party has a chance to straighten you out. Don't overdo this technique, of course; you don't want to come through as some kind of idiot. Add or subtract a number from a figure supplied by the person called, or misspell a name just given you as you spell it back. The correction doesn't have to be a significant one, but make certain you furnish a couple of opportunities early in the call.

FACT-FINDING QUESTIONS

What do I want to learn from this call?

In prospect qualification the basic objective is to establish that there is a real project—or the probability that one or more projects will be coming up in the next six months or so. To obtain the information you need to decide if the project is worth pursuing, you must ask searching questions which demand a detailed response.

The next point of interest is whether consultants have been retained. If they have been, is there still a possibility of picking off some piece of the project?

After those two points are cleared up, there is no particular order of importance for the remainder of the information, but it could include questions such as

1. When will the job go ahead?
2. How will it be funded—through a bond issue, from funds on hand, by sale of stock, or what? If it is to be a bond issue, when is the election, and what is the past history of bond votes in the city, county, or state?
3. Will funds from other government entities—state or federal—be involved? To what extent?
4. How will selection be made?
5. When?

6. Who is on the selection board?

7. Who is the primary decision maker?

8. Scope and size of the project (whatever is known now)?

9. What other projects will the client have coming up in the near future?

10. What has been the use of local firms in the past?

11. Prospect's use of out-of-town or out-of-state consultants?

12. Is the project part of a larger complex? If so, what is the status of the remainder of the complex?

Other questions, based on the specific prospect and the specific project, will suggest themselves as the conversation flows along.

It is important to have some organized process for recording and archiving the information gathered. Figure 5-1, a combined call report and qualification worksheet, is similar to those used in many design firms.

KEEP IT OPEN-ENDED

Remember to use open-ended question words during the first part of the conversation in order to initiate and maintain the information flow. As a reminder, the five Hs and a W of journalism are the open-ended words to use:

Who
What
Where
Why
When
How

There is absolutely no way the person called can answer questions beginning with one of these six words with yes or no.

Examples of closed-ended question words are:

Are	Will	Has
Was	Should	May
Were	Could	Does
Did	Can	Shall
Have	Is	Would

A quick mental review will demonstrate that every word in this list demands no more than yes or no from the person on the other end of the line.

GLYPCO ARCHITECTS & ENGINEERS

Rushton, Ohio

TO ATTENTION OF

PROSPECT QUALIFICATION WORKSHEET AND CALL REPORT

Date _____ ☐ Visit
                          ☐ Telephone

Name of company or agency _____
Street address _____
City _____ State (Province) _____ ZIP _____
Telephone _____ Type of business _____
                          Type of project _____
Name of person(s) contacted _____ Title _____
                            _____ Title _____
                            _____ Title _____
Subject _____
_____
Remarks and action required _____
_____
_____
_____
_____

PROJECT INFORMATION
Approximate cost _____ Approximate size _____
General scope of services required _____
_____
_____

AS APPLICABLE
Source of lead _____
Names of competition _____
_____
_____
Date for proposal return _____ Date for formal presentation _____
Date for contract award _____ Construction start wanted _____
Occupancy date wanted _____

Contact made by _____
Next contact (date) _____ Type of contact _____

Figure 5-1 *As soon as a cold call is completed, some type of internal record of the information obtained should be made. The prospect qualification work sheet and call report shown here are designed to hold pertinent facts about the prospect and the project.*

I've seen cases where the prospect tired of giving strictly affirmative and negative replies to closed-ended questions and, in effect, rescued an inept cold caller by voluntarily expanding on their answers and giving open-ended answers to closed-ended questions. But you can't count on prospects' being helpful enough to question themselves, as it were.

Pick a word from each column; by combining an open-ended word with a closed-ended one, we get

Who will . . . ?
When are . . . ?
How should . . . ?
Why has . . . ?
What does . . . ?
Where is . . . ?

As information accumulates during the cold call and as you move into the closing stages of the conversation, it's all right to shift to closed-ended questioning. By then your main interest will be in verifying and refining earlier answers.

CONTROLLING THE CALL

As in a formal presentation, you should control and direct the qualification call. As recommended earlier, establish rapport as soon as possible. Once you feel you're on a friendly basis with the prospect, gradually take command.

For instance, don't ever let a secretary or anyone else switch you to someone else without getting the full name and organization title of the person you'll be talking to. Be alert to pick up any other tidbits of information about them you can—how long with this organization, where they came from, nicknames, and the like. Ask for all names to be spelled out. If you aren't sure you got it right the first time, ask until you are sure.

On a cold call I usually ask to speak to the chief executive officer even when I have a name within the organization I am pretty sure of. For a private company this would be the president or executive vice president; for a public client, the mayor or city manager, the governor, agency administrator or director, and the like.

When you ask for the top executive, you are normally put through to his or her executive secretary or administrative assistant. I immediately identify myself by name and city (no more information about me than this in the beginning) and by my interest. At some early point I get the name of the person answering the phone. After that person knows what

I want, I act as if I'm having second thoughts about whether I need to bother his or her boss with my questions, particularly if the person has already made it clear the executive is busy or otherwise unavailable. Ask who else in the firm might be able to help you. Nine times out of ten you'll be transferred to exactly the right person. As we said a few paragraphs back, people are basically polite and *want* to help. As soon as the secretary or assistant realizes he or she is not going to have to tell you that there is no way you are going to talk to his or her boss, the secretary or assistant will become much more helpful and friendlier.

All of the preceding is nothing more than a charade, played out to enable you to get to the right person with the least waste of time. If you tell switchboard operators what you want, they will be polite and try to help—and you may end up talking to seven or eight wrong people.

On the premise that whoever answers in the head office is paid well to know the organization's internal structure, I always opt for that route. Occasionally, you can pick up some useful information there, but I have no interest in talking to the president or administrator or governor in this early project qualification stage.

Presumably, many executive secretaries know what you are up to, but if you come through as a pleasant, friendly, but businesslike person, they have no reason not to play out their part.

When the party you've been referred to comes on the line, you *can* say, "Mr. X (the president or other top executive) referred me to you for information ———." If this slight stretching of the truth causes you any discomfort, say "Mr. X's office referred me to you."

If all you want on the first call is a referral to the right person, try calling around 12:30 P.M. Someone else usually is covering the chief executive's phone while the secretary is out to lunch, and once in a while you'll pick up interesting and helpful information from such a source.

My style in cold calls is to go directly to first names; it helps my comfort level. If your style is to stay with a more formal form of address, fine—be yourself. (I suspect the immediate use of first names is a function of advancing age. Were I 22 again, I'd probably stay with last names.)

An important point to keep in mind when calling corporate clients—particularly when the inquiry is about projects planned for some time in the future—is that the executive you end up with usually will hesitate to volunteer much new information. Remember that corporations, unlike most government agencies, do not have to tell you anything about their plans. There may be considerations of secret site acquisition, expected local resistance to the project, and employee and stockholder relations. The qualifier, therefore, should give the impression that he or she knows most of the details and is only calling for verification of the information in hand. Corporate contacts thus approached will not necessarily feel that they are violating company confidences—and may end up providing much new and useful information about projects.

KEYS TO BEING A GOOD LISTENER

Once the conversation appears to be going well and the information you need is forthcoming, have the good sense to shut up, sit back, and take a lot of notes. These thirteen keys cover the main points of good listenership:

1. *Prepare in advance.* Remarks and questions prepared before you place the call free your mind for the important task of listening. You won't have to worry about what you're going to say next and can focus on the prospect's answers.

2. *Think like the prospect.* His or her requirements and needs are important. And you'll understand and relate to them better if you keep the prospect's point of view in mind.

3. *Limit your own talking.* No one can talk and listen at the same time and derive anything from the conversation. Listening should account for most of your time in a cold call because you are after information.

4. *Listen for ideas—not just words.* Get the whole picture rather than isolated bits and pieces.

5. *Concentrate.* Focus on what the prospect is saying. Practice shutting out distractions that you cannot control before placing the call.

6. *Don't interrupt, and don't rush in to fill silences in the conversation.* A pause—even a long pause—doesn't necessarily mean the person on the other end of the line is through. Jumping in too quickly can rattle some people or cause them to lose their train of thought.

7. *Take notes.* This will help you recall important points later. Be selective; trying to take a verbatim transcript can result in your being left far behind and missing important points.

8. *Ask questions.* If you are unsure about something, ask the prospect to repeat it. Being certain that you have everything correct as you go along is a sign to the person you're talking to of your interest and professionalism.

9. *Use reflective phrases.* When you want someone to elaborate on a point, pursue the thought with a reflective phrase such as "You said . . ." or "You mentioned a moment ago . . ." After repeating the statement,

follow up with an open-ended question: "What else can you tell me about . . . ?" or "How will you . . . ?"

10. *React to ideas—not the person.* Never argue mentally. Don't allow momentary irritation at something said—or the prospect's manner—to distract you from getting the information you need.

11. *Don't jump to conclusions.* Avoid making unwarranted assumptions about what he or she is going to say—or mentally trying to complete sentences for the prospect. Otherwise, your concentration and listening ability will be reduced.

12. *Use listening responses.* An occasional interjection—"Yes," "I see," "Uh-huh"—shows the person you are still with him or her and paying attention. Don't overdo this: it can throw someone off the track to have to talk over a continuing series of grunts.

13. *Listen for overtones.* You often can learn a great deal about the prospect from the way he or she says things and from his or her reaction to what you say. At the same time, be alert to all opportunities to branch—to follow a comment from the prospect into new areas of lead potential.

AND SEVEN STEPS
TO TELEPHONE SUCCESS

1. *Time calls appropriately.* This usually just requires common sense and a little judgment. But sometimes it involves knowing a prospect's particular working habits. You would not call a doctor in his office on a Wednesday afternoon, for example. A rule of thumb is to avoid Monday mornings and Friday afternoons—especially for prospects in the federal government.

On the other hand, if everyone follows that rule, there may be millions of people sitting at their desks during those hours who are wondering why the phone doesn't ring so they'll have something to do. If they are busy when you call, you can always fall back on the question: "When *is* the best time to call Mrs. Smith?"

2. *Get to the decision maker.* If it is a current or past client, information about who makes the decisions should be in your files. The "right" person can vary with the stage the project is in, of course. A senior vice president or the president may make the final decision as to the consultants to be retained—or at least have veto power over someone else's decision—but right now the early decisions may be made by an executive three or four levels down from the top. It never hurts to ask, "Who is in charge of the project at this time?"

3. *Speak clearly and distinctly.* We've mentioned this point before. If you are not sure how you sound, get a tape recorder, and speak into it. Better yet, record a telephone call. Find out how you sound to others.

4. *Don't give any more information at the outset than is absolutely necessary.* This is admittedly a controversial concept, but since you are gathering information—not selling anything—at this stage, there is no valid reason for loading the prospect down with a lot of unnecessary and irrelevant information about your firm, its specialties, branch office locations, past clients, and the like. If your specialties or major disciplines are part of your firm's name—XYZ Structural Engineers, ABC Interiors, Brown & Green Architects—the prospect most likely will screen out projects he or she doesn't think apply to you. As the marketer, I want to make those decisions. If the firm name is that important, the prospect will ask at some point. The tenor and direction of the ensuing conversation certainly will hold many clues to your professional background and interests. Come on as a professional doing research, not as Willie Loman trying to peddle trinkets.

5. *Use good language; avoid crude or annoying expressions.* Slang and blue language offend many people. Test yourself by trying out your telephone approach on friends and fellow workers. Do it on the phone. Insist on candid critiques.

6. *Generally, stick to one piece of business per call.* And make every call more productive by showing interest in the other party, either with a personal greeting or with offers of help.

7. *Be courteous, polite, and helpful.* When was the last time you bought anything from a salesperson who tried to bully or con you? The hard sell does not belong in professional services marketing. I'm not certain where it really does belong, since I am always turned off by it. Don't forget to punctuate your conversation with those magic words and phrases: "Thanks," "I appreciate that," "Thanks for returning my call so promptly," "I like that idea," and "Glad to have been of help." They are simple techniques, guaranteed to help you put your best marketing foot forward.

TELEPHONE TECHNIQUE EVALUATOR

A form similar to that shown in Figure 5-2 is used in some firms to upgrade the information-gathering skills of cold callers. The evaluator listens in on an extension phone or a loud speaker, so that both sides of the conversation are audible.

```
TELEPHONE TECHNIQUES EVALUATOR

                            Excellent                    Poor
     Opening statement      10  9  8  7  6  5  4  3  2  1

     Personal rapport       10  9  8  7  6  5  4  3  2  1

     Areas of mutual interest  10  9  8  7  6  5  4  3  2  1

     Non-fluencies used     10  9  8  7  6  5  4  3  2  1

     Follow-on questions    10  9  8  7  6  5  4  3  2  1

     Branching and spin-offs  10  9  8  7  6  5  4  3  2  1

     Open-ended questions   10  9  8  7  6  5  4  3  2  1

     Grammar and diction    10  9  8  7  6  5  4  3  2  1

     Voice timbre           10  9  8  7  6  5  4  3  2  1

     Inflection             10  9  8  7  6  5  4  3  2  1

     Animation              10  9  8  7  6  5  4  3  2  1

     Rate of speech         10  9  8  7  6  5  4  3  2  1

     Note taking            10  9  8  7  6  5  4  3  2  1

     Interest and empathy   10  9  8  7  6  5  4  3  2  1

     Information verified   10  9  8  7  6  5  4  3  2  1

     Thanks for help        10  9  8  7  6  5  4  3  2  1

     Further contact left open  10  9  8  7  6  5  4  3  2  1

     Closing                10  9  8  7  6  5  4  3  2  1

     Signs of nervousness   10  9  8  7  6  5  4  3  2  1


     Best points _____

     Worst points _____

     Other comments _____

                    _____

                    _____
```

Figure 5-2 *Form for self-critique (or critique by others) of your telephone techniques.*

YOUR TELEPHONE WORKING TOOLS

Qualifying leads and making appointments by telephone may be compared to calling on a blindfolded prospect. Unlike most sales situations, where such presentation aids as charts, slides, signs, pamphlets, and models can be used, in cold-call qualification you have only three tools to work with:

Your voice
Your story
The way you use the first to tell the second

A person's voice conveys a mental image of his or her entire personality to the listener. A physical image often is conveyed as well, but the image and the reality can be poles apart. Make certain that the image you convey is friendly and self-assured. Give the prospect reason to have confidence in you and your firm.

The manner in which you get across your story is an indication of your skill and intelligence and interest. Everything you say should be further evidence that doing business with you will be a pleasant experience.

THE COLD-CALL PROCESS SUMMARIZED

1. From all sources, including those discussed in Chapter 4, develop a list of prospects to qualify.

2. Develop a list of general and specific question subjects upon which to structure the call. Subject areas might include
   - The facilities planning process of the prospect organization
   - Current and future prospects
   - Previous facilities development experience—organization *and* individual
   - Selection criteria and the process
   - Structure of the prospect organization
   - The called individual's role in the organization
   - Selection and project schedule
   - What others in the same general business (the prospect's competitors) are doing in the way of facilities development

3. The goal of the call is to identify one or more specific jobs—jobs far enough into the future that the liklihood of a design firm's already having been selected is nil or small. By the end of the call, reach some agreement with the prospect contact about what, if any, specific action you will take to obtain consideration for the project or projects quali-

fied. If appropriate at this stage, set up a meeting time. As a minimum, have the prospect agree that a meeting in the near future is desirable.

4. As a general rule, send a follow-up letter of appreciation that will also confirm major points of information gathered during the telephone discussion. This should be a *selling* letter.

5. Record all pertinent information from the call on the report form used by your firm—to ensure that consistent, reliable followup is the rule.

REFERENCES

[1]From *Talking Between the Lines* by Julius and Barbara Fast. Copyright © 1979 by Julius and Barbara Fast. Reprinted by permission of Viking Penguin, Inc., p. 19.

[2]Jack Schwartz, *How to Get More Business by Telephone*, The Business Bourse, New York, 1953, p. 49.

[3]Michael Korda, *Power! How to Get It, How to Use It*, Random House, New York, 1975, p. 185.

Chapter 6
MARKETING COMMUNICATIONS: INDIRECT

This chapter and the following one on direct marketing communications correspond loosely to Chapters 5 and 6 ("Promotional Tools and Strategy" I and II) in the first edition. The term "marketing communications," now almost a buzz phrase among design service marketers and marketing consultants, is somewhat more descriptive of the total process than terms such as "promotion" or "public relations."

Here are my definitions of *indirect* and *direct* marketing communications:

1. *Indirect communications* are aimed at a firm's total market or at relatively large (and specific) market segments, consisting of any number of prospects. Indirect communications, if you will, are broad, general marketing attention-grabbers and door-openers—sometimes referred to as "venture marketing."

2. *Direct communications* are normally sole-project oriented and are pointed toward a single prospect (individual or group). They are intended to presell a design firm, its management, and staff by establishing credibility, responsibility, and acceptance in the prospect's mind.

In the case of past, present, and lost clients, direct communications are geared more to keeping already opened doors at least slightly ajar. Indirect communications also must take into account those prospects with whom the firm has had a past client relationship.

For purposes of this discussion we break down indirect communications into four major headings:

Public relations
Printed marketing tools

Direct mail
Advertising

The public relations category includes corporate identity programs, internal communications, exhibits and design competitions, self-serving seminars, and the catchall subhead, publicity. Under printed tools we'll consider brochures, newsletters, reprints, annual reports, job histories, self-publishing, and photographs—plus a few other related items.

COMMUNICATIONS AUDIT

Not so long ago, internal and external communications were viewed as relatively simple processes. Write out the message, send it out as a press release, or post it on a company bulletin board, and the job was done. If you got it into print, the message was communicated!

But the last decade has seen the introduction of myriad new technologies in communications, ranging from "smart" typewriters (with certain self-editing capabilities) to personal computers and satellite transmission of picture and text. Most marketers now realize that the information channel or system used can influence content, along with impact, retention, and action generated. Consider the difference in quality and quantity of information conveyed by a fifteen-minute videotape and the same amount of audiotape.

In view of the fact that modern communicators essentially can deliver messages on command—anywhere, anytime, to any public—assistance is needed to help them decide how, where, when, why, what, and to whom to communicate. The cornerstone of such aid to communications discrimination is known as a "communications audit" or a "needs analysis." As a rule, a firm's needs analysis is closely related to the statement of professional and business goals and objectives in its marketing plan.

Publics to be communicated with are both internal and external. Inside a firm are these publics:

Management
Staff
Stockholders (if publicly owned)
Spouses of employees

External publics include

Clients (lost, past, and present)
Prospective clients

Banks and other financial institutions
Attorneys
Suppliers
Unions
Minority groups
Consumer groups
Environmental groups
Historic preservation groups
Conservation groups
Planning commissions
Zoning boards
Governments (local, county, state, provincial, national)
Political parties
The media
Peers and competitors, including consultants used and professional
    associations

This does not mean that every message must be tailored to seventeen different external publics. But it should remind you to be aware that each of these groups has specific interests and needs and motivations—and that at least occasionally customized communication is advisable.

MANAGEMENT SUPPORT

Out of the needs analysis should emerge internal agreement as to what external image a firm wants to project to its publics, along with suggested schedules, recommendations for media mix and concentration, strategies, and staffing plans. Goals and objectives from the market plan will guide much of the decision making about the firm's self-image.

Whether your marketing communications plan will be fairly passive in nature or aggressively active or perhaps somewhere in between, unequivocal support from top management is of critical importance to its success. Support includes an adequate budget to cover estimated staff and materials costs.

Overall marketing budgets were covered in Chapter 3, where we saw that typical budgets will range from 4 to 11 percent of gross billings. Based on our own surveys among subscribers to *Professional Marketing Report,* the average allotment from marketing budgets to fund marketing communications programs ranges from 10 to 30 percent—with the average at slightly more than 20 percent. "Allotment" is perhaps too specific a term for it; to our knowledge few firms make much of an effort to break such items out of the overall marketing budget.

PUBLIC RELATIONS

Public relations is an extremely important support activity for every firm's marketing efforts—so important that I wrote a 279-page book on the subject a few years ago *(Public Relations for the Design Professional,* McGraw-Hill Book Company, New York, 1980). Because it is still the only book to address public relations from the design professional's standpoint, I strongly recommend that you review it in conjunction with these two chapters on marketing communications.

"Image" is a word loosely used by some PR practitioners. Everyone and every firm has an image, of course, but the rather fuzzily stated goal of certain public relations people is to "establish an image." What is meant, we assume, is to improve or strengthen the already-in-place image.

In a 1978 special issue of *Professional Marketing Report* ("Marketing Principles and Tips") was this item:

> *Image.* Begin with the assumptions that the personal dress and grooming of staff and principals leave nothing to be desired—and that your office looks like a place of business and the telephone is always answered promptly and properly. Now, pull out samples of your business stationery. Alongside them lay out copies of contract and invoice forms. Take out one of your business cards. Add a copy of the firm's general capability brochure, a representative proposal, and a mailing label. Complete this graphic sampling with copies of the last three letters to prospects and a copy of the most recent newsletter, if you publish one. This collection of printed materials should reflect and communicate the same polished professional image your personal appearance does; every item on your desk mirrors you and your firm to the public, for better or for worse.[1]

And, for further proof that image-building begins at home, these items for the same special issue:

> ■ If you appear to be insensitive to such details as the general appearance of your office, how the telephone is answered, the overall image generated by your graphics, presentations, proposals—even dress codes—clients may properly conclude that this is also your approach to design and to progressing the job.
>
> ■ Some firms make good use of their reception areas as part of their marketing program, with displays of framed design awards along with renderings and photographs of projects. A continuous, repeating slide show, with views of projects completed and underway, can also be an effective, low-key promotion vehicle. Give a lot of thought to the selection of slides for this type of showing. Include title and explanatory slides to take the place of the usual narration. Charts, maps, and graphs will also help viewers understand the photographic slides. Although I haven't seen this done, I'd recommend the preparation of a small (number 10 envelope size) folder, listing the slides and

offering a few facts about each project. Your receptionist can make sure visitors get a copy of the folder.

■ Related to the above tip, in one architectural office all of the awards, citations, plaques, and honorary degrees conferred on the principal during some 30 years of practice were framed and mounted in a stairwell leading to the client conference area. The effect on clients and prospects of this massing of professional honors and awards was always a very positive one.[2]

Corporate Identity Programs   Once your "front room" is in order, it is time to look further afield; to consider a full-fledged corporate identity program.

A corporate image, or personality, is the total public perception of a company. This image results from the perceived quality of a company's services or products, its activities in the public and business communities (and policies affecting such activities), and how information about these factors is communicated through public relations and advertising.

Corporate identification programs, utilizing technical manuals and graphics standards guidelines, can bring wider, more immediate recognition of the desired corporate image. There should be a recognizable continuity throughout a company's graphic family. Visual identity programs can be established to cover

Stationery supplies
- letterheads
- envelopes
- memoranda forms

Business Cards
Mailing labels
Checks
Purchase orders
Statements
Decals
Press release heads
Stock certificates
Publications
- brochures
- newsletters
- annual reports
- proposal covers

Title blocks in drawings
Computer printout covers
Office decorations
- entrance doors
- walls
- ashtrays

Field equipment, including hardhats
Job signs
Vehicle identification[3]

Internal Communications   Although many administrative, financial, and personnel items fall under the broad head of internal communications, here we are concerned only with marketing subjects. By now, most principals and marketing directors have accepted the idea that marketing, at some level, is the business of everyone in the firm.

Unless this principle is communicated often, emphatically, and enthusiastically, the average staff member will find other things to occupy his or her time in the office. Periodic reports on the status of prospects—especially those turned up by nonmarketing staff—are one method of helping to focus internally on the importance placed on marketing in your firm.

The use of meetings (scheduled or casual), bulletin board notices, widely circulated memos, and items in the in-house newsletter all help to put marketing into the proper perspective. If your firm has a policy of giving rewards for successful prospect leads, publicize those recipients.

Exhibits   Marketers for design firms have become more aggressive in their promotion efforts, while, at the same time, most of the professional restrictions on exhibiting in trade and association meetings have been relaxed. As a result, many firms are spending more of their marketing communications budget for exhibits.

Anything shown or used in an exhibit should advance the exhibiting firm's self-image, be of interest to those attending the meeting, and be based on an active marketing and promotional medium. The goal is to go back to the office with a list of good prospects, not to spend your time with the curious or just-lookers. As in a telephone cold call, qualify visitors to the exhibit quickly. If they hold no promise, thank them for stopping and move along with your prospecting.

Design Competitions   Design awards of all types can be good promotional tools for the professional. Competitions are sponsored by professional organizations, magazines, suppliers, business development associations, and departments of state and federal governments. One must enter these competitions, obviously, before he or she can hope to win any awards. While a list of the winners almost always is publicized, the list of losers is not, so the secret is to keep entering until your work is recognized by an award.

If the design competition route to publicity is new to you and your firm, a good information source is *The Design and Building Industry's Awards Directory*. The directory, published by the *A/E Marketing Journal* and Lord & Welanetz, Inc., carries complete information about some

200 award programs and their sponsors, from the Acoustical Society of America to the Western Society of Engineers.

In addition to the listings, the sixty-page booklet has several pages of helpful hints and useful tips on preparing submissions plus a checklist for award entries. As of this writing, the awards directory is published annually.

Self-promoting Seminars   Under this heading the emphasis will be on self-serving or self-promoting seminars, with some attention given to other staged events such as open houses, career days, and the like.

There are almost unlimited opportunities for public appearances open to the design professional. Unfortunately, many of these involve talking to fellow professionals—a notoriously bad source of prospects. The trick here is to uncover lecture and other speaking possibilities where the audience is apt to include potential clients.

Since I first wrote about the possible benefits of self-promoting workshops and seminars in the last edition, many firms have picked up on the idea. The earlier edition carried an account of a firm with a large share of its practice devoted to hospital design. This firm regularly offers qualified speakers from its staff to university classes in hospital administration. Students in the audience always are in at least their fifth year of study, and many soon will be going into hospital administration work with a master's degree.

The design firm donates bound copies of the documentation of past projects—master plans, programs, and small-scale copies of plans—to the school's library. Guest lecturers provide each student and the professor with a large folder of material gathered from many sources, including, of course, the firm's own brochures.

The class discussions cover such subjects as planning, development, and construction, illustrated by a motion picture made by the firm for showing to hospital and health field prospects. Since this usually is the initial exposure of the students to a design firm—and their first opportunity to discuss some of the practical matters involved in renovation and new facilities construction—a friendly and interested reception is always assured the lecturers. Best of all, it is a chance to get the name of the design office firmly implanted in the minds of up to forty future hospital administrators in a single presentation.

The results of this type of contact do not manifest themselves overnight; indeed, five or ten years may pass before any one of the students is in a position to influence selection of an architect or engineer. It must be viewed as a long-term investment of time and materials, but most design firms fully expect to be in business five to ten years from today.

William Feathers, director of development in the Los Angeles office of mechanical-electrical engineers Syska & Hennessey, Inc., schedules monthly seminars on building and design subjects for the firm's clients and prospects. The seminars have quickly become an "in" occasion—with clients calling in to make certain they are on the invitation list.

The two-hour, early evening seminars are held in the firm's offices. A cocktail hour runs from 5 to 6 P.M., followed by the seminar from 6 to 7 P.M. The speaker normally takes about thirty minutes of the hour, with the remainder of the time given over to discussion and questions. The Syska & Hennessey office director opens each session with a few words of welcome—the only direct S & H involvement in the program.

A majority of the leading architectural offices in the area—Syska & Hennessey's primary clients and prospects—have been represented in most of the seminars to date. Corporation clients and prospects are also invited.

The Nashville A-E firm of Gresham & Smith has planned, sponsored, promoted, and produced several successful 1½-day seminars on "The Emerging Role of Marketing in the Health Care Industry." For the first seminar one of the firm's goals was to break even on costs, and a fee of $145 was charged each of the hospital administrator participants.

For their fee attendees heard from ten experts, got breakfast, lunch, refreshment breaks, and a cocktail hour—and took home a packet of reference material. Out of the thirty-five in attendance, several good prospects resulted, and the principals decided to hold several more programs in cities in the firm's marketing area.

Open houses and career days held by design firms are not as focused toward prospect development as workshops and seminars, but they do offer community involvement and publicity opportunities.

The Hillier Group, in Princeton, N.J., sponsors an annual career day for local high school seniors and their parents. Nancy Duperrault, Hillier's public relations director, makes the point that a lot of advance planning—including for such mundane items as parking and toilet facilities—is the only way to ensure a successful event of this type.

Following tours of the office and viewing exhibits, students and their parents meet with a Hillier architect to discuss educational goals and personal concerns. Admissions officers from nearby professional schools are on hand for follow-up interviews.

Open houses may be pegged to a significant anniversary or take the form of annual art shows and other types of exhibits and seasonal parties (Christmas is a favorite time) or serve as host for various kinds of civic affairs.

Many offices regularly schedule exhibitions of staff paintings, sculpture, photography and other art forms. In medium- to large-sized cities local galleries are often open to the idea of lending works of art for temporary display. One large architectural-engineering firm in Pennsylvania holds its annual employee art exhibit during the two-week period preceding Christmas, capping the event with the office Christmas party, to which several hundred local friends and clients are invited to join the staff and principals for refreshments and tours of the office.

Certain civic groups are always interested in unusual meeting places, and a designer's office, if he or she has a large conference room, is an ideal location. Scouting groups and others include architectural and engineering subjects in their achievement programs. These young people will always welcome the opportunity to tour design offices and hear an explanation of the operation.

PUBLICITY

As most readers will know, publicity and public relations are *not* synonymous. Much as public relations is strongly supportive of marketing, publicity is the strong support arm of public relations.

Publicity has been defined as "telling the story." Publicity is news—and sometimes vice versa. It traditionally comes in one of two forms: manufactured and natural (planned and accidental). Good PR practitioners try to avoid natural or accidental publicity for their firms.

More than a dozen years ago, in an article in the *Public Relations Journal*, Donald T. Van Dusen set out four rules for handling publicity. They are still pertinent.

1. Find the story. No reporter ever did a good job just "taking news" he got over the phone and the public relations man has to dig even harder.
2. Determine the story's worth to the company, editor, and reader. This is not as simple as it sounds. There are compromises all the way along the line.
3. Think the story out, exploring every angle, twist, interest level, etc. Avoid the mechanical "bored reporter" approach that gets the facts right, but always looks like filler copy.
4. Shape the release, selecting tone, language and structure according to the subject matter and various editorial interests. There are so many variables determining the way a release is written that any "rule" is dangerous, but, in general, an exciting style helps any release as long as the "excitement" is balanced by "content."[4]

With practically every project, the design professional has at least five story possibilities. In chronological order they are

Signing of the design contract
Bid opening and construction contract award
Groundbreaking
Topping out
Dedication

In addition to the plus coverage that truly imaginative groundbreaking, topping out, and dedication activities can bring, there are a number of feature-type articles related to the basic list of stories. They include

A historic or unusual site
Construction site activities and events
Progress stories
New or unusual design features
New or unusual construction techniques

Although every project does not lend itself to the bigger-than, more-than, longer-than, deeper-than approach, the comparative tie-in is applicable to many building stories. An example was in *The New York Times* on June 6, 1969, "Trade Center Doing Everything Big."

> In addition to coils of wire that could be unravelled and stretched from New York to Seattle and more steel than is in the Golden Gate Bridge and enough air conditioning equipment to cool 15,000 homes, the World Trade Center now rising in lower Manhattan will need doorknobs.
>
> Forty thousand doorknobs. . . . the six buildings will have 230 acres of rentable space, nine more than the 18 buildings of Rockefeller Center, and their demand for electricity will be equal to that consumed by a city the size of Schenectady, N.Y.[5]

Another method for developing concrete examples from abstract concepts was illustrated in *Professional Marketing Report* for July 1981. The article was about the then-approaching trillion-dollar U.S. national debt.

> In Marketing Management Workshops on formal presentations, participants are advised to try to relate estimated construction costs and design fees to concrete examples easily grasped by interview committees. Since a trillion dollars ($1,000,000,000,000) is rather an abstract figure (some of us even view a billion dollars as an abstraction), here are some figures and examples to help you visualize those enormous sums of tax monies.
>
> According to the Bureau of Engraving and Printing, a single U.S. note or bill is 0.0043 inches thick and measures 6.125 inches long and 2.562 inches wide. Therefore, a stack of one million $1 bills is 358.33 feet high—say about the height of a 40-story building. If you would rather picture the million bills laid end-to-end, then you are looking at a strip of dollars 96.67 miles long. For every $1 million you can save a client, tell them to think of a stack of $1

bills about two-thirds as high as the Washington Monument—or a string of bills reaching from the outskirts of Philadelphia to New York City.

Even concrete examples of how much a trillion dollars is become somewhat abstract. Staying with the $1 bill stack example, you'd need a ladder 67,865.53 *miles* high to put the last note in place on top of the pile. On the end-to-end basis, you'd have a string of $1 bills 96,669,820 miles long. Mean distance between the earth and the moon is 238,857 miles, so with a trillion dollars in $1 bills you could create a paper highway to the moon more than 86 feet wide; the equivalent of an eight-lane superhighway.[6]

You may occasionally run across editors you think might be interested in how far people will be able to see from the top of their new high-rise office building or apartment house. Under twenty stories in height, the figures are not too impressive, but from 200 feet up, the statistics provide an interesting bit of trivia to drop into a presentation or a news story.

Here is the simple formula for computing how far one sees from how high, taking the earth's curvature into account:

$$VM = \sqrt{A} \times 1.22$$

VM is the view in miles, and *A* is the altitude in feet. Multiplying the square root of *A* by the constant of 1.22 gives the answer (within a foot or so). Using the Washington Monument with its well-known 555-foot height as an example, we get

$$VM = \sqrt{555} \times 1.22$$

$$= 23.56 \times 1.22$$

$$= 28.7 \text{ miles}$$

In theory, a person with normal eyesight standing at the top of the monument can see 28.7 miles in any direction on a clear day. Finding the clear day in Washington is the trickiest part of the equation.

To save you the trouble of looking up a lot of square roots, here are the figures for various altitudes. (The last three are representative VMs from aircraft in flight).

Altitude in feet	View in miles
100	8.2
300	21.1
700	32.3
1000	38.6
10,000	122.0
20,000	172.5
30,000	211.0

Media Relations and Press Releases

ATD = PRTGU = GMR.

Attention to detail = press releases that get used = good media relations.

It's almost that simple. Just about any print editor and broadcast news director will identify the daily flood of useless press releases as one of their greatest headaches.

In 1978, Charles Honaker, a former UPI staffer who had moved into medical association public relations, surveyed newspaper editors about their use of news releases. His findings, written up for the *Public Relations Journal*, suggested that actual use of press releases by media ran from 0 to perhaps 5 percent of those received.

In April 1981, Honaker conducted a follow-up study. Editor-respondents characterized the great majority of releases as "poorly written, fatuous . . . [with] absolutely no news value."[7]

The most glaring shortcomings in press releases, leading to disastrous media relations, seem to be

1. The use of out-of-date mailing lists. Releases are addressed to people who haven't been on the staff for ten years. Some have died.

2. Information is missing.

3. Illiteracy. Of all professionals, journalists are credited with having the largest vocabularies; in the United States, approximately 20,000 words. They have little patience with writers who obviously have not mastered their crafts.

4. No local angle to the story.

5. Cute leads. (Just the facts, ma'am.)

6. Too wordy; too long. According to an *Editor & Publisher* poll, most editors prefer releases of not more than 300 words—about 1¼ double-spaced pages—while 16 percent of those responding consider a 100-word release (three paragraphs) about right.

7. The release arrives late—either after the release date or after the event no longer is news.

Publicity results are often measured (and treasured) in column inches of print media space and in minutes (even seconds) of radio and television time devoted to a story. A one-time staff aide to a U.S. Representative (whom we'll call John Doe) was assigned to clip and save all newspaper and magazine references to his boss. Eventually, the aide turned over to the congressman an inch-thick pile of tiny clippings, each bearing only the words "Rep. John Doe." Or so goes the story around the National Press Club.

Media Lists   These are some of the most useful listings of media contacts and outlets:

1. *Ayer Directory of Publications.* Compiled and published annually by Ayer Press, One Bala Avenue, Bala Cynwyd, PA 19004. The 1981 edition listed more than 21,000 newspapers, magazines, and trade publications in the United States, Canada, the Caribbean, Panama, and the Philippines.

2. *Bacon's International Publicity Checker.* From Bacon's Publishing Company, 14 East Jackson Boulevard, Chicago, IL 60604. Lists over 8000 publications in fifteen countries. Published annually.

3. *The Design and Building Industry's Publicity Directory.* Available from *A/E Marketing Journal,* P.O. Box 11316, Newington, CT 06111, this directory describes the editorial requirements of some 250 national magazines and journals of particular interest to those in the design profession.

4. *Standard Periodical Directory.* From Oxbridge Publications, 1345 Avenue of the Americas, New York, NY 10019, this is a complete guide to U.S. and Canadian periodicals; more than 62,500 listings.

5 *TV News.* A 300-page guide to television news department contacts, this specialized directory is published by Larimi Communications Associates, Ltd., 151 East 50th Street, New York, NY 10022.

6. *Working Press of the Nation.* This five-volume directory, listing more than 23,800 publicity outlets, is published by the National Research Bureau, 310 South Michigan Avenue, Chicago, IL 60604.

7. *U.S. Publicity Directory.* From Norback & Norback, 353 Nassau Street, Princeton, NJ 08540. Published annually in two volumes: business and financial editors in one and radio and TV program and news directors in the other. Regional editions of the radio and TV directory are available.

Another helpful list of reference sources is on pages 57–59 of *Public Relations for the Design Professional.* To get your own media list underway, you might look into current editorial needs of these twenty-five publications:

AIA Journal
American Schools & University
Apartment Life
Architectural Record
Building Design & Construction
Building Progress
Buildings

The Buildings Journal
Canadian Consulting Engineer
Canadian Office
Civil Engineering
Consulting Engineer
Contract
Engineering News-Record
Hospitals
Housing
Inland Architect
Interior Design
Interiors
Landscape Architecture
Modern Office Procedures
Parking
Professional Engineer
Progressive Architecture
Shopping Center World

Keep in mind that *where* an article appears originally is not as important as *what* is done with it after it is in print. You select your audiences for reprints, moving from a shotgun (the original publication) to a rifle approach (sending reprints to your own mailing list). That the article appeared in a leading publication obviously gives it a little more credibility with most reprint recipients, but never turn up your nose at opportunities to be published in even the very small circulation papers and magazines. (I used to cite *Peanut Journal & Nut World* as an example of a relatively obscure publication, but after a former peanut grower and governor of Georgia moved into the White House, the little goober magazine's circulation escalated to the point where I had to find another example of nonhousehold publication names. My current favorite is the *Macaroni Journal*.)

Crisis PR The point was made in *Public Relations for the Design Professional* that "public relations, just as marketing, should never be reactive. Proper planning for crises and disasters can avoid many problems. And the few truly unpredictable situations that arise will seem easier to handle because internal thinking has been directed to the general considerations of crisis public relations."[8]

The last several years have seen a variety of disasters and near disasters involving the design profession and the building industry. Arena roofs collapse and blow away; fires consume luxury hotels and high-rise office buildings; walkways collapse into a hotel lobby; windows in high-rise structures pop out and fall to the sidewalk. Design firms caught up in government bribery and corruption cases face another type of crisis PR as media rush to publicize all such accusations.

Whether it's a loss of a roof, windows, lives, or tax monies, a lot of organizations and individuals get caught in the backlash of such publicity. Even when principals of the design firms involved are finally exonerated, a public perception of something's being not quite right usually lingers on.

A few firms have developed crisis PR procedures. At least one large office has a manual to guide internal reaction in the event of a crisis. What can you do *before* the crisis arises to prepare for an unknown disaster?

1. Get agreement among principals or management as to who will serve as company spokesperson. As insurance, draw up a ranked list of several people qualified to speak to the media. If the primary spokesperson isn't available, number two takes over, and so on.

2. Put together skeleton releases to cover several possible disasters:
   ■ death of a construction worker on the job
   ■ partial or full collapse of a structure under construction
   ■ an injury or death to someone passing by a construction site— from dropped materials and the like
   ■ charges about someone in the firm paying off government officials for any reason

We're talking about a fill-in-the-blanks type of release, which might strike some as a little cold-blooded and calculating, but it is possible to think and reason much more effectively when not under media and official pressures for an immediate statement about the tragedy or charge.

With any luck, you'll never need to pull out the crisis PR file and fill in an outline release. But if the occasion ever arises that sends you to the file, you'll be glad you have at least that much available.

Speeches   A young speech writer once pointed out the difference between the Epistles and the Gospels and their relation to effective speech writing:

> The epistles are letters from the apostles to their brethren warning them against sin and urging them to do good; little sermonettes which most of us need—but abstractions.
>
> But the gospels are stories. Nothing abstract about them. They start out like stories, and anytime you come across an opening sentence like: "Now in the fifteenth year of the reign of Tiberius Caesar . . . ," you know that something is going to happen.

Most people can't remember much from the epistles. Everyone remembers the gospels. That taught me a lesson. If I had my way, every speech would be a succession of stories. As it is, I go to a great deal of trouble hunting actual examples to illustrate the points I make.[9]

One of the reasons for making a speech is the possibility it will have publicity value beyond the audience present to hear the address. If the speaker or the audience is important enough, just the fact that a speech will be given is often worth an advance story.

Once the speech is delivered, it still has one or more PR lives left. You might reproduce the entire speech and send copies (with appropriate transmittal notes) to a select mailing list. Or quote sections of it in your newsletter.

But one of the most productive (and often overlooked) extra lives for a speech is to use parts of it as the basis for news releases to selected publications or as a general release to all news media. If the details connected with getting a release such as this prepared and distributed seem overwhelming, consider turning to one of the PR news services.

North American Precis Syndicate (NAPS), for example, will cut down a speech text to press release length, submit the new version for your approval, and then distribute it to almost 4000 suburban newspapers. NAPS will even produce art to illustrate the article. Cost for a one-column by 7-inch release is $1150, plus $65 per drawing. If you don't get at least 100 clippings, the next release is on NAPS.

If you'd rather use television, a release sent to 325 newscasters and talk show producers costs $1875. The package includes art, slides, scripts, reply cards, mailing, postage, a computer printout of audience data, and a station usage map. The slides and scripts are put together from the text of the speech.

Television and Radio A survey approach to the several types of indirect communications unfortunately does not allow for detailed coverage of any one type. This is particularly so of a complex subject such as the broadcast media.

With the number of public and cable television stations expected to begin operations during the 1980s, the opportunities for getting at least snippets of a firm's marketing message aired on news and talk shows should be greatly improved. For television, anything you do must, above all, be visual; it's that kind of medium even though some network producers seem to overlook the fact on occasion.

Find a contact in local TV and radio stations (the procedure is not unlike locating sponsors in a prospective client group), and help them to help you by sending along interesting program ideas as they arise. Develop credibility, be patient, study the medium—and you will eventually make your own breaks.

PRINTED TOOLS

Brochures   A brochure is the primary printed tool for the majority of design firms. Most principals feel comfortable about brochures, and a general qualifications booklet traditionally has been one of the first things to be put into the hands of prospects.

Brochures may be either the most productive or the least effective items in the professional's kit of promotion tools. After reviewing hundreds of brochures from architects, engineers, planners, contractors, and others in the design and building fields, plus a general familiarity with many other brochures from the same groups of design professionals, one might, as I did in the first edition, venture some general observations. Unfortunately, things haven't changed much in the intervening years.

1. Design professionals' brochures, by and large, are poorly done. Perhaps 20 percent are truly effective.

2. Many brochures come through as a kind of ego trip for the principals of the firm—and little more. In addition to the obvious narcissism, other frequently noted faults are wordiness leading to excessive length (and reader exhaustion), professional jargon, rambling and often meaningless expressions of design philosophy, and insufficient space (and thought) given to client interests about personnel, direct and related experience in the project type, and attention to budgets.

3. One of the secrets of good brochure production is to spend whatever is necessary to produce an effective marketing tool for a firm and its services without giving the client-reader the impression that it is gold-plated. Conspicuous extravagance usually backfires, particularly where the client's project is a modest one or on a tight budget or both. It is also possible to spend a great deal of time and money on a brochure and have it turn out to resemble the cheapest of discount store throwaways, but that is another matter.

Qualities to strive for in a firm brochure are relatively simple and should be self-evident to any professional: clarity, brevity, excellence in graphics, straightforwardness in presentation and text, and a demonstrated awareness of client interests.

In the past, probably the most-used approach to getting a new brochure produced was to ask an advertising or public relations firm to put it together. The writer and other specialists assigned by the consultant to the brochure project usually came to it fresh, open-minded, and completely objective—in that it was the first time they had worked on a brochure for an engineer or architect.

I am happy to report that in the years since the first edition was published a number of good-to-excellent brochure consultants have developed—consultants specializing, in many cases, in working with design professionals. These consultants tend to be clustered on either coast, with a few scattered from Chicago to Houston, which is a disadvantage to firms located in between. However, the good consultants will travel.

We'll close out this brief section on brochures with a few basic design principles, most of which apply to all printed marketing tools. In the Western world we read from left to right; in normal reading, readers always look first at the top of the left column of the left page. In design and layout work, make it easy for readers to begin where they are used to starting.

1. Watch eye movement in design. Keep readers moving in the right direction through a page or spread.
2. The best design is never noticed.
3. Good design reinforces words and helps comprehension and retention.
4. Capital and lowercase letters are easier and faster to read than all caps.
5. Shorter lines of type are easier to read than longer lines.
6. We look at color before we look at black and white.
7. Use subheads, bullets, dingbats, ballot boxes, and other graphic devices to break up copy and make it more readable.
8. Leading (space between lines of type) helps readership.
9. Black type on white stock reads almost 12 percent faster than reverse type (white type on a black or colored background).
10. Quantity comparisons are better illustrated by bar charts than by line graphs.

Photos   When there are several pictures on a page, one should dominate all the others. People look at larger objects first. Humans look at other humans first, then animals, then objects.

Color   Color is a very personal thing; it always attracts attention, and it should always help legibility. All colors have certain associations. Red attracts the most attention and gives the illusion of closeness. Blue gives an illusion of distance. Green reminds people of the outdoors, but green and orange are tricky to use because some people are offended by the two colors. Blue seems to be the least offensive, which accounts for its wide use in direct mail.

Newsletters and News Magazines (The lead piece in *Professional Marketing Report* for January 1977 was called "How to Start a Newsletter." Since its publication the article has been reprinted many times and is used as primary source material in workshops on how to produce newsletters. This section is based on that article.)

Newsletters, with their unique journalistic format, began in the sixteenth century to serve commercial, social, and political interests. After a relatively long period of disuse, they came back from obscurity early in this century, primarily to fill information gaps left by business publications and newspapers.

Variations on the newsletter format include mininewspapers (tabloid size or smaller), magazines, special booklets, and updates to general capabilities brochures on a fairly regular basis. (See Figure 6-1.)

One advantage of a newsletter is its relatively low cost, compared to that of other types of marketing publications. We'll get into detail about costs a little further on. As a marketing tool, a newsletter is particularly well suited to specialized, customized communication: the rifle, rather than a shotgun, approach.

A newsletter can

1. Keep open a direct line of communication between a design firm and its clients and prospects. It also serves as a public relations device—showing your concern for, and interest in, individual clients.

2. Interpret and analyze important forces at work in the design profession and the construction field, alerting readers to significant developments now and in the future.

3. Guide reader decisions on what to do, how to do it, when to do it—based on sound, current advice from authorities in the field.

4. Soft sell. Newsletter experts say that once reader rapport is established, items about a service or a product produce a solid response. But a newsletter should never use hard sell or appear to sell directly; otherwise, it becomes an obvious piece of self-serving promotion.

In the book *How to Produce Professional Design Brochures*, I pointed out that starting a newsletter closely parallels the customary early steps in designing and producing a new office brochure. Some thought should be given to the publics a firm wants to reach and what the objectives of the newsletter are. Likely audiences or publics to zero in on include

Figure 6-1 *Variations on the newsletter theme. The montage of publications represents the hundreds of newsletters from design offices and construction firms.*

most of those listed in the section entitled "Communications Audit" at the beginning of this chapter.

The objectives usually are a little harder to define. They might include the following:

1. To explain new services offered by your firm
2. To reflect staff changes and added capabilities
3. To aid internal staff morale
4. To serve as a continuing contact (bridge) between your firm and its clients and prospects
5. To reflect your firm's experience and competence, through the use of case histories, letters from clients, and other means

The target groups are made up of people who, for the most part, are already bombarded by media messages almost every waking moment. So anything new to be added to their reading load *must* be good—well above average in content, style, and design—even to get their attention.

In 1977 a survey was conducted among the hundreds of newsletter publishers in the Washington, DC area. Some of the results of that survey are pertinent here.

1. Of the 448 newsletters responding, 87 percent use the standard vertical 8½ × 11 inch format.
2. Slightly more than 40 percent of the newsletters gave four as the "usual" number of pages.
3. Almost half (44.1 percent) of those replying publish on a monthly basis. The next most popular publishing frequency is bimonthly, with weekly issues coming in third (11.7 percent).
4. Seven out of ten are typewritten, about a third have type set by photocomposition, and the remaining 3.5 percent are printed from metal type. (Typeset text allows you to get from 10 to 14 percent more material into a four-page newsletter.)
5. Three out of five newsletter publishers prefer white over colored stock, and the same proportion mail the newsletter in an envelope as opposed to sending it as a self-mailer (no envelope). Remember that white stock is always available.
6. Two or three columns in a vertical format are preferred over a single column.
7. Typeset newsletters mostly use a 10-point body type (a point is approximately 1/72 of an inch) in a 20- or 22-pica wide column (a pica is 12 points or .166 inches).
8. In summary, the majority of respondents put out a monthly, four-page newsletter with typewritten text in one color of ink on white paper.

Content   The ideal situation is to have two newsletters: a purely internal one for executives, staff members, and their families *and* an external newsletter for the other publics listed earlier. Some larger firms do have such twin newsletter publishing ventures, but it is not a practical approach for smaller firms. So keep the content of your newsletter as client-oriented and unparochial as possible; otherwise, it may become an early casualty to an overload of staff marriages, new babies, photographs of the principals, and bowling league scores.

Of potential interest to outsiders (particularly to lost, past, and present clients) are items about staff promotions, project case histories, new work, and honors won by principals and staff. Occasional service articles about new trends in design and construction or a different (money saving, if possible) approach to a specific project type usually enjoy good readership.

Use plenty of photographs, drawings, diagrams, and charts. Such visuals, along with short, active headlines, allow busy executives to grasp the main thoughts more quickly and help them decide whether or not to take time to read into the text.

Frequency of Publication   Our recommendation is to begin a new newsletter on a quarterly publication basis. Even four pages can become difficult to fill with interesting material when the editor is on a part-time schedule. Some newsletters use a number instead of a date of publication, avoiding any tie-in with the calendar. (One firm began its newsletter as number 100, achieving a kind of instant publishing history. Luckily, no one ever asked for back copies of numbers 1–99.)

Because there is no consideration given by the receiver for the type of newsletter under discussion, you are not legally bound to maintain any kind of regularity in its publication. There is a certain amount of credibility and reader loyalty to be gained from a regular publication schedule, however—on a monthly or quarterly basis.

Procedure   Once the news and illustrations for an issue are in hand, the routine steps in publishing a newsletter are

1. Prepare a dummy (usually a rough dummy) of the issue.
2. Have the type set, or type it on a typewriter.
3. Get photographs made into halftone prints—called Velox prints. Get other artwork reduced or enlarged to the proper size (as shown on the dummy).
4. Paste up all of the elements (type, photos, heads, page numbers) in their proper positions on a "mechanical"—illustration board or heavy paper sheets—ready for the printer.
5. The printer makes paper or metal plates from your "camera-ready" art and runs the job.

We are considering only the offset printing process for a newsletter, since that undoubtedly is the way it will be printed.

One other procedural matter is the method used to get the newsletter produced. Some firms opt to have an outside consultant take full responsibility for the job. Others manage to find the right people in-house. Still others use a combination of consultant and in-house staff. If yours is a quarterly publication, it should not require more than a couple of days a month of some staff member's time.

Perhaps the best initial arrangement is to have a consultant work with the in-house person, doing layout, editing, preparing mechanicals, and dogging the printer's heels. After experience with preparing a few issues, the staffer should be able to do most of these things. Since *everyone* needs an editor, use the consultant or someone from your staff who is competent to do a final reading of all copy before it goes to the printer.

Costs   The expense of a newsletter normally comes out of a firm's marketing budget. If the publication is produced entirely in-house, all costs should be identified and charged back to the proper budget item.

If the newsletter is to be set in phototype, with justified (even) right and left column margins, the type will cost around $1.25 per column inch or $25 to $30 a page to set. Paper and printing costs for 400 copies will add another $150 to $200 in most areas.

Mailing the newsletter at first-class postage rates can get expensive if your mailing list is extensive. If you mail to at least 200 persons, you might want to check out third-class bulk mail costs. Third-class mail requires a special annual permit from the U.S. Postal Service, filling out forms for each mailing, zip-coding the pieces in order, and delivering the newsletter to a post office. Cost of third-class bulk mail, as of this writing, is 10.4 cents per piece, for up to 5.04 ounces (the rough equivalent of a twenty-four-page newsletter). There would be theoretical annual savings over first class (at 20 cents each) of $113.60, assuming you mail an average of 400 copies per quarter. That $113.60 saving would no doubt be offset by internal costs for the handling just described.

Totaling up the costs for typesetting, printing, and postage for a four-page, 400-circulation newsletter gives us a range of from $302 to $400 for one issue depending on whether the newsletter goes first or third class—or a unit cost of from 75 cents to $1. None of these calculations include the time of inside staff to write, layout, and mail the newsletter, of course, or the cost of a consultant.

Newsletters as Marketing Support   *Design Profile*, the newsletter published by A. Epstein and Sons International, Inc., a Chicago-based design, construction, and development firm, brings a number of interesting features to its prospect and client readership on a continuing basis.

One issue of the newsletter (see Figure 6-2) illustrated the marketing benefits, actual and implied, of third-party endorsements. The article, "We're Making Headlines!" shows the covers of eight business and professional magazines that carried articles about the firm, along with a brief description of the coverage in each case.

The Epstein and Sons' newsletter is an excellent example of the possibilities of publicity recycling:

1. The original articles were seen by readers of the eight magazines.
2. Reprints were obtained and sent to the firm's client and prospect lists.

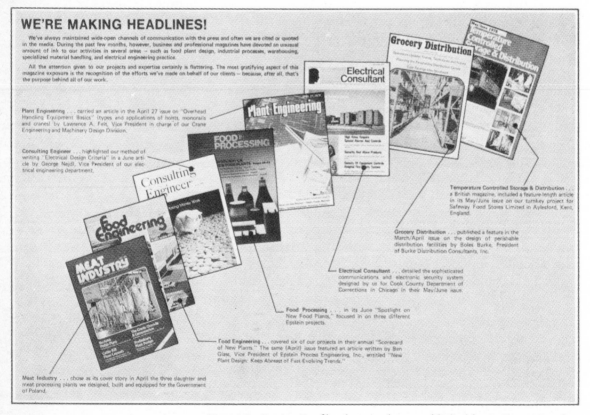

Figure 6-2 *Design Profile, the newsletter published by A. Epstein and Sons International, Inc., features covers of the magazines that carried articles about the firm and its projects.*

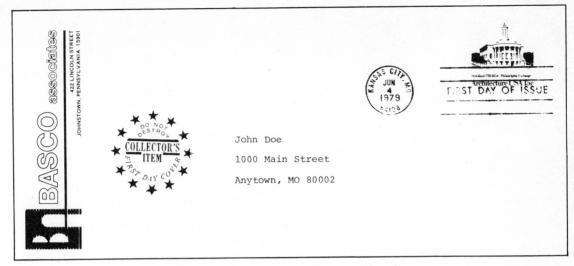

Figure 6-3   *A first-day cover sent by BASCO Associates to clients and friends of the firm.*

3. In a final reprise, a roundup story is carried in the newsletter.

That's about as far as anyone can take the original material.

Imaginative Uses of Newsletters   BASCO Associates, the York, Pennsylvania, subsidiary of Pace Resources, Inc., capitalized on the special June 1979 postal service commemorative stamp honoring American architecture. First, BASCO President Richard E. Shields sent first-day covers, with the stamps affixed, to clients and friends on the firm's mailing list (see Figure 6-3). The letter enclosure explained the significance of the stamp and first-day cover to collectors. Shields suggested that, if the recipient were not a collector, he or she pass along the cover to a philatelic friend.

Then the company newsletter, *Pacesetter,* carried a front-page story about the commemorative stamp issue and the first-day cover gifts (see Figure 6-4).

The first-day cover mailing is an excellent promotion tool even if of limited application. No recipient could possibly object to such a "gift," and the letter enclosure and follow-up newsletter article capitalized on the original mailing.

Reprints—and Piggybacking   In discussing the additional mileage to be gotten from speeches a few pages back, we talked about one form of "piggybacking." Piggybacking, to some public relations practitioners, is the practice of squeezing every possible promotional drop out of any one article or situation.

For example, one of the firm's principals might address a group on some fairly newsworthy subject (first publication). When properly merchandized, the talk will be covered in the local or even regional press (second publication). The entire text of the talk might be picked up by a magazine (third publication). Then, a friendly representative or senator could read the magazine article into the *Congressional Record* (fourth publication). While this doesn't exhaust all of the piggybacking possibilities in this case, it is evident that the original material had three good additional exposures beyond the speaker's original audience. The total audience thus reached could be in the tens or even hundreds of thousands rather than the original 100 or 200 people who may have heard it in person.

A few more words on the *Congressional Record* as a promotion tool for design professionals. Regular readers of the *Record* will know that many of the back pages of each issue are given over to a potpourri of material which representatives and senators have been granted per-

Figure 6-4 *The first-day cover distribution was then described in the BASCO newsletter, Pacesetter.*

mission to "read" into the *Record.* Obviously, they don't really read this mass of material on the floors of the House and Senate. It is only necessary to have an aide deliver it to the House or Senate clerk. The clerk adds the material to the actual record of the day's deliberations, and it ends up as part of the official record.

Getting a quantity of reprints of the appropriate pages of the *Congressional Record* for distribution to clients and prospects is highly recommended (fifth publication—and probably the most effective because of the medium it's in and the rifle approach). The best types of articles to suggest to your congressional representatives are those from architectural or engineering magazines which give a general overview of your firm and its operation or a story about a particularly significant design solution on a major project.

Needless to say, the *Record* is not open to design professionals on a will-call basis. No real rule-of-thumb can be suggested, but insertions should probably not be requested more often than once a session—and even that may be pushing it a bit. Naturally, a great deal depends on an individual's personal relations with his or her senators and representatives.

The staff of the senator or representative involved will appreciate it if you also provide the draft for the introductory remarks in the *Record.* Someone has to write it, and you should know best what should be said (and what you would like to have said) in the introduction to this promotion piece.

Figure 6-5 is an example of the *Congressional Record* reprint approach. Excerpts from the keynote address by Ezra Ehrenkrantz, F.A.I.A., at the awards dinner of the New York Association of Architects, were inserted in the *Record* of November 9, 1979, by Congressman Richard Ottinger, who represents the district Ehrenkrantz lives in. As recommended, the *Record* section with Congressman Ottinger's remarks was pasted up below the masthead of that day's issue—for quick identification of the source and date of the material.

Annual Reports A few design firms that are publicly owned must publish annual reports, but a growing number of privately held firms now publish an "annual reportage" on the previous year's most important events—significant projects won or completed, individual and firm professional honors and awards, important staff acquisitions, mergers or buy-outs of other firms, and the like.

In a way, the voluntary yearly reports are a form of once-a-year newsletters or news magazines as opposed to the monthly or quarterly frequency of publication. They might also be viewed as an annual update of the general capabilities brochure. With the requisite attention to detail, such reports are desirable additions to your kit of printed marketing materials.

Job Histories   Job histories might seem like a mundane subject to include under marketing communications, but few in-house records are so universally neglected by otherwise conscientious design professionals. Job histories, when complete and up-to-date, can play an important role in marketing and promotion.

A format must first be developed that will serve the needs of many

Congressional Record

PROCEEDINGS AND DEBATES OF THE 96*th* CONGRESS, FIRST SESSION

United States of America

Vol. 125   WASHINGTON, FRIDAY, NOVEMBER 9, 1979   *No. 158*

House of Representatives

ENERGY ZONING IN LAND USE PATTERNS

HON. RICHARD L. OTTINGER
OF NEW YORK
IN THE HOUSE OF REPRESENTATIVES
Friday, November 9, 1979

● Mr. OTTINGER. Mr. Speaker, in the keynote address to the fourth annual awards dinner of the New York State Association of Architects, Ezra Ehrenkrantz, a constituent of mine from Mount Kisco, N.Y., raised some fascinating questions about the energy implications of local land use planning. Mr. Ehrenkrantz is the president of the Ehrenkrantz Group, a national architectural firm, and is a fellow of the American Institute of Architects. Some excerpts from his speech follow, and I commend them for my colleagues' consideration:

ARCHITECT PREDICTS NEED FOR "ENERGY ZONING" IN LAND USE PATTERNS

"We have destroyed much of our urban fabric, wasted our farm lands and created an inefficient industrial machine. Our mortgage policies, our tax laws and our Federal funding programs have all emphasized the single family suburban house. The ever-expanding suburban ring has been largely dependent on the free-flow of the Federal dollar."

"Today, we seek to make our automobiles a little more efficient in gas mileage. Today, we seek to make our new houses more energy efficient by emphasizing solar application and insulation techniques. Shouldn't we want to question whether we are building these houses in the wrong place at the wrong time?" * * * "Shouldn't we question land development patterns which require us to drive children to school, to commute long distances, to use cars for everyday shopping? Inevitably we will be faced with the need for 'energy zoning.' "

"At the same time that we were encouraging the suburbanization of our housing, we were moving toward the centralization of agricultural production. Unfortunately, in many urban areas, the result has been to cover the surrounding farmlands with single family houses. Often this was done at great potential national cost, as for example the incredibly fertile lands of the Santa Clara Valley, south of San Francisco, today covered with rambling single family houses and single story high-technology industrial plants."

"For years, our energy costs for industry have been well below those of our foreign competitors. Our industrial plants have been designed to take advantage of that fact. As a result, our plants use about one-third more energy than similar production facilities in Britain, France and Germany, a Massachusetts Institute of Technology study showed. But now we must take a hard look at industrial wattage of energy if we are to compete in the international market place."

* * * "Chinese philosophy has a principle of 'Ying and Yang,' that for everything, there is an opposite. And so too the energy crisis. It will force us to revitalize our cities, to revitalize our agricultural base and to revitalize or industrial machine. We have no other alternative, if we are to survive in the years which lie ahead."●

Figure 6-5 *Congressional Record reprints of speech texts and articles make good promotion pieces for design firms.*

individuals and departments in a firm: administrators, planners, pro-
grammers, designers, accountants, specification writers, estimators, *and*
the marketing and promotion staffs. A number of guides exist, including
the Specification Outline developed by *Architectural Record* a number
of years ago.

Accurate and complete job histories are important in compiling information required for design competition entries. The public relations
staff makes use of much of the information in a comprehensive job
history when writing releases about a project. And new staff members
can get a fast orientation to the firm's important work by reviewing
job histories. So, whatever format is decided upon for your firm, make
certain that job histories are being compiled regularly, accurately, and
fully—as they progress. No one can put together a job history ten years
after the fact.

The narrative job history that follows was developed for use on projects
by architect Edward Durell Stone's office. Having the material organized in this fashion proved to be helpful internally and to editors and
reporters who wanted background information about Stone's larger
projects. The history is not intended to be a press release; it is deliberately overwritten to include something for practically everyone.

JOB HISTORY—FACT SHEET

Garden State Arts Center
Telegraph Hill Park (Holmdel)
Monmouth County, New Jersey

OWNER:	New Jersey Highway Authority Sylvester C. Smith, Jr., Chairman Garden State Parkway Woodbridge, New Jersey
ARCHITECT:	Edward Durell Stone
CONSULTING ENGINEERS:	Engineers, Inc.—Mechanical T.Y. Lin—Structural
LANDSCAPE ARCHITECT:	Edward D. Stone & Associates
CONSULTANTS:	Ralph Alswang—Theater Bolt, Beranek & Newman—Acoustical
GENERAL CONTRACTORS:	Building Contractor: Sovereign Construction Co., Ltd. Site Contractor: Middlesex Concrete and Excavating Co.

The Garden State Arts Center in Telegraph Hill Park on New Jersey's Garden State Parkway will feature an open-sided amphitheater providing covered seating for 5000 people. An additional 5000 people can be accommodated
on the sloping lawn surrounding the amphitheater.

The New Jersey Highway Authority, which operates the Parkway, has planned this project on its roadside site in Holmdel Township, N.J., for opening next June (1968). Construction of the amphitheater is scheduled for completion several months before the opening.

The Arts Center amphitheater will be accessible only from the Parkway, which runs north and south along the length of New Jersey.

A unique feature of the design is the cable-hung catenary* (dish-shaped) roof, with a clear span of 200 feet over the seating area. Except for this upper suspended roof, which is formed of pre-cast post-tensioned concrete planks, the amphitheater is all cast-in-place white concrete. The stagehouse slab is also post-tensioned.

Site preparation included the excavation of more than 400,000 cubic yards of earth, as a hill was removed and the bowl created for the amphitheater. The lowest footings are 94 feet below original ground level. The excavated dirt was used as fill for the 2000-car parking area between the theater and the Parkway. The parking lots will be screened from both the Parkway and the Arts Center. Future parking is planned for an additional 2000 cars on the opposite side of the Parkway, with shuttle bus transportation to the theater.

Eight fluted hollow white concrete columns, five feet six inches in diameter, support the roof structure. The columns also carry lighting and sound amplification systems and drainage conduits.

The stage, 120 feet wide and 45 feet deep, is designed for flexibility. An acoustical shell for presentation of symphonic music is readily moved for other forms of entertainment. The proscenium is 60 feet wide and 49 feet high and the stage is convertible from a conventional proscenium type to a thrust stage.

A two-section orchestra pit allows one or both sections to be used, depending upon the type of program being staged. When the stage itself accommodates the orchestra—as in a concert—audience seating can be expanded to fill the entire orchestra pit area.

Lighting is handled by a combination system from slots in the supporting columns and special light booths incorporated in the roof. Spotlight placement is at the rear and directly above the stage, while a total of 36 theatrical lights will focus on the stage from the four nearby columns.

The four rear columns contain recessed speakers to supplement the main amplifiers, for spectators seated on the grassy slopes adjacent to the theater.

A complete sound control center for recording of performances, special television outlets, understage dressing rooms, storage areas, restrooms, and refreshment stands are other design features.

For patrons in wheelchairs and other handicapped persons, access to the amphitheater is possible from all areas without going up or down stairs. Reserved unloading spots will minimize wheelchair travel. Special restroom facilities for the handicapped are provided.

The unusual roof of the Center is an adaptation of architect Stone's award-winning design for his circular U.S. Pavilion at the Brussels World's Fair. The main Pavilion building in Brussels had a cable-suspended free-span roof

Catenary—the curve assumed by a perfectly flexible inextensible cord of uniform density and cross section, fastened to fixed points at both ends and subjected only to the additional force of gravity.

350 feet in diameter. At the time the World's Fair Pavilion was constructed the only historical prototype for a free-span roof of that magnitude was the Colosseum in Rome, which employed a canvas covering hung from ropes radiating from a circular opening in the center.

A cantilevered, poured-in-place lower roof ring 260 feet in outside diameter rests on the eight columns and the stagehouse structure. This doughnut-shaped roof section is approximately 20 inches thick over the columns, tapering to a six-inch thickness at its outer edges, and cantilevers out 30 feet and in 17 feet from the fluted columns.

A nine-foot-high concrete box girder ring, which is also supported by the eight columns, in turn supports the 200-foot diameter compression ring.

From the outer compression ring 784 high-strength steel cables run inward from 56 stressing stations to a small tension ring 25 feet in diameter. More than 5600 miles of wire were used in fabricating the ½-inch diameter cables.

The central concave roof section is made of 224 prefabricated wedge-shaped concrete panels, each 25 feet long and precisely tapered to fit over the supporting cable network. The lower roof and dome together extend over an area equal in size to a football field.

The inverted dome principle has several advantages; it is more appealing esthetically and is considerably less costly to build than a truss-supported or other type of roof which might have been employed to span the wide area. Still another advantage is an improvement in acoustics. The enclosure and the natural bowl provided by the surrounding topography serve to contain this sound.

Parkway authorities plan a full season of artistic activities, including opera, ballet, drama, and music, beginning in June 1968.

Photographs Almost every story about people and most stories about things are enhanced by a good photograph or two. According to one free-lance photographer, there are three very good reasons to use photographs in a publicity program:

1. To communicate information quickly
2. To create excitement without easily recognized bias
3. To offer graphic proof of intangibles, such as market acceptance, style leadership, quality production, modern manufacturing techniques, and dynamic management[10]

Advance planning, an occasional change of angle, and intelligent cropping are all important in getting the right kind of publicity shot. Good storytelling photographs must be technically perfect and make a definite contribution to the story.

When non-project-specific pictures are in order, many people think only of the better-known commercial stock photo sources—Black Star, Bettmann Archive, the photo libraries of AP and UPI, and the like. In most cases, commercial photo libraries should be the last resort rather than the first.

The best starting place for a photo search is the nearest—local chambers of commerce, local and state development commissions, and city, state, and regional recreation and tourist promotion offices. Don't overlook local newspaper morgues (libraries) and the public relations offices of nearby corporations. All of the sources have good-to-great photo libraries, and copies may be had for little or no payment beyond a credit line when you use the photograph.

Federal agencies, bureaus, and departments have literally millions of photographs in their files—for your use on request and, occasionally, a small fee. The Library of Congress sells a 297-page book, *Pictorial Resources in the Washington, D.C., Area,* by Shirley Green. The book is available from

Information Office
Library of Congress
Washington, DC 20540

The Library of Congress itself is perhaps the most logical starting point in a photo search at the federal level. The library's special photo collections cover most subjects known to humankind, including architecture and engineering.

In *How to Prepare Professional Design Brochures,* I referenced the fine, low-cost satellite and airplane photos available from the Earth Resources Observation Systems (EROS) Data Center in Sioux Falls, SD. For all types of aerial photos, taken from various altitudes in black and white and in color, the best one-stop source is

U.S. Geological Survey
National Cartographic Information Center
Federal Center
Box 25046 STOP 504
Denver, CO 80225

The General Service Administration's National Archives and Records Service is one of the better sources for all types of historic photos—stills, slides, and motion pictures. Since our interest is in still pictures, contact

Still Pictures Division
National Archives and Records Service
7th & Pennsylvania Avenue, N.W.—18th Floor
Washington, DC 20408

And we haven't yet touched on such sources as the Agency for International Development (mostly foreign scenes), Environmental Protection Agency, Department of Commerce, National Aeronautics and

Space Administration or NASA (heavy, naturally, on space views), Department of Transportation, the Smithsonian Institution, and the National Park Service.

If the sheer quantity of potential federal photo sources is a little overwhelming and if you are not quite sure where to begin, contact the office of your congressional representative or one of your senators. Explain your photo requirements, and ask for their help. And expect to get it. You could end up with some much-needed pictures for free instead of paying from $4 to $10 to a government agency—pictures you would expect to pay from ten to twenty times as much for on the commercial market, assuming your photographer could even get the shot.

Self-Publishing   More and more design professionals are writing books— both as creative outlets and as marketing tools for their practices. Your own words, hardbound in printed form with a colorful dust jacket, achieve instant professional credibility.

Just turning out a manuscript is no guarantee of instant immortality, of course. Someone must publish and distribute it. The bad news is that of the some 40,000 new books published annually in the United States, up to half will not sell enough copies to break even. The good news for first time writers is that nonfiction books from unknowns have a much better chance than fiction of finding a publisher.

If you think you have an idea for a book, make up a lengthy outline, write two or three sample chapters, and try it out on several trade publishers. It's always better to let someone else take the gamble on what can easily be a $30,000 to $50,000 investment. If no interest is aroused among the trades, you can (1) forget it, or (2) proceed to a vanity publisher. Under option (2) you take all the risk, of course, since you pay the vanity publisher.

There is a third possibility if you believe your firm can use at least 3000 copies of the book for marketing purposes—and you are prepared to place an order for that quantity upon signing a publishing contract. If the book meets the trade publisher's requirements as to style, subject, and quality of writing, a bargain usually can be struck.

The economics of this arrangement are simple. For most publishers the nut or front-end investment is met when sales reach 3000 or so copies. After that point the publisher must make money. (The break-even sale on my book about brochures was number 3612, according to the McGraw-Hill computer. On number 3613 the publisher began turning a profit.)

One last piece of advice; don't scurry around trying to find an agent for your first book. Few literary agents will even talk to you until you have at least a couple of successful books. Some agents set an income floor—usually around $12,000 annually—and until your royalties exceed that figure, there is little or no interest in you as a client.

DIRECT MAIL

As backup to this section, read the excellent booklet *Direct Mail* from the S. D. Warren Company, 225 Franklin Street, Boston, MA 02101. The publication is free, as is access to Warren's "Idea Exchange." The exchange stocks at least 75,000 different printed samples of marketing communications under more than 200 industry and graphic categories. Write to the same address for information about the Idea Exchange.

The following brief working definition of direct mail is from *Direct Mail:* "Direct mail can be a letter, a booklet, a folder, a catalog. You can use it to advertise, produce sales leads, offer information, sell magazines and merchandise, or solicit valuable market research data. The key is to get your message to the right people."

Commit that last sentence to memory—"The key is to get your message to the right people." With printing and postage costs in an ever-increasing inflationary spiral, direct mail is an expensive promotion and sales tool, particularly when improperly or badly used. On the other hand, well-planned, creatively done direct mail can produce outstanding results. It can be as sophisticated in application, penetration of markets, coverage of potential audience, and selling ability as any other promotion medium.

The list (or lists) to which your direct mail goes can be at once the most important and the weakest part of the process. The best layout, copy, paper, and graphics in the world won't sell church design expertise to a prospect for a sewage treatment plant, nor is the head of a state highway department apt to be impressed with your firm's design awards for hotels and shopping centers. In putting together a mailing list, try to stack the odds in your favor as much as possible by maximizing hot prospects and minimizing cold ones. List refinement or narrowing is just as important as list building.

For example, if you are located in Atlanta and if your real expertise is in designing clean rooms for industry, there are several targets for a direct mail program to prospects:

1. All U.S. corporations
2. The top 1000 U.S. corporations
3. The top 500 U.S. corporations
4. Corporations from list number 3 who must manufacture or assemble products in controlled environments

5. Corporations from list number 4 located east of the Mississippi River

6. Corporations from list number 5 located east of the Mississippi River and south of the Mason-Dixon Line

7. Corporations from list number 6 within a 200-mile radius of Atlanta

Each successive list is narrower and theoretically better than the one it follows.

List Maintenance   The first step in maintaining your own list (called a "house list") is to have it ZIP-coded in order. This can be done in-house with a ZIP code directory, or the postal service will do it for a fee. If yours is a large list—say, more than 20,000 names—you may want to consider putting it into a computer. The computer operation is fully automatic and weeds out duplicates by matching new names against your master list. The new nine-digit zip code (not yet implemented as of this writing) promises a few new frustrations for direct mailers. The USPS claims use of the expanded ZIP will be voluntary. Time will tell.

Few design firms have lists large enough or active enough to warrant computer handling. Most in-house mailing lists are kept on stencils or metal plates. A Xerox list system combines some of the best features of stencil cards with computerization. The address goes at the top center of the long dimension of a $7\frac{3}{8} \times 3\frac{1}{4}$ inch card, leaving most of the card's face free for keying and other notations. The cards are fed through a special machine in the mailing house, which prints "one-up" cheshire or pressure sensitive labels (see Figure 6-6).

The U.S. Postal Service will help in list cleaning. For a few cents a name, local postmasters will check your list against their master list. Names and addresses must be on 3×5 cards or data-processing cards, one name and address per card. If you have "Address Correction Requested" printed on the outgoing envelope, you'll get the undelivered mail back (or a Form 3547) with a new address or the reason for nondelivery. There is a charge for each piece returned.

Once you developed a house list, consider it an important business asset. Keep it clean through regular weeding, and keep it growing by feeding in good new names.

ADVERTISING

The first edition of *How to Market Professional Design Services* devoted just fifty-five words to the subject of advertising, covering a general definition of the term. The omission is understandable in light of the fact that the manuscript was written almost six years before design professionals were allowed to advertise by their respective professional societies. (The AIA, for example, approved the use of certain forms of advertising by its members on May 24, 1978, during its national convention in Dallas.)

By 1980, when *Public Relations for the Design Professional* was published, it seemed appropriate to devote a fifteen-page chapter to advertising for design firms. Since this chapter on indirect marketing communication tools is a survey approach rather than any attempt at an in-depth study, you are again directed to the material in Chapter 14 of *Public Relations for the Design Professional* for a complete discussion of advertising by and for design professionals. Much additional information is in the two-part series "Advertising: New Kid on the Marketing Block," by Vilma Barr. The series appeared in *Professional Marketing Report* for November and December 1977.

The experts generally agree that advertising has two primary functions:

1. To inform a firm's publics about the availability of goods or services.
2. To encourage those publics to make use of the goods and services available.

An understanding of just those two basic points—and what they can mean to your firm's total marketing program—will put you far ahead of most design professionals at this point.

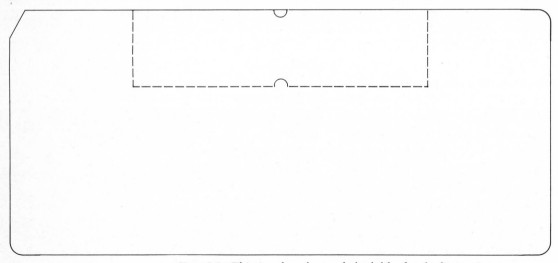

Figure 6-6 *This is what the cards look like for the list maintenance system described in the text. When the cards are run through a special machine, the address area within the dotted lines at the top is transferred to a mailing label.*

In the relatively short time since professional associations relaxed restrictions against advertising, architects and engineers have not exactly knocked one another over in a headlong rush to break into print (or onto the airwaves and television screens) with advertising campaigns.

A few design firms (and their nondesign companion services such as construction management) have been advertising in various media for many years. Most of them have continued to do so. A relative newcomer to the world of advertising is SHWC, Inc., the Dallas-based architectural, engineering, and planning firm. Some of the results of a print advertising campaign were discussed in the firm's newsletter, *Concepts:*

> SHWC was one of the first architectural firms in the nation to implement a repetitive advertising campaign when the American Institute of Architects lifted the bans on advertising in 1978. SHWC's ads for 1981 have a new look with the addition of bold graphics.
>
> Architects, like others in professional fields such as law, medicine and accounting, have been reluctant to advertise. The objective of the first two years of advertising was name recognition. Results are hard to measure for such a campaign, but one project is directly attributed to an ad that ran in *Houston Magazine.* Eugene Ybarra called SHWC, Houston, for help after seeing the ad. SHWC prepared a land-use study, feasibility study and has prepared schematic designs for Ybarra's chain of El Toro Mexican Restaurants.

See Figure 6-7 for a sample of the type of print ad campaign SHWC used in 1981.

SUMMARY

Most of the tools and techniques of indirect marketing communications discussed in this chapter are not even remotely peculiar to professional design services marketing. In that sense, the subject perhaps could have been covered to almost the same degree in the previous edition. But ten short years ago, few firms were intellectually or philosophically prepared to mount the type of marketing program that is almost commonplace among architectural and engineering firms today.

In fact, a fairly large number of the marketers I know rightfully will consider much of the material in this chapter to be rather basic. In that connection, I am reminded of a marketing consultant and friend who decided a few years ago to discontinue his workshops on such basic (but important) subjects as making telephone cold calls for prospect qualification, how to put together a marketing plan, and preparing for formal presentations. He believed that everyone who needed the information already had been exposed to it.

If marketing professional services were a static concept *and* an exact

Define your project before you design your project.

SHWC believes in extensive research and client consultation to determine exactly what your needs are and how they can best be met before you consider a design. We'll work with you to develop your program and present it to you in complete written form. So your project's requirements are on paper before the design is.

SHWC has learned through 35 year's experience that we can present the most functional design when the project is first programmed in detail. From our designs for office and commercial complexes to condominiums to schools and more, SHWC has made it a policy to ensure the project's design fulfills the project's purpose.

SHWC. Because a project is only as good as its planning.

SHWC, INC

Architects   Engineers   Planners

Houston   Dallas   Corpus Christi   Harlingen   Brownsville   Washington, D C
713/444-0114 214/691-6299 512/991-8160   512/423-3044   512/546-5511   703/442-7930

Figure 6-7 *One of the ads in the SHWC, Inc., series. In the original ad, the irregular slashes on the left side and the SHWC initials in the logo at lower left are printed in red.*

science *and* if those doing the marketing all had achieved the equivalent of a marketing MBA *and* there were no movement in and out of the specialty, my friend the consultant might have been right. But people are coming into marketing at the entry level even as you read these words, and the truly conscientious marketer will always seek more knowledge and greater experience. The point is, I suppose, that no matter how many times a thing has been said, there's a large group out there who have yet to hear it for the first time. Some consultants might not know that; most educators do.

REFERENCES

[1]*Professional Marketing Report* special issue, September 1978, p. 5.
[2]Ibid.
[3]Gerre Jones, *Public Relations for the Design Professional*, McGraw-Hill Book Company, New York, 1980, p. 191.

[4]Donald T. Van Dusen, "Is Publicity a Neglected Art?" *Public Relations Journal*, December 1969, p. 17.

[5]© 1969 by *The New York Times* Company. Reprinted by permission. June 6, 1969, p. 45.

[6]"FY 1981 Federal Budget Breakdown," *Professional Marketing Report*, July 1981, p. 3.

[7]Charles Honaker, "News Releases Revisited," *Public Relations Journal*, April 1981, p. 25.

[8]Jones, *Public Relations*, p. 39.

[9]Vincent Drayne, "How to Lose an Audience," *Public Relations Journal*, March 1969, pp. 18–19.

[10]Mel Snyder, "How to Get the Best in Pictures." *Public Relations Journal*, March 1969, pp. 18–19.

Chapter 7
MARKETING COMMUNICATIONS: DIRECT

Indirect marketing communications may be viewed as a form of controlled shotgunning; as a kind of discriminate spraying of identified publics and markets to project the primary message and to help in communicating the firm's overall professional, design, and client relations images.

Direct communications, on the other hand, are rifle shots. After a prospect's attention is obtained, it is time to zero in on as many sensitive areas as marketers can identify. Careful targeting means going in for the kill (sale). Marketers speak of their "hit rate" in much the same connotation.

Most marketers agree that direct communications involve

1. Marketing correspondence
2. One-on-one meetings (for a continuation of the project intelligence-gathering process as well as for the early selling efforts)
3. Qualifications submittals
4. Proposals (including Standard Form 255s)
5. Interview preparation (including the design and production of customized presentation aids)

One writer-consultant suggests that market planning also belongs under direct communications. Technically, just about all marketing communications are in support of marketing efforts directed by and growing out of the market plan. Marketing communications should be spelled out and tasked to specific staff members in the market plan, but one cannot make the whole a part of one of the segments of the whole.

For our purposes, market planning is a separate entity and was so treated in Chapter 3.

Persuasive Communication The operative word here is "communication." Everyone communicates something, of course, but how often and how well you can communicate persuasively determines the degree of your success in selling. Examples of flawed communications and ineffective messages are everywhere. There are probably several examples among the correspondence and other papers now on your desk.

Professor David Ricks, chairman of Ohio State University's International Business Program, collects communications blunders made by big business. Many such blunders occur when manufacturers or distributors overlook cultural differences in foreign markets. Colors, for instance, can be culturally significant: white is the color of death in Japan while green is the color of disease in many parts of Africa.

A few samples from Ricks' growing collection:

1. In Southeast Asia blackened, discolored teeth (from chewing betel nuts) are a symbol of status and prestige. Pepsodent's advertised promise of pearly white teeth from using its products fell on deaf ears.

2. Until a Spanish-speaking employee broke the news to them, Chevrolet executives were unable to figure out why the company's popular Nova model wasn't moving in Latin American markets. In Spanish, "*no va*" means "doesn't go."

3. What began as a promotional blunder by McDonald's in Canada turned into a blessing—albeit an embarrassing one—in disguise. "Big Macs" in French-Canadian slang are big busts, and the oversized hamburger is doing very well in Eastern Canada.

4. Sales efforts of a baby food company on behalf of its product in an African country moved not a jar. The label pictured a cute, cuddly baby, and the mostly illiterate natives thought the contents were ground-up babies.

5. A final example from Professor Ricks' collection concerns an American firm that ran ads for refrigerators in the wealthy—but mostly Moslem—Middle East. The ad pictured an open refrigerator full of delicious-looking food—including a giant ham.

CORRESPONDENCE

Effective selling letters are

Direct
"You"- and "your"-oriented

Specific and concrete
Believable
Interesting
Clear
Grammatical
Cliché-free
Brief

As I wrote in *Productive Proposal Preparation,* the application of two simple writing rules vastly improves most correspondence, especially marketing correspondence.

1. Omit the first paragraph.
2. Write to the *MOM/Y*^{2} ratio.[1]

Omit the First Paragraph   Most of us prepare to speak to an audience by running through a psyching up process we've developed over the years. We clear throats, check out voice pitch and timbre, and generally try to clear all extraneous thoughts from our minds so that we can concentrate fully on the subject at hand.

Unfortunately, beginning a letter seems to call for a similar mind-clearing exercise—and all of the jargon, legalese, and gobbledygook comes pouring out in the first paragraph. By the time we get to the second paragraph, our mental system has been purged of the dull, stumbling, stuffy, nonselling words and phrases. The remainder of the letter is usually good written "salestalk."

In short, most correspondence is vastly improved and strengthened in its selling and persuasiveness by simply dropping the first paragraph. The attractive thing about this particular writing principle is that no one has to modify or unlearn long-standing writing habits. Write, type, or dictate as always, *but* remember to delete the first muddled, weak paragraph just before you hand the letter over for final typing.

I have occasionally encountered hard cases where letter writers run on for two paragraphs—even three in rare situations—before they've rid themselves of the pent-up, noncommunicative verbiage. When this happens, you must drop out as many of the early paragraphs as are necessary to ensure that the letter opens with a selling, persuading orientation.

Should a good thought creep into the first paragraph (an unlikely event), don't panic. Simply incorporate the fragment into the second (now the first) paragraph when you rewrite. Apply the "delete the first paragraph" principle to some of your recent marketing correspondence, especially letters transmitting proposals. Unless you are a writing rarity or have heard the principle described previously, you should immediately see improvement.

This process, incidentally, is known as "editing," and no written product should ever be considered finished until it has been thoroughly edited.

Observe the *MOM/Y²* Ratio The *MOM/Y²* principle of writing will also help you write more interesting and persuasive letters. It is based on a truism we tend to honor all too often by its misapplication: the most important person in the world is me! That does *not* mean the letter writer; "me" is the recipient.

The *MOM* side of the ratio represents all of the inward-directed pronouns—me, our, my, we, us, mine, our, and especially I. Y^2 is to remind you of the three receiver-directed pronouns—you, your, and yours.

Apply the ratio to most of what you write by playing down *MOM*-type pronouns while using as many of the Y^2 words as often as possible. When you finish a letter draft, go back and count the *MOM* words. Put that figure, which might be 10 for a two-page letter, down as the dividend. Then go back and count the "you" words. Unless you already practice the *MOM/Y²* principle of writing, the latter figure may well be 2 or less in the same two-page letter. Your calculation will look like this:

$$\frac{MOM}{Y^2} = \frac{10}{2} = 5$$

A 5 is high; with a little effort and concentration you should reach the 1–2 range in a short time. Considerably more effort is required to change your writing style to the point that you consistently score between 0.3 and 0.5. If you are wondering, it *is* possible to score 0, which can be either very good or very bad news. Obviously, a zero Y^2 count will give you an answer of zero; that's bad. But a zero *MOM* count is the zero answer to aim for; all Y^2s and no *MOM*s.

Examples The following paragraphs illustrate the application of the *MOM/Y²* ratio.

An opening paragraph:

> Please consider the firm of Jones, Smith, Brown & Green, Inc., in your selection process for the above-referenced work. Our firm has in-house capability in all design and engineering disciplines, and we offer the following qualifications, which we believe to be appropriate to merit consideration for your project: [A list of qualifications follows.]

Analysis: The paragraph is awkward and stiff; it communicates badly, if at all. (Technically, as the first, mind-clearing paragraph, it probably should be deleted.) The *MOM*/Y^2 count: our (1), we (2), you (0), your (1).

$$\frac{MOM}{Y^2} = \frac{3}{1} = 3$$

Rewrite: The firm of Jones, Smith, Brown & Green, Inc., offers in-house capability in all design and engineering disciplines—an important consideration in view of the complexity of your project and the desired completion schedule you set out in your RFP. We have these additional qualifications to process your project on time and within your budget: [List of qualifications follow.]

Analysis: Generally a more positive statement. Another rewrite probably would improve it. The *MOM*/Y^2 count: we (1), you (1), your (4).

$$\frac{MOM}{Y^2} = \frac{1}{5} = .2$$

A closing paragraph:

We welcome this further opportunity to assure you of our continued interest in the project and to present our combined qualifications. We look forward to your favorable action in this matter.

Analysis: A rather weak close to what should be an aggressive, persuasive sales letter. The *MOM*/Y^2 count: we (2), our (2), you (1), your (1).

$$\frac{MOM}{Y^2} = \frac{4}{2} = 2$$

Rewrite: JSB&G welcomes this opportunity to assure you of our continued interest in your project. After you've had a chance to review our combined qualifications and the outstanding nominated project team, please let me know how JSB&G may be of further help to you at this time.

Analysis: The count; our (2), me (1), you (3), your (1).

$$\frac{MOM}{Y^2} = \frac{3}{4} = .75$$

The second example revision illustrates one type of legitimate fudging to avoid using a *MOM* word—where the firm's initials are substituted for the original "we." Use of the firm's full name, its initials, or "the firm" in place of *MOM* words will improve the *MOM*/Y^2 ratio appreciably.

Other Examples Although direct-mail selling letters make use of a somewhat different writing style than many of us would feel comfortable with in general marketing correspondence, there are some outstanding examples of the *MOM/Y*^{2} principle in such letters. Read over some of the direct-mail offers you get in the next few weeks rather more carefully than usual, especially letters attempting to sell expensive ("big ticket") items through the mail. You should pick up a few ideas you can use.

Writing Since many aspects of successful direct marketing communications (and almost all of indirect communications) depend on one's writing ability, a few writing tips are in order. This section makes no attempt to be a short course in creative writing; there is no such course, for one thing, because there are no shortcuts to experience.

Teaching or making a point by negative example has a long and proud tradition. If a little humor can be introduced into the reverse example educational process, so much the better; the lesson sometimes stays with us longer.

On page 125 of *Public Relations for the Design Professional* was a list of thirteen not-so-serious rules for writers—my contribution to the negative example school of writing. An anonymous author has since expanded the list of rules to twenty-eight. Here is the expanded version:

1. Subjects and verb always has to agree.
2. Make each pronoun agree with their antecedent.
3. Just between you and I, case is important, too.
4. Being bad grammar, the writer will not use dangling participles.
5. Join clauses good, like a conjunction should.
6. Parallel construction with coordinate conjunctions is not only an aid to clarity but also the mark of a good writer.
7. Don't write run-on sentences they are hard to read, you should punctuate.
8. Don't use no double negatives. Not never.
9. Mixed metaphors are a pain in the neck and ought to be thrown out the window with the bathwater.
10. A truly good writer is always especially careful to practically eliminate the too-frequent use of adverbs.
11. In my opinion, I think that an author when he is writing something should not get too accustomed to the habit of making use of too many redundant unnecessary words that he does not actually need in order to put his message across to the reader of what he has written,
12. About them sentence fragments. Sometimes all right.

13. Try to not ever split infinitives.

14. Its important to use your apostrophe's correctly.

15. Do not use a foreign term when there is an adequate English quid pro quo.

16. If you must use a foreign term, it is de rigor to use it correctly.

17. It behooves the writer to eschew archaic expressions.

18. Do not use hyperbole; not one writer in a million can use it correctly.

19. But, don't use commas, which are not necessary.

20. Placing a comma between subject and predicate, is not correct.

21. Parenthetical words however should be enclosed in commas.

22. Use a comma before nonrestrictive clauses which are a common cause of difficulty.

23. About repetition, the repetition of a word is not usually an effective kind of repetition.

24. Concult to dictionary frequently to avoid mispeling. Corect speling is esential.

25. In scholarly writing, don't use contractions.

26. Don't abbrev. unless nec.

27. Proofread your writing to see if you any words out.

28. Last but not least, knock off the clichés. Avoid clichés like the plague.

Number 11 reminds us that the English language is about half redundant, setting a trap for unwary writers. There are at least three redundancies for the word "redundancy": pleonasm, tautology, and superfluous. Doublets—a kind of synonym for redundancies—are phrases that say the same thing twice. Doublets are among the worst offenders in a lot of writing.

Doublet	*Correct*
absolutely complete	complete
auction sale	auction
basic fundamentals	fundamentals
blended together	blended
connected together	connected
crazy maniac	maniac
dead corpse	corpse
descending down	descending
false pretenses	pretenses
forward planning	planning
lift up	lift
mental telepathy	telepathy

necessary requirements	requirements
pare down	pare
past history	history
recessed in	recessed
retreating back	retreating
share together	share
unintentional mistake	mistake

One writer's pet name for doublets is "baby puppies."

Most messages properly reflect a point of view, but one judgmental adjective, in the right context, can color fact. Herbert Baus, in a book called *Public Relations at Work*,[2] used the case of a governor's refusal to meet with a delegation as an example of how a single word can give distinct editorial coloration to plain fact: "The governor refused . . ."

The governor {
frankly
stubbornly
bluntly
weakly
bravely
sourly
blithely
impatiently
hastily
shrewdly
cautiously
timidly
foolishly
} refused to . . .

The obverse of the judgmental adjective coin is the simple device of quoting someone verbatim. Even the most mellifluous orator can be turned into a fumbling, ungrammatical mushmouth through a direct quotation. Senator Ted Kennedy's moving speech to the 1981 Democratic National Convention is remembered as an outstanding oratorical achievement. Here is the same Senator Kennedy verbatim in a preconvention CBS interview:[3]

> I think we need a foreign policy which is tied to our national security interests, which are tied to intelligence interests for the United States, which are tied to energy interests, which in turn are tied to a sound economy here in the United States and an energy policy that is going to free us from heavy dependence on the Persian Gulf States and to OPEC which is strongly . . . which has the strength and support of the American people and which is predictable and certain, which has a down side to it in terms of disincentives

to the Soviet Union for actions which are contrary to the, to uh, a standard of both international behavior and also has incentives to the Soviet Union, uh, to try to work in a way that can at least some, uh, create at least a world which is going to be freer from uh, the nuclear nightmare which hangs over the world.

Clichés   We all know that persuasive writing is based on precise writing and that readers can be rendered catatonic by too many stale metaphors and clichés. Professors Lois and Selma Debakey (sisters of the famous Houston heart surgeon Michael Debakey) are prolific writers on the subject of clear writing. Herewith, a list of clichés compiled by the Professors Debakey, all of which, to help make the point, should be shunned as the plague.

acid test
all in all
along these lines
at this point in time
be that as it may
belabor the point
bottom line
cutting edge
each and every
easier said than done
exciting new results
fact of life
fall-out benefits
few and far between
for all intents and purposes
goes without saying
hard data
I submit
if you will
in-depth study
in the final analysis
last but not least
leaves much to be desired
matter of course
more often than not
new dimension
play an important role
real challenges
richly rewarding
safe to say

step in the right direction
tip of the iceberg
ways and means
worthy of trial

You probably winced a few times as you reviewed the list; I did. Just because a worn-out phrase is included is not a permanent ban on its use, of course, but it should remind us to apply a little more imagination to how we write and say things in the future.

ONE-ON-ONE MEETINGS

Chapter 5, on qualifying prospects, might profitably be reviewed at this point, especially the material on fact-finding questions. The question forms and examples listed there are just as pertinent to one-on-one interviews as they are to prospect qualification by telephone.

A productive interview is part information gathering (fact-finding) and part selling.

1. Effective interviewing is an art.
2. Successful interviewing is based on the application of a variety of psychological principles and techniques.
3. Research by behavioral scientists has formalized—even formularized—many productive approaches and principles, enabling marketers to use certain tested and proved techniques to improve their interviewing skills.

Nonverbal Communication Communication takes place in several modes and at various levels. We communicate orally, in writing, graphically, and kinesthetically (so-called body language). According to Dr. Albert Mehrabian, UCLA psychology professor, some 55 percent of all communication is nonverbal. This means that interviewers must be at least as good at observing as they are at listening during one-on-one sessions.

Notice that speaking was not mentioned as an attribute of good interviewers. After initial rapport has been established (which does require several communication skills, including speaking), other than to pose brief questions at the right times and to periodically give some sort of verbal feedback to indicate continued interest in what the prospect is saying, a good interviewer will have little to say in most meetings. He or she must be in obvious control of the interview, but that control must be imposed through other means than nonstop talking. It is the prospect who is being interviewed.

Nine different types of nonverbal communications have been isolated by Professor Michael Argyle of Oxford University:

Body contact
Proximity
Orientation
Appearance
Posture
Head nods
Facial expressions
Gestures
Eye contact

Body Contact Aggressive and nonaggressive touching includes everything from the spine-shattering clap on the back to feathery stroking. Body contact often begins and ends with a handshake, and some practitioners profess to be able to read a variety of signs and signals in the initial position of the hand offered and in the firmness of the handshaker's opening grip.

Proximity The proximity element of body language deals with how close to others people stand, sit, or lie. People tend to position themselves closer to people they like. Maladjusted people usually stand farther from other people.

Orientation The angle at which people stand or sit in relation to others, ranging from side-to-side positioning to direct face-offs, comes under orientation. Side-by-side orientation (while standing, sitting, or walking) indicates friendliness, cooperation, and trust. People face each other when confronting, bargaining, and negotiating.

Appearance How a person looks to another person sends important messages about social status, occupation, social group or groups identified with, the self-image level—even political orientation. Faded, ragged cutoffs, uncombed shoulder-length hair, and an untrimmed beard nonverbally tell us a person probably is not a corporation president. Formal or nonformal dress codes address the appearance factor of nonverbal communications. The safest rule of thumb for proper dress for interviews and other selling activities is to reflect in your dress and grooming what you believe professionals should look like. If your own comfort level is high when dealing with a doctor or lawyer who affects a ten-gallon hat, no shave, a T-shirt inscribed "I rode the mechanical bull at Gilley's," cutoffs, and scuffed cowboy boots, then perhaps you are justified in using that model for your own public appearances.

Posture Communication through the manner in which people lie, stand, or sit is a result of posture. Different postures reflect friendliness, hostility, superiority, expectancy, and the like, and others usually can interpret these postures correctly.

Head Nods Head nods are reinforcement, cues for another person to speak, and signals that the nodder wants to speak. Head nods at specific behavior—verbal or physical—serve to increase the frequency of the behavior. During a conversation a head nod by the speaker gives another permission to speak; several rapid head nods are a sign the nodder wants to speak.

Facial Expressions Human facial expressions appear to be independent of learning and to occur across cultures. Facial movements and expressions provide continuous reaction (feedback) between interviewer and interviewee. We tend to try to conceal negative emotions more than positive ones.

Gestures Gestures include the movements of the hands and other extremities. The most expressive gestures are delivered by the hands, but the head, feet, and other parts of the body are also used. Some gestures signal general emotional arousal while gestures such as a clenched fist are a sign of more specific emotional states. Gestures go closely with all communications to emphasize a point and even to replace speech (gestural language).

Eye Contact Eye contact is an important means of establishing the desired interviewer-interviewee relationship. Looking at another person signals interest in what is being said. Researchers have found that people *look* at one another during conversation between 25 and 75 percent of the time. Making *eye contact*—as when both parties in an interview gaze into each other's eyes—happens much less frequently than mere looking. Depending upon the distance between people, true eye contact occurs between 20 and 50 percent of the time. The farther away from the other person you are, the more you maintain eye contact. Some believe that breaking eye contact signals disinterest, guilt, and other negative attitudes; but the fact is that sustaining direct eye gaze over too long a time is uncomfortable and distracting—and unnatural.

Listening We spend about 80 percent of our waking hours (some thirteen hours a day) communicating—in listening, speaking, reading, and writing. Listening accounts for roughly half of that time. In spite of the fact that listening is the most-used communication skill, it is the skill least taught. See Table 7-1.

Interview Organization As was pointed out in the discussion of features and benefits in Chapter 2, the experienced, skilled presenter helps prospects make a series of small but related commitments. Movement is step-by-step toward the sale (close) rather than a headlong rush into the big question—the prospect's final decision. (See Figure 2-5.)

Table 7-1. **Analysis of Communications Skills**

Skill	*Used*	*Learned*	*Taught*
Listening	45%	First	Least
Speaking	30	Second	Next least
Reading	16	Third	Next most
Writing	9	Fourth	Most

QUALIFICATIONS SUBMITTALS AND PROPOSALS

Because qualifications submittals and proposals will be discussed in Chapter 8, we will note here only that they are both technically part of direct marketing communications.

INTERVIEW PREPARATION

Chapters 9 and 10 take up presentations in detail, so at this point we'll be concerned primarily with the direct marketing communications function of designing and producing customized presentation aids.

The operative word is "customized." The substantial investments in time and money made by design firms to get themselves into short-list status—and the opportunity to make a presentation to a selection board—often are negated through a pinch-penny management attitude when it comes to putting together a first-class show for the prospect. (If that word "show" bothers you, be assured it will all be cleared up in Chapters 9 and 10.)

Interview committees and selection boards will always be more impressed by what they perceive to be a presentation customized to their project and interests and slanted to them as individuals. Presentation aids, including audiovisuals, give you an outstanding opportunity to put across a customized approach. (Following interviews, I have heard client groups discussing what they believed were stock presentations—"dog and pony shows"—and how unimpressed they were with the approach. On the other hand, when the group feels a presentation had at least some elements of customization, the residual attitude is a positive one.)

As general guidance, presentation aids should always be supportive of the ideas that precede them and *never* used in a primary role. Aids have these eight primary functions:

Clarification
Proof

Generation of a mood
Definition or identification
Time savers
To strengthen or reinforce
To increase retention (aural *plus* visual stimuli increases retention of a message by up to several hundred percent)
To increase or recapture attention

The Colorado Society of Certified Public Accountants offers these tips for preparing presentation aids:

- Concentrate on making one point or comparison per visual.
- Remember that the eye habitually moves left to right and from top to bottom. Lay out visuals in that pattern. [Remember, also, for ease of audience viewing, that the normal human field of view measures about 30 degrees up, 45 degrees down, and 65 degrees to each side.]
- Avoid decorations (borders, patterns, figures, color spots, and the like) that are not directly related to the subject being visualized.
- Maintain consistent size and shape throughout a single presentation. [Don't mix horizontal, vertical, and square image formats.]
- During the presentation, hold an image on the screen only long enough for an audience to grasp the meaning. [Usually 20 to 30 seconds per image.]
- Control attention and avoid distractions by turning off projectors (slide and overhead) when they aren't in use.
- Distribute handouts only when they are to be used. If passed out too early, the interview group will read them while they should be listening to your presentation.

Graph Distortion   Figure 7-1 demonstrates the potential for information distortion in a 35-mm slide or an overhead projector transparency. The graph at 7-l(a) might represent gross fee sales of a design firm for a thirteen-month period, as

January	$200,000
February	100,000
March	600,000
April	100,000
May	300,000
June	400,000
July	700,000
August	500,000
September	100,000
October	800,000
November	300,000
December	100,000
January	300,000

The peaks and valleys apparent in a conventional axis treatment (vertical equals $100,000 to $1 million; horizontal represents January to January) might leave the impression of a lack of consistency in a marketer's selling efforts. The obvious alternatives: control sales efforts and smooth out the curve somewhat, or make a new graph.

In Figure 7-1(b), the horizontal (time) axis represents six rather than thirteen months (from January to June) and minimizes the peaks and valleys of 7-1(a) to some degree. Another solution is shown in 7-1(c); keep the time axis at thirteen months, but take the vertical axis up to $5 million. That approach damps and disguises vertical changes.

Altering both axes, as in 7-1(d)—which is a combination of 7-1(b) and 7-1(c)—stretches out the curve and condenses it at the same time. This results in almost a straight-line graph. In 7-1(e), graph d is laid over graph a to illustrate the differences caused by axis stretch in both directions.

Types of Visuals   Aids take many forms—blackboards, slides, printed handouts, flip charts, motion pictures, mounted photographs, film-strips, models, closed circuit television, and overhead projection of transparencies, to name a few of the more popular ones.

Participants in Marketing Management Workshops over the past several years know of my personal fondness for flip charts. One of the greatest advantages of a flip chart is the presenter's ability to create visuals as he or she goes (automatically putting action and color into the presentation) and to *destroy* the flip charts as part of the proceedings. The latter action assures prospects that it is *their* presentation, not a canned or off-the-shelf show that you give to all prospects.

(If you have not attended a Marketing Management Workshop on presentations, a word of explanation is in order. The "destroy" reference in the last paragraph is to marking up sheets of the flip chart as you go. With a list of five reasons why the prospect should retain your firm, for example, that you have just written on the chart, do something to each brief statement as you review the list. Circle each statement, or put a check mark or a bullet in front of it. This is a clear signal to the interview committee that they are getting a custom presentation. You would hardly take the scribbled-on chart into a future interview.)

One of the prime advantages of a flip chart is that you use it in a fully lighted room. (Obviously, the main disadvantage of a slide presentation is that it must be shown in a dark room.)

A major disadvantage of flip charts is the presenter's need to turn away periodically while lettering or drawing on the pad, foregoing eye contact. One might conclude from observation and experience that the ideal visual aid

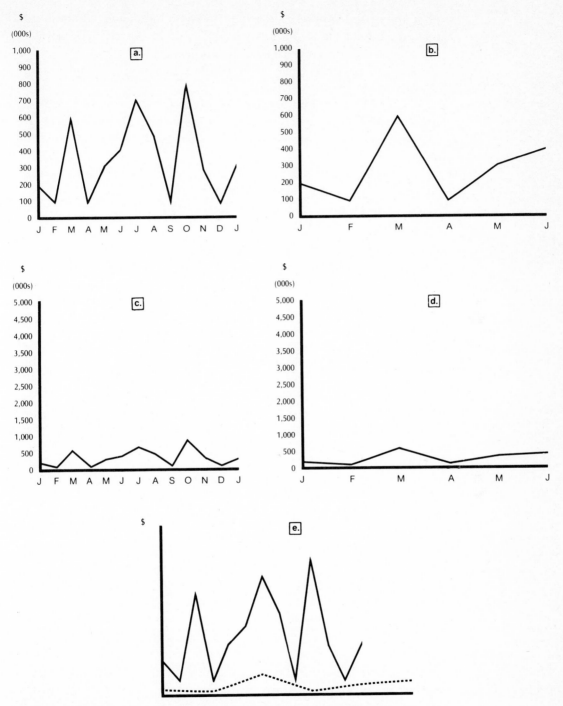

Figure 7-1 *Changing the value of either or both axes on a graph leads to a distortion of the information presented.*

169

1. Can be used (and seen) in a meeting room light enough to maintain good eye contact—and to allow viewers to make notes if they wish

2. Allows the presenter to face the audience at all times

3. Enables material to be displayed large enough and high enough for everyone to read it with ease

4. Is flexible in format so that the presenter can use material prepared in advance, as well as create images during the presentation

5. Is basically portable—perhaps close to standard briefcase size and weight

6. Allows for changes or updating of material to be made in a location remote from your office—rapidly, simply, and inexpensively

7. Uses quiet, nondistracting projection equipment

8. Is simple to operate

If that sounds like a list of user benefits and features for an overhead projector, you aren't far off the mark.

The Overhead Projector Definition: An overhead projector places an image on a screen by passing light through a transparent acetate or other cell that lies on the face of the projector. Overhead projectors commonly have a 10-inch square projection surface (the stage), but frequently use transparencies with a $7\frac{1}{2} \times 9$ inch field, usually in the horizontal position. (See Figure 7-2.)

Film such as 3M's type PPC 671 is available to make overhead transparencies from your originals on most office copying machines. (PPC stands for "plain paper copier.") Type 671 gives a black image on a clear background, but with color adhesive or color transparency film sheets you can add an overall color background or highlight in color selected elements of the transparency.

Single transparency sheets can be projected as they come from the copier, unmounted. For more heft, easier handling, and to provide a place for notes, it is recommended that cardboard frames be used to mount the transparencies. If you add color transparency sheets, the frame must be used to carry the film sandwich. Write-on film (plain transparent sheets) can be used to create visuals, much as the created flip chart sheet. The write-on film is placed on the projector stage, and the presenter, using colored-ink pens, draws the image as he or she talks.

If you prefer more latitude in color use on an overhead projector, a number of infrared films are available. These films, which must be exposed on a special copier, give

1. A black image on red, yellow, blue, or green backgrounds
2. A color image (red, green, blue, or purple) on a clear background
3. Clear (reverse) images on black, red, or blue backgrounds

In all cases, color adhesive or color transparency films may be added to the infrared film transparencies for additional color impact.

Several companies, including Bell & Howell and 3M, make a full line of overhead projectors—from large, not-at-all portables to completely portable machines. 3M's 6202 Executive Presenter weighs about 17 pounds and folds into a briefcase 10½ inches wide, 12½ inches long, and 4¼ inches thick. The projector is air-cooled and silent in operation, which means a little care is required on the part of the operator; leaning on the hot projection head could be hazardous to the skin.

Our recommendation: look at several makes and models of portable overhead projectors. Try them out. Study the sales literature. As of this writing you won't find a smaller machine than the 3M 6202, but there are cheaper portables. You might want to write 3M for copies of a

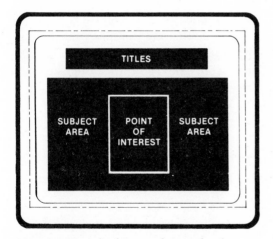

Figure 7-2 *Standard image format for the overhead projector. Both vertical and horizontal formats may be used, but horizontal images are considered best for audience viewing. Titles generally should be at the top of the original and information kept within the bottom two-thirds of the transparency for the best visibility. With a frame, the image area is 8 × 10 inches, but the best results are obtained when the image area is confined to 7½ × 9 inches.*

couple of helpful booklets, *A Guide to More Effective Meetings* and *Transparency Preparation Guide.* Write to:

Visual Products Division
3M Center
St. Paul, MN 55101

One last point—overhead projectors are more prone to noticeable keystoning than are slide projectors. (Keystoning is caused by an indirect angle of the projector in relation to the screen.) This is curable by using a keystone eliminator—a little arm which juts forward from the top of the upright standard that supports the screen. A hook on the top of the screen is brought into position on the arm, tilting the image forward and eliminating the keystone effect. Another cure for keystoning is to use a cardboard frame, with the opening forming a reverse keystone and attached to the projector stage. The image is actually projected as a reversed keystone, and when it hits the screen, the two keystone effects cancel each other.

For additional information about the preparation and use of presentation aids, you may want to refer to Chapter 8, "Audiovisuals," in *Public Relations for the Design Professional* (McGraw-Hill Book Company 1980) and to the 1977 Glyph Publishing Company marketing manual, *Effective Audiovisual Presentations.* Another helpful booklet is *Overhead Projection Guide*, available from Arkwright, Inc., in Fiskeville, R.I. Arkwright makes overhead transparency materials.

REFERENCES

[1]Gerre Jones, *Productive Proposal Preparation*, Glyph Publishing Company, Washington, D.C., 1981, pp. 12–13.

[2]Herbert M. Baus, *Public Relations at Work*, Harper & Brothers, New York, 1948, p. 127.

[3]"Teddy," Interview with Roger Mudd, *CBS-Report*, Nov. 4, 1979.

[4]*Conference Speakers' Guide*, Colorado Society of Certified Public Accountants, Englewood, Colo., n.d., p. 6.

Chapter 8
PREPARING PRODUCTIVE PROPOSALS

For most design professionals, learning how to win at the proposal game is a time-consuming, frustrating, and basically learn-from-experience process. Relatively little has been written about the subject that has realistic application to the marketing of professional design services. A few books will be of some help to engineers, architects, and planners trying to improve their proposal writing skills—and most of them are referenced in this chapter.

Some evidence of the increasing importance attached to productive proposal writing is the fact that over the past several years one of the most popular Marketing Management Workshops has been "How to Write Winning Proposals." And in periodic surveys of *Professional Marketing Report* subscriber interests, solving the perceived mysteries and intricacies of the proposal writing process ranks near the top on everyone's list.

THE FIRST STEPS

Basic to your understanding and use of the information that follows is the realization that all proposal efforts begin with a thorough analysis of the *request for proposal* (RFP). If you don't understand the client's requirements, as set out in the RFP, then your proposal is apt to lack one or more of these three things:

Focus
Specificity
Responsiveness

And nothing disqualifies a proposal more quickly than a perception of nonresponsiveness on the part of proposal evaluators. Such perceptions arise for one or all of these reasons:

1. You do not seem to understand what the client wants.
2. Your proposal appears to call for meeting objectives different from—even alien to—those set out in the RFP.
3. Deliberately or unconsciously, you ignored or glossed over items of obvious importance to the RFP writer.

Proposal consultant Herman Holtz suggests that these five points must be made in all proposals:

1. A demonstration of your clear understanding of the project
2. An offer of a reasonable plan, backed up with a logical, persuasive rationale
3. Evidence that your plan is likely to work out all right
4. The offer of a well-qualified staff for the project
5. A reasonable estimate of costs, presented in an understandable form

Holtz says these are the five most evaluated items, and they are listed in their usual order of increasing importance to most evaluators.

When required by a prospect, submission of a proposal must be considered the first subgoal in the marketing process; it is a key way station on the road to winning the job. The second subgoal is attained when prospects include your firm in their short list for formal interviews, with the latter selling plateau increasingly reached through answering an RFP. Final victory is achieved, of course, when you are selected for the project.

Writing a good proposal might be viewed as a form of establishing and proving your firm's *provenance* in experience, staff, and organization. Collectors of all types of things, antique and contemporary, will be familiar with the term "provenance" as it applies to collectibles.

The source or origin of a sixteenth-century Persian rug, an eighteenth-century netsuke, or a nineteenth-century oil painting (indeed, of even 1940-era baseball cards and comic books) traditionally is established by written documentation from the seller, along with notations about previous collections the item has been a part of in the past.

The proposal's primary purpose, then, may be realistically viewed as a vehicle for setting out in detail why and how your expertise is greater than that of others who may propose for the project and also what the derivation of your expertise is—in short, the proof of your professional provenance for *this* project.

Among the subjects to be covered in this chapter on proposal writing are

In-depth analysis of the RFP
Planning and organizing
Makeup of the proposal team
Required or justified levels of effort
Strategies and tactics in proposal writing
Internal assignments
Scheduling
Budgets
Controlling the process
Internal evaluation of the finished product
Basic elements of a proposal
Writing the proposal
- Research
- Outlines
- Establishing a theme
- Editing
The use of graphics and visuals

Several checklists—specific and general—will be provided, along with useful tips from successful proposal writers and from those who evaluate your proposals.

HOW NOT TO DO IT

Winning proposals are not written in a few spare half-hour periods or by those unskilled in composition, good grammar, and organization of material and time. Nor are winning proposals pulled together in a day or two from off-the-shelf components and by overly generous use of word processors.

If the go or no-go decision is to "go," then the final product should reflect all the positive factors and attributes of your firm, staff, management, direct and related experience, attention to detail, and design capabilities. Anything in the least negative or tentative does not belong in a proposal. If that fiat gives you a problem, you probably should take it as a message to pass up this RFP.

Attempts to scrimp and save at the proposal stage of marketing are misdirected, inane, and practically guarantee failure. If it is "go," then go first class; bid to win or don't bid.

ANALYZING THE RFP

Selectivity and objectivity are important early considerations. When a firm's principals insist that the marketing staff respond to every RFP that comes along and consistently refuse to assess the firm's chances against the potential competition, profitless years are in the future. Some firms have perfect track records for proposal submissions: 0 jobs for thirty-eight proposals, 0 for 103, and the like.

As for the decision to pursue a prospect, two now-familiar questions must be answered for every RFP received:

1. Is it a job?
2. Is it a job for our firm?

In a determination of whether or not the RFP describes a real job, such questions as sources of client financing, local codes and regulations, and the possibility of the project's being wired must all be disposed of.

Actually, the RFP evaluation begins much earlier. After an RFP is logged in upon its arrival in the office (more on this later), it is routed to the editor-coordinator or proposal manager for dissection. The initial evaluation ideally is based upon a point-by-point—almost a sentence-by-sentence—review of the entire document. The editor or manager writes a memo of findings and recommendations and circulates it to those who will decide on whether to go after the project. If possible, this should be done a day or so before the first review meeting.

Here are some of the questions for participants in the review meeting to discuss and answer:

1. For all areas of the RFP, do we have specific, identifiable, and marketable capabilities?

2. How many—and of what quality—competitors are we apt to face for this project? (Does the prospect really need *us*?)

3. Is the required staff available, and do we have the financial capability to progress the project?

4. Does the prospective client have funds—or the ability to get them—to pay for the services required?

5. Do we have a real interest in working in the project's geographical location?

6. Do our expertise and our direct and related experience rank us third or higher among the probable competition?

7. If the project described in the RFP isn't of interest in itself, should we submit a proposal on the basis of the potential follow-on work for this client?

Or you may prefer to run through a list of key points—items that you know must be covered thoroughly and positively in any proposal, but relating them to the subject RFP. Each of these points may be rated "negative," "neutral," or "positive."

1. Quality and extent of your marketing intelligence about the prospect and the project
2. Probable competition
3. Proposed project team
4. Direct and related experience with the
   - client type
   - project type
   - geographic area
5. Requirements for consultants, associates, and subcontractors—and their probable availability
6. Your ability to meet all identified RFP requirements
7. Sufficient time, staff, and budget to propose properly and professionally for the project
8. Your ability to establish a profitable, competitive pricing strategy
9. Your general interest in the project

Jack Robertson, in his book *Selling to the Federal Government*, suggests these six guidelines for making the go or no-go decision about an RFP:

1. Has your firm done its homework? (Did you have enough advance information about the project to begin preparing a proposal months before the RFP was issued? If a firm starts its response as of the day the RFP is received, it's probably too late.)
2. Is this a real project that will meet an actual need? (Could the prospect just be testing the market, in a form of design consultant tire kicking? Project officers sometimes request proposals long before budget funds are committed.)
3. How well does the prospect know your firm? (Will you have to begin at ground zero in your marketing to the prospective client? Is there time?)
4. Is the RFP itself defective? (Some RFPs are so defective that a firm should seriously consider passing them up on that basis alone. A few RFP red flags:
   - Criteria for proposal evaluation are omitted or are vague and ambiguous.
   - Related, high-stake costs are ignored in the RFP.
   - No expected award date is given, leaving proposers wondering how long they should keep staff and other resources committed.)

5. Is the RFP wired for a favored firm? (Even the most experienced design professionals occasionally get suckered into proposing on projects slated to go to a favorite consultant. Overly optimistic—or desperate—marketers ignore such telltale signs as

- Very short deadlines to submit a proposal—or very short delivery schedules.
- The RFP seeks equipment, special features, or consultants not readily available.
- Special tests are required.
- Performance specs that sound suspiciously as if they had been written by a competitor.)

6. Does the project really fit the company's marketing plan? (Does the firm have the resources to perform the contract if it wins? Can it acquire the necessary talent and equipment? At what cost?)[1]

Related to Robertson's last point is this consideration: no design firm principals in their right minds will badly overcommit staff. Remember that your first obligation always is to clients already on your books. Play as fair with present clients and their projects as you expect to be treated.

Here is yet another set of guidelines for deciding when to and when *not* to enter a proposal. You *should* compete when

1. The profit potential is good to excellent
2. The project will allow broadening of staff skills in desirable areas
3. Your firm has identified, unique capabilities
4. There is an opportunity to acquire equipment or facilities as part of the contract
5. It offers company make-work, to spread overhead in slow times

You probably should *not* compete under the following circumstances:

1. The project is truly foreign to your past experience.
2. You've had *some* experience, but it really is too light. (Don't overlook the current client syndrome of more is better; if the competition has done fourteen or twenty-five or 120 jobs just like the project in the RFP and if you can claim only three or five or nine, it will be a very uphill fight.)
3. The job is wired and you are able to identify it as such early enough.
4. The competition is too strong (but don't be faked out by fast-talking competitors on this point).
5. Winning the job would stretch staff capability to the danger point.

(Remember the brief lecture of a few paragraphs back on being fair to your current clients.)

6. You know that your proposal will be a cover or convenience entry to make the procurement section "look good"—or to make the selection process legal. (Some jurisdictions require a minimum number of proposals before an award can be made. Not only is this approach non-productive of work, it is also probably illegal under the Sherman Act.)

Summarizing this section on RFP analysis:

1. Resolve to read and understand every part of an RFP.
2. Set up your own go or no-go criteria for internal guidance in decision making. You may want to include or adapt some of the check points set out above.
3. An ignored RFP may be your best marketing move of the week.

DEFINITIONS

As we move into the planning and organizational stages for answering RFPs, some definitions may be helpful. There are two fairly common types of proposals used in the design profession:

1. *Qualifications proposal.* Often an unrequested proposal, the qualifications proposal usually reflects a firm's qualifications for doing a certain kind of project or a specific part of the project. Many qualification proposals are little more than expanded general capabilities brochures. They are used mostly in interprofessional marketing.
2. *Requirements proposal.* A requirements proposal is used to respond when clients set out their requirements, usually in the form of a request for proposal. Fee proposals are a form of the requirements proposal; they are exactly what the name suggests.

Here is a suggested definition of the type of proposal we'll concentrate on through the remainder of this chapter: a written response to an RFP, with explanations and documentation of

What the proposer or bidder offers to do
How it will be done
With whom
On what schedule
At what estimated cost
The proposer's qualifications to do the job
The reasons the proposer should receive the contract

PLANNING: THE PROPOSAL TEAM

Nothing worthwhile is ever achieved without a plan. And the better the plan, the greater your chances for success. In successful proposal writing perhaps the only common denominators are detailed planning and organized teamwork. Every proposal is—or should be—a customized, unique effort from the best qualified team you can assemble for the job.

A few successful proposal submissions will convince you of the importance of internal organization and intensive planning. You will also realize that a winning proposal is seldom, if ever, an individual creation. It depends on cooperation, teamwork, and contributions from management, accounting, technical and production staffs, and the proposal writers.

Makeup of the proposal team usually is governed by the requirements and nature of the project covered by the RFP and by the availability of in-house personnel. A typical proposal team could include these specialists:

Editor-Coordinator or Proposal Manager He or she takes full responsibility for the final product. This role may be filled by a principal who has primary marketing responsibility, the marketing director, or the nominated project manager. Since every successful undertaking, in war and peace, operates under a single commander, full responsibility for the total effort must be vested in the editor-coordinator. And since responsibility must be accompanied by the necessary clout to get things done, something close to full authority must also be extended to the editor-coordinator. The person who fills this key spot must

1. Have a good to encyclopedic knowledge of the organization
2. Be knowledgeable about proposals
3. Be able to make assignments to technical and production people and to follow up on staff assignments effectively
4. Know how to set up and follow schedules
5. Be able to work well under increasing pressure and short deadlines
6. Know how to do research, plan, and write.

Because proposals ultimately win through their ability to persuade and sell—as a written form of selling—in many firms marketing or communications specialists become the editor-coordinator.

Proposal Writer In smaller firms the proposal writer will be the same person as the editor-coordinator. If yours is a fairly large office, given to generating and answering numerous RFPs, you may well have a writing specialist or two who spend almost all of their time on proposals.

Contract Manager Strictly speaking, the contract manager is not a member of the proposal team, but since he or she has obvious control and administrative responsibilities for the contract, when won, it makes sense for this staff member to play a role in the initial RFP analysis.

Graphics Adviser or Consultant Again, in many firms the graphic direction and input will be from the person who coordinates or manages the proposal. Graphic standards are important to winning proposals; establish them for your proposal output.

Estimator The estimator is responsible for all cost and pricing information included in your proposals.

Various Technical and Production Staff Members The need for their input is as determined to be necessary by the proposal manager—on a schedule established during the first review meeting.

Consultants For a particularly significant or desirable project, some firms retain proposal consultants. Such consultants are more commonly found in nondesign firms, for example, aerospace companies and military equipment suppliers. Consultants should be able to advise on both the cosmetic and content approaches.

Proposal teams may be set up as permanent units or as special groups organized for each RFP. Most firms—particularly the smaller ones—prefer the ad hoc approach, drawing on all departments and specialties for staff and information as necessary.

PLANNING: THE SCHEDULE

Early strategy for producing winning proposals includes

1. A definition of the strategy to be used in *this* proposal
2. Assignment of responsibilities
3. Creation of the master control and planning schedule

A sample master plan is shown in Figure 8-1. The schedule is set up for a preparation time of eighteen working days, but it is important to remember that the schedule is compressible or expandable to fit the situation.

Relatively few proposal managers have the luxury of an eighteen-day turnaround for RFP responses. But as you get organized internally, so that each RFP does not result in crisis action and a crash program, you should find that purely reactive proposal writing becomes the exception rather than the rule in your firm.

Every activity shown on the schedule is important and must be accomplished at some point. In extreme cases the entire schedule can be compressed into a few days—even into a few hours—but few winning

Proposal Master Schedule (for 18 working days)				
Days to Go	Meetings	Research and Information Input	Writing	Art	Production
18	First review meeting				
17	Strategy and coordination meetings	Begin background research		Selection of type and paper stock	Order paper if necessary
16			First draft of transmittal letter		
15		Background research cutoff		Begin design of cover, tabs, B.P., charts	
14	Status meeting	Begin assembly of technical, management, and cost information			
13			Final draft of transmittal letter	Cover, tabs, charts due	
12		Technical, management, cost information due	First proposal draft due		
11					
10	Status meeting		First proposal draft review cutoff		Print cover, tabs, charts
9					
8			Final proposal draft due		
7					
6			Final draft review cutoff		
5	Final review meeting				Print proposal
4					Assemble proposal
3					Check final assembly
2					
1	Proposal due				

Figure 8-1 *Suggested working schedule for proposal anaysis and preparation.*

proposals are produced under such time constraints. The proposal master schedule should call out these milestones:

Date for completing background research
Dates on which technical, management, and cost information are due
Date for completing first draft
Cutoff date for first draft review
Date for completion of final draft
Cutoff date for final draft review
Proposal production deadlines
Final review, sign-off, and delivery dates

As all proposal managers learn early in their careers, clear initial guidance to technical staff members is extremely important. Control and planning of staff input can be difficult, but they must be handled by the proposal manager. Some managers use assignment sheets or proposal directives to define

1. Specifics required (often set out as a series of questions).
2. What each internal discipline, division, or section is to provide in the way of essential elements—from a suggested working title to detailed descriptions of text segments required.
3. The number of pages, number and types of illustrations, charts, tables, and the like. Don't pad; don't be too brief.
4. The sequential time frame schedule, with due dates for all information required.

Just as you will do a dry run of formal presentations, provide time for a thorough internal evaluation of proposals before they go to prospects. Whenever possible, select evaluators from among those who did not work on the proposal—for obvious reasons of objectivity. Finally, review the proposal with the aid of a checklist you've developed. Some of the important points to be covered by such a list will be given later in this chapter.

LOGGING IN RFPs

What happens to an RFP when it reaches your office has a lot to do with efficient scheduling of the preparation process. If no specific procedures have been established, it's possible for the RFP literally to float around in a firm for days—even weeks. In some firms the person who opens the mail knows vaguely that RFPs should be routed to one of the principals. If the principal is out of town or otherwise occupied, the RFP tends to get buried on a desk after a day or two. From there on it's all downhill. This haphazard method of receiving RFPs is the primary cause of panic production at the last possible minute, which, as I pointed out above, results in few winners.

Make someone in the firm responsible for receiving anything that even resembles an RFP and for logging it in. It should then be quickly and automatically forwarded to the editor-coordinator for action. From here on the schedule dictates the followup. Over a period of time, the logging-in technique will gain many days at the important front end of the proposal preparation process.

SETTING UP STRATEGY

These are the three key, early steps to producing a proposal:

1. Define the strategy.
2. Assign responsibilities.
3. Put together a master control schedule.

Winning at anything requires a strategy. In their book, *How to Create a Winning Proposal*, Jill Ammon-Wexler and Catherine Carmel suggest this approach to strategy development:

1. *First*—analyze what prospects *say* they want in the RFP.
2. *Second*—decide what the competition probably will offer.
3. *Third*—decide what your firm can offer.
4. *Finally*—decide on the best strategy for assembling the proposal most likely to win. Develop a cohesive theme with an effective selling impact.[2]

The essence of making a successful proposal is strategy—in programming, in costing, and in overall presentation.

THEME DEVELOPMENT

Some proposal writers compare the importance of a proposal theme to the plot of a novel. Without a plot—no novel; no theme—no proposal.

Remember that proposals initially are read and evaluated by people who are humans not unlike yourself. Effective proposals always benefit from an identifiable theme. To make it easy for readers to grasp your primary salespoints, make it crystal clear that you

1. Really understand the problem
2. Have a practical solution
3. Have backed up your solution with an implementing program

4. Have selected the best qualified, most professional team to accomplish all of these goals

After you've decided what it is you want to say in the proposal, say it in the clearest possible way. And don't be afraid to restate your theme throughout the proposal.

1. *Identify* the theme.
2. *Write* a topical outline around the theme.
3. *Plan* where the theme will go in the proposal.

A basic theme for any proposal is the assurance to the prospect that he or she will be "in good hands" with your firm—and especially with your nominated project team. As you'll recognize, this is borrowed from the Allstate Insurance Company's theme.

RECORD KEEPING

Strange to report, some design firms have no idea of their success or kill rate with proposals. Seemingly, they have a bottomless well of funds to tap at will, and proposals (and Standard Form 255s) are ground out endlessly with no concern about the project return rate. Most of what has been written about proposal preparation overlooks this dollar-and-cents consideration, so practitioners will find little guidance in the matter. Diane Creel, in a paper for the Society for Marketing Professional Services, wrote:

> It is good to keep up with your proposal "track record"—how many pre-qualification packages are getting you to a short list, how many qualification packages are getting you to an interview, and how many fee proposals to the project. By keeping this record, you can obtain insights that will give you the opportunity to make immediate changes to increase your success rate.

The only change I'd make in the quotation would be to substitute "mandatory" for "good" in the first line.

Elsewhere in her monograph, Diane Creel mentioned that the firm she then worked for achieved a 53 percent win record (out of some 100 proposals submitted) during the previous year. No one in marketing should have to be told that taking 53 percent of the projects on which you propose is a record to be emulated. More important than the number of proposals won is the total dollar volume represented. The latter should not be a problem if proper standards of selectivity are applied in early stages.

What *is* an acceptable win record? Dollar volumes involved, individual firm goals and objectives, your general client mix, and the number and quality of your competitors are some of the considerations in deciding whether or not your proposal activities are paying off. Anything less than a 20 percent kill rate would be a danger signal. Firms with special skills and relatively few competitors probably should hit in the 40 to 60 percent range. Therefore, a win rate of from 25 to 35 percent is acceptable—but it is a rate always to be improved upon.

ANATOMY OF A PROPOSAL

Most proposals contain three primary elements:

Technical information
Management information
Pricing information

Without pricing information, the proposal technically is a qualification statement; when fees are included, it becomes a fee proposal, of course.

Some (occasionally all) of these twenty-two sections may be included in a proposal:

Cover
Letter of transmittal
Title page
Table of contents
List of illustrations and tables
Executive summary
Terms of reference; scope of services; or statement of work to be accomplished
Proposed execution (methodology)
Schedules
Exceptions to RFP (if any)
Company history
Facilities
Related past experience
Project management
Staff resumes
Associates, joint ventures, subcontractors, consultants
Visual aids (charts, graphs, maps, photos, diagrams, copies of design awards, and the like)
Costs
Terms and conditions
Explanation of cost-estimating techniques used
Certifications and representations
Draft contracts (when required)

Summaries should be used freely throughout the proposal. In the preceding list a technical summary might appear after the tenth item (exceptions to RFR, if any); a management summary following the sixteenth item (associates, joint ventures, subcontractors, consultants); and a summarization of the cost information after the twentieth item (explanation of cost-estimating techniques).

The list is not necessarily in any order, and not all of the twenty-two possible elements will be used in every proposal. Let's now consider each of the twenty-two sections in some detail.

Cover   While the entire proposal must be regarded as a selling instrument, three elements—the cover, letter of transmittal, and executive summary—should be viewed as the primary sales pieces.

The cover *always* should be customized to some degree. Usually, the more customization, the better selling job it will do. As a minimum, the cover should carry the client's name, city and state, project title, and the name of your firm—or association or joint venture. Add a logo, official seal, or some other form of graphic identification of the client. If the client has no logo or seal (a rare occurrence), design one. It may take all of fifteen minutes; you aren't trying for gallery-class art forms.

Photographs and other art can be used—of a local scene or object related to the client and project. Here are a few examples of cover art seen in recent years:

1. A photograph of an Atlanta bus loading passengers, with the intersection street sign visible; for a proposal to MARTA in Atlanta

2. A regional map showing the location of the prospect's job *and* locations of all projects done by members of the proposing joint venture in the area

3. For a recreational park study, a view of a scenic wooded area on the site

4. A series of several small photographic views of areas related to the project

When the cover elements have been assembled, give the final layout some graphic attention. A pleasing design, with clean readable type faces and a judicious use of white space, has never been known to hurt a proposal's chances. Give some thought, too, to the selection of cover paper stock, especially its color and texture. Too dark a stock color will cause type and artwork to fade into the background.

Letter of Transmittal   A few basic considerations are these:

1. Make certain the letter is addressed to the right person.

2. Be sure the addressee's name, title, organization, and address are spelled correctly.

3. Try to keep the transmittal letter to less than two full pages.

From the strategy approach already agreed upon, select the two or three main reasons your firm is uniquely qualified to do the project. Be concise and factual, but be convincing. Since a transmittal letter is incorporated by reference into the proposal, it becomes part of the formal offer from your firm; from both psychological and legal viewpoints the letter should be professional, persuasive, and complete.

Some letters of transmittal I've seen appeared to have been carefully worked over so as to become dull, uninformative, and uninteresting. Actually, as much time and effort should go into writing the transmittal letter as is devoted to any of the other major sections of the proposal—perhaps more.

Some of the items usually included in a transmittal letter follow:

1. A reference to the RFP—usually by title and number. Pull this reference out of the body of the letter, and put it in the upper right section of the first page, as

Re: Boylton National Park Study
No. FM-320-14-B

2. An indication as to whether you are responding to the RFP as it was issued. If you are proposing alternatives, taking exceptions to some parts of the RFP, or submitting an alternative proposal for any reason, mention it in the transmittal letter.

3. Any conditions in your proposal; the offer is contingent upon award on or before a certain date, or you give an expiration date beyond which the proposal is invalid.

4. The type of contract proposed.

5. As much information about the firm's and the nominated team's direct and related project experience as you can squeeze in without making the letter longer than two pages.

The page-and-a-half to two-page limitation can be violated, but there should always be a good and compelling reason for doing so.

At this point you may want to review the material on marketing correspondence in Chapter 7, particularly the recommendations for omitting the first paragraph and writing to the MOM/Y^2 formula.

Title Page   Title pages in proposals are not always appropriate; they are probably best used when it is a lengthy proposal for a complex project. Some firms use the title page for a disclosure statement to prevent recipients from passing along proprietary information to competitors. A disclosure statement recommended by some federal agencies is this:

> The data contained herein shall not be disclosed, duplicated, used in whole or in part for any purpose other than to evaluate the proposal, provided, that if a contract is awarded to this offerer as a result of, or in connection with,

the submission of these data, the client shall have the right to duplicate, use, or disclose the data to the extent provided in the contract. This restriction does not limit the right to use information contained in the data if it is obtained from another source without restriction.

Whenever a disclosure statement is used, on the title page or on some other early page, it's a good idea to follow the statement with a list of the sections or pages to which it applies. Then, at the top of each protected page, a brief statement along these lines should appear: "Use or disclosure of proposal data is subject to the restriction on the title page of this proposal." Many firms use a rubber stamp for the supplemental statement.

Table of Contents   Not many proposals boast a table of contents. For shorter documents—say up to twenty-five pages—a table of contents would seem superfluous, if not ostentatious. The primary reason for including a table of contents is to make it easier for evaluators and other serious readers to refer back to key points or sections. Obviously, the proposal pages must be numbered consecutively in order to benefit from a listing of the contents. (Some proposal pages are not numbered in any fashion!)

List of Illustrations and Tables   If the proposal includes more than a half-dozen illustrations, charts, and tables, a listing probably is justified—again for the purpose of making life a little easier for evaluators.

Executive Summary   An executive summary should follow the letter of transmittal (or appear after the title page, table of contents, and list of illustrations and tables, if those elements are used). Since by its nature the section is a *summary* of the entire proposal, it must be one of the last elements written, that is, after the rest of the proposal is complete and has been through all of the editing, rewriting, and polishing stages.

The executive summary should be viewed as an abstract or condensation of the total proposal that follows it. Use the summary to highlight unique and significant ideas and to restate for emphasis the three or five or seven strongest reasons for hiring your firm. Don't forget to spotlight the nominated project team.

Charles B. Thomsen, architect, author, and marketer, explains and defines the executive summary:

> [An executive] summary, always at the front, should convey 98 percent of the message using 2 percent of the words so a busy executive can get the message without falling asleep and so the person who actually reads the whole proposal has a framework of understanding upon moving into the full version.[3]

Some more of Thomsen's advice about writing winning proposals:

> Short proposals are almost always better proposals. It's hard to be brief, but your clients will appreciate it. . . . Simple words, graphics, and a distin-

guished cover letter are the essential components of a good proposal. Most of the time you have to force yourself to be original and fresh, using good material only when it applies. The important parts of a proposal are the sections on (1) services, (2) qualifications, and (3) price. The rest is boilerplate. The most important thing is not to let the support material smother the communication. Keep the issues up front and the backup where it belongs.[4]

Jack Robertson, in *Selling to the Federal Government*, has this to say about executive summaries:

> Whatever else [is included] in the proposal, it should contain an executive summary. This key section gives an overview of all the parts of a proposal, summarizing the major information and details. It outlines the program scope, expected results, state of the art, and how work will be accomplished. It summarizes the company experience, program, staff, and resources. The executive summary should make explicit reference to the other parts of the proposal, and each theme should be documented and presented in detail. Finally, it should end up with the sales pitch; the reasons why the firm should be awarded the contract.[5]

Herman Holtz and Terry Schmidt point out that the executive summary

> . . . may be (and in our view should be) pressed into service to aid in selling. That is, while the Executive Summary should offer an abstract of the proposal, it should be so constructed as to present the chief appeals—reasons for acceptance, using the most persuasive language and presentation possible. One recommended way of doing this is to organize it as a series of points, each a brief paragraph with a number, bullet, or other device to dramatise it. It should, however, be kept as brief as possible—probably not more than ten items, unless the proposal is an extremely large one.[6]

In addition to the executive summary (one of the three primary sales tools in a proposal), summaries should be used freely throughout the proposal—to restate, reemphasize, and resell. Do not be concerned about the obvious repetition this approach calls for; repetition is a proven, traditional, and effective sales technique.

The executive summary will be the first part of the proposal proper to be seen by evaluators and members of the selection group (some will read no farther). It should be brief (two to eight or ten pages, depending on the length of the proposal itself), graphically attractive, and interest-arousing. Use subheads, bullets, ballot boxes, underscoring (or through-lining with a transparent ink marker), white space, charts, photos—anything to pull the reader into the text. Some proposal designers call extra attention to the executive summary by shifting to a different paper color and even to a different paper weight and texture.

Terms of Reference; Scope of Services; or Statement of Work   Pick one of the three phrases used here—the one you feel best describes this section.

The extent and complexity of this part of the proposal is best decided after a thorough analysis of the RFP—and with some idea of the technical background of potential readers (clients occasionally retain a technical specialist to supplement the efforts of staff evaluators). Use simple graphics to explain and expand on technical points wherever possible. Try to limit task descriptions to a brief paragraph for each.

Proposed Execution (Methodology)   Some of the information in this section—sometimes referred to as the program plan—may repeat or refer to data in the previous section on scope of services and statement of work. This is the section in which you describe how the activities and personnel of your firm will be organized to get the job done. Usually included in this part are

Master schedule and plan for the project
Manpower estimates and staffing analysis
Work breakdown analysis
Proposed makeup of the project team
Related experience
Implementation and control plans

All six of these items should be explained graphically as well as described in the narrative.

Schedules   The subject of schedules may be treated as a separate item (it usually is in lengthy or complex proposals), or it may be included under "Proposed Execution." The project master schedule details time frames for completion of each major project task and for the entire project. A program evaluation and review technique (PERT) chart often is employed to present the master schedule. Each subsequent project task is scheduled so that the required completion date is met.

Exceptions to the RFP   If the proposal team believes that some parts of an RFP should be modified, they have these alternatives:

1. Take an exception to the questioned item or items. Detail the exceptions in a special entry in the technical section of the proposal. This method can be risky because an evaluator may decide the proposal is nonresponsive, especially if the exceptions are lengthy.

3. Respond to the RFP as it stands; then submit an alternative proposal based on your exceptions.

Either way, you must be able to justify all exceptions as soundly based and designed to save time or money for the client.

Company History   Do not give a month-by-month developmental account of the growth of your firm since its founding. Summarize such information as

1. When the firm was founded and by whom
2. General nature of the practice
3. Anything that will establish and reinforce your credibility for *this* project; similar projects for similar clients, design awards, publications, and the like

General capabilities brochures sometimes are bound into the proposal to cover this section.

Facilities Describe what you have, including branch offices—with special emphasis on those facilities which may be used during project design and construction. Particularly where joint ventures or associations are involved, you might consider including a diagram showing locations of

Where the design work will be done
The project
The client's office

Distances between each of the locations should be shown in minutes of travel time and drawn proportionate to the actual time involved, as in Figure 8-2.

If a diagram like this would weaken your case, it obviously should not be supplied. (The same diagram enlarged can be used on a flip chart during a formal presentation or projected from a 35-mm slide or an overhead projector transparency.)

Related Past Experience Some of the material about related past experience may appear elsewhere in the proposal; remember, repetition is an accepted promotion technique. Here you want to demonstrate past experience with the same or closely related project type for similar clients. Cover experience in such items as

Estimating accuracy
Budget control effectiveness
Management contributions
Staff and facilities utilization
Diversity and depth of experience
Field support

Writing techniques, which we'll take up later in the chapter, can make all the difference in how your message gets across. Take the case, for example, where your staff, as individuals, have certain appropriate experience for a project, but your firm has no track record with the project type. Unless the RFP demands that you discriminate between staff experience and organization experience (some RFPs carry such a requirement), you can state "The staff of ABC Design, Inc., has experience with seventeen projects of a similar nature . . . ," thus compensating in some degree for the firm's own lack of experience with the project type.

Project Management   If this is not set out as a separate topic, it may be included in the section entitled "Proposed Execution." Featured under this heading is a full description of the nominated project management team, with the greatest emphasis on the proposed project manager's background, qualifications, and direct and related experience. Management control procedures should be discussed at least in general terms; the more specific you can be here, the better. Organization charts should be used freely.

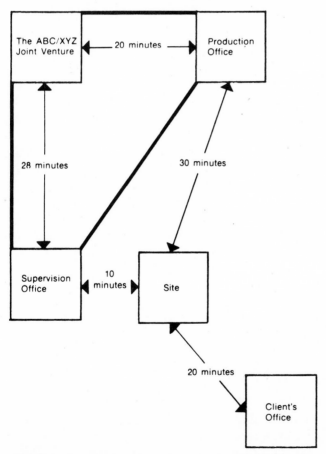

Figure 8-2 *Location diagram showing relation of project site to A-E offices, the production office, and the client's office.*

Staff Résumés   The section on staff résumés should be the clincher for the proposal. Ideally, every member of the proposed project team will have had many years of direct experience with the same type of project being proposed for—all equal or greater in scope. Since this ideal is seldom, if ever, realized, the proposal manager should make sure that everyone on the team appears in the best possible light. If, for example, someone has heavy experience in both grain silo and bridge design—and the project is a bridge—naturally you'll lead off with the bridge experience.

Résumés seldom are reworked for every proposal, a fact which can present the proposal manager with problems. Some firms make up three or four basic résumés for each of their technical people, emphasizing different experience and capability backgrounds in each version. This form of trying to outguess RFP requirements is successful perhaps 50 percent of the time.

A better approach is to leave two to four inches of the résumé page blank under a heading "Experience." A list of the total work experience of each staff member is kept in marketing's files. After the proposal manager indicates which jobs and the order in which they should appear on the résumé, a typist or word processor can quickly type in the relevant experience data. This method works best (and looks better) if the typewriter type matches the rest of the résumé.

Try to keep résumés to a standard length and in a standard format (one page seems preferable; two pages are acceptable if there really is that much relevant information about one person).

Of the greatest importance to the prospect is the individual's experience with the building type under consideration. Next in importance is the staff person's experience in the position he or she occupies in the organization chart. Among the kinds of information usually found in résumés are these:

Birthplace
College and university degrees and graduate study
Length of employment with your firm
Special education courses completed (when related to the project)
Personal and professional honors and awards
Publications, especially books
Teaching experience
Registrations (if numerous just give totals, but making sure to call
    out registration in the state where project is located)
Professional organizations of which staff person is a member; offices
    held, if any

Foreign travel and work experience
Foreign languages person is fluent in
Patents awarded

The data on publications, teaching experience, foreign travel and languages, and patents held may relate only indirectly, if at all, to the project being proposed for. Although this might sound like a violation of the "nothing but project-relevant information" rule, the information usually is worth including because some clients are impressed with such activities and achievements, particularly those clients who have had fairly unexceptional and ordinary careers themselves.

The use of a photograph in the upper left or right corner of the résumé is becoming more popular in most firms. The picture should be fairly recent—never more than three years old—and preferably showing the individual in a work environment.

Throughout the proposal, and especially in résumés, use specifics wherever possible. Instead of "many" say, "twenty-one;" rather than "numerous" say, "seventeen," and the like. Where you are weak, however, it is usually better to generalize. "Several" or "numerous" sounds better than "one" or "three."

Résumés also benefit from graphic attention. Develop a good format, and be consistent in its use.

Associates, Joint Venturers, Subcontractors   When other firms are brought in to work with you on a project, the prospective client must be convinced that each outside member is the best obtainable for the job and that the total entity offers at least as much as the sum of its parts.

Put associations and joint ventures together very carefully. There must be a justifiable and convincing reason for every firm in the package. One of the best selling points for an association or joint venture is that each of its components has worked together in the past on projects at least as large as the present project.

One proposal consultant believes that the appearance of your staff's capabilities can be profitably broadened by including well-known, competent people from college and university faculties. These consultants should cost you nothing until you get the project. Some firms make good use of advisory or review councils, both in general marketing and for specific projects.

In the proposal you might state that "for the six-month (or nine- or twelve-month) design review we will bring together a panel of experts drawn from among the following. . . ." You obviously are safe in putting almost anyone living on *that* list.

Always try for consistency throughout the proposal, even when you have to marry information and brochures from five or six firms in a joint venture. At least for significant projects—for sophisticated clients—make the proposal appear as an entity, with typefaces and type sizes, paper stock, and format the same throughout, except where you purposely change them for emphasis. And try to avoid including third and fourth generation Xerox copies of material in a proposal; it is not the sign of a class operation.

Visual Aids   While content will always be important, the appearance or style of your proposals can count heavily with those responsible for making up the short list of firms for further consideration. Careful graphic attention, as we've said elsewhere, must be given everything that leaves your office. This is especially true for proposals, since marketers are precluded from most personal selling at this point in the process. The proposal, therefore, must carry messages about your attention to graphic and design detail, along with information about your experience and technical expertise.

One method of setting your proposal apart from the crowd is the use of visuals to explain, emphasize, and expand on the narrative material. Scatter professional-looking illustrations, charts, graphs, and other types of art throughout the proposal.

Related to the use of illustrations and other art is a creative typographic approach. Use the graphic devices listed under "Executive Summary" throughout the proposal to give it visual interest and to lead readers into particularly important information.

Anything you can do to relieve the mass of gray typescript that most proposals become will be in your favor. Open up the pages; make them more inviting to evaluators and, later, to those who decide on selection.

Covering something less than the full width of the page with typing helps. Some firms have adopted a proposal page format featuring a vertical rule (line) about one-third of the page width in from the left side of the sheet. Another method of narrowing the typing area (which, incidentally, makes the material easier to read) is to prepare proposal pages with a screened area on the left side (see Figure 8-3). In both cases, the setoff left column can be used for subheads and other graphic devices.

If between 2 and 2½ inches on the left side are left open by one of the spacing methods and if approximate 1-inch margins are taken from the remaining 6 to 6½-inch page widths, you are left with a typing area of 4 to 4½ inches in width. For best readability, the ideal column width is about 3½ inches, so you are in the reading ease ball park.

Charts and Graphs   A mandatory chart is the organization chart. This key visual aid should be a simple, graphic representation of what the prospect is buying from your firm. Be honest, clear, and thorough in the organization chart, and always show the client in the top box! (See Figure 8-4.)

Another useful graphic is the human resource chart, showing staff required and available to do the project by month or job phase (see Figures 8-5 and 8-6).

This formula will remind you of the importance of scattering good graphics throughout the proposal: *HOG = > COW.* (Heavy on graphics *equals* a greater chance of winning.) It is a fact that any type of illustration is noticed ahead of plain text. One survey found that thirty-eight out of 100 people who are stopped by an illustration in a magazine, book, or newspaper will read the entire text. Many of the remaining 62 percent will read at least part of the text because the illustration got some part of their attention.

Some proposal editors now lay out the graphics first; then they write the narrative around the visuals decided on. This method also makes life a little easier for the proposal manager, who often must deal with less-than-professional writers from the firm's technical staff.

Remember that it is possible, through intelligent use of charts and other visual aids, to compress many pages of narrative into one page of graphics and, at the same time, to make the information transmitted more interesting, or at least more palatable, to the reader. And when it's more interesting, comprehension will go up.

For a quick review, the three main elements of a proposal are to explain

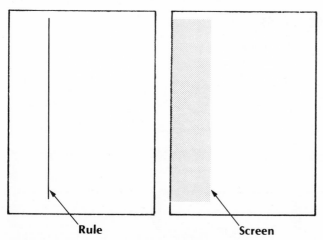

Rule   Screen

Figure 8-3 *Use graphic devices, such as rules and screens, to make proposal pages more inviting to readers.*

WHAT must be done? (The requirements)
HOW will your nominated team meet the requirements?
WHY you have selected the approaches set out in the HOW section.

Most of the WHY element has to be covered in the text. Much of the
HOW and up to about half of the WHAT can be handled with some type
of graphic format.

Make a strong claim in the headline of each graphic page—in full
sentence form:

1. *ABC engineers provide expert cost control, based on a quarter-century
of practical experience.*

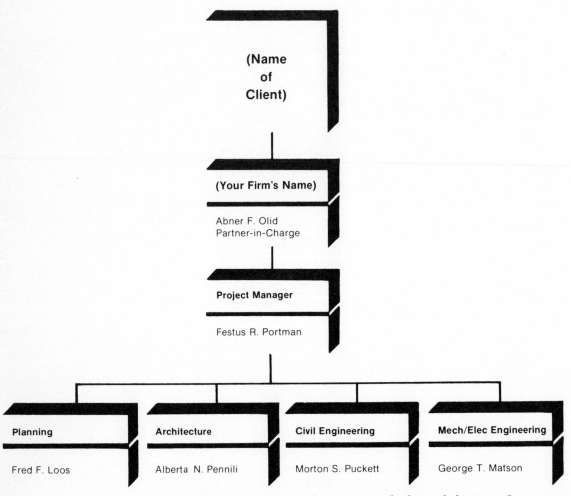

Figure 8-4 *Organization charts are standard visual elements of most proposals.*

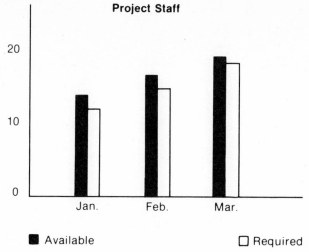

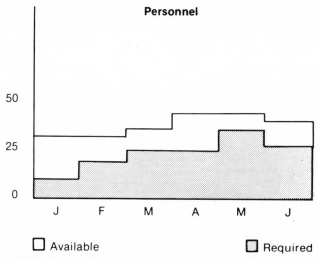

Figure 8-5 *Staffing charts help to prove you'll have the staff required when they are needed on the job.*

   2. XYZ Engineers have a well-defined organizational structure to handle the design of Big City's water treatment plant.
   3. The aerial survey capabilities of ABC Surveyors are unsurpassed.

Follow up the initial complete sentence strong claim with boxed information, lists, graphics, PERT charts, and the like. Give each supplemental entry on the page an equally strong caption (subhead)—*ABC Architects have completed twenty-five health care projects since 1978; ABC's*

Figure 8-6 *Another version of the personnel availability chart.*

hospital projects win design awards. Make the claim in the headline; then prove it in the graphic exhibits that follow.

Cost   The cost proposal section can exert a strong positive influence on proposal evaluators when the material is accurate and in sufficient depth.

Usually included in this section are

1. Statement of work (actually, a restatement—taken from the technical proposal material). A formal listing of tasks you agree to undertake upon award of a contract. The information should be summarized in a table.

2. Completion schedule. In a tabular format repeat the basic project schedule (from the project master schedule). Show beginning and terminating dates for each major item in the statement of work.

3. Cost summary. For most government proposals this information is submitted on agency supplied forms.

4. Cost breakdowns.

Terms and Conditions   This is the section for exceptions to the proposed terms and conditions in the RFP, if any. In proposals for commercial prospects, list *your* proposed terms and conditions in this section.

Estimating Techniques Used   The "Truth in Negotiations Act" makes an accurate description of how you arrived at your prices important. A tabular format is the most efficient way to display this information.

Certifications and Representations   This section consists primarily of government supplied forms to be filled in and signed by a responsible person in the firm. Be completely honest and exceedingly accurate when completing these forms.

Draft Contracts   Supply draft contracts when the client requests them in the RFP. Have *all* contracts drawn up or at least reviewed by your attorney.

Appendixes   Charles Tomsen advises us to "stick [proposal] boilerplate in the back where it won't hurt." One proposal consultant recommends putting technical details in an appendix—"if you have to include them at all."

While size as a criterion for responsiveness is now pretty well ruled out in most cases, an occasional client (and RFP) will indicate bigger is better. In such cases, appendixes can be used to fatten the final product to almost any desired thickness.

In making out the U.S. Government Standard Form 255, consider section 10 as an appendix to the form. Any enclosures with S.F. 255s should follow block 10.

And while it might be appropriate to consider appendixes as a sort of dumping ground for most proposals, a little creativity can lend impact to the final section. You might include copies of design awards, letters from satisfied client references, and copies of technical papers written by your staff and news clippings about your firm's achievements. *Never* send originals of any of the enclosures. In a sense, the appendix section thus becomes a kind of scrapbook for exhibits of all types—all attesting to the general worth, professionalism, staff capabilities, and related experience of your firm. Most such attachments should be referenced in the text, with readers directed to the appropriate appendix.

POST MORTEMS

If you lose, find out why. And don't be put off or engage in self-rationalization by letting a prospect tell you your proposal was ranked second or third out of those received. There is only one winner; every other firm who submitted a proposal is one of the losers.

Client Expectations A recent study of corporations with major building programs, from Texas A & M's Department of Management, researched the selection and use of A-E consultants. When a proposal submission is part of the selection process, the survey respondents said these are the five most important evaluation considerations:

Experience lists or completed project lists
Résumés of the proposed project team
The organization chart for the project
Fee structure
Photographs of previous work

Proposal consultant Albert Shapero uses this checklist to measure the relative success of a proposal submission:[7]

1. *Success in proposal writing.* Winning the award under conditions where you can deliver the technical product on schedule within the budget.

2. *Less than success—but short of failure.* When you don't win, but your proposal makes a lasting, positive impression on a prospect who buys a lot of your kind of services.

3. *Failure.* You don't win, and you fail to make *any* impression on the prospect. You might as well have skipped the whole process.

4. *Worse than failure.* While losing the award, you manage to make a *bad* impression on the prospect.

BUDGETS

During the initial RFP analysis, some firms now attempt to set a cap on how much they will invest in preparing a given proposal. One firm uses 2 percent of the stated or estimated fee as the first-stage alarm. When it appears that the cost of obtaining the project will exceed 2 percent, a policy committee must approve a higher investment; in effect, decide whether or not to continue pursuit of the project.

Two percent seems a little low; I'd recommend a first-stage limit of closer to 4 percent, based on average marketing costs for all firms of around 6.5 percent.

A large engineering firm in New York City routinely runs a computer analysis of RFPs it receives. The printout shows the probability of winning, based on a number of key factors and variables, plus the amount of money that logically might be spent to prepare the proposal.

Perhaps the most important ingredient of budget control is the selectiveness exercised at the front end of the RFP analysis. Unless there are sufficient compelling reasons for your firm to go after the project, pass up the RFP.

WRITING

Diane Creel, in her 1978 paper on proposal preparation for the Society for Marketing Professional Services, offered these three key elements of a winning proposal:[8]

1. Clear, concise, accurate writing.
2. Clean, illustrative graphics.
3. Individualization or specialization of information *which focuses on the individual project at hand.* [Emphasis added.]

By now, there should be no question about the importance of the proposal writer's expository skills.

Before you begin to write, be sure these three preliminary tasks are out of the way:

1. Total familiarity with the RFP has been achieved.
2. A detailed proposal outline has been prepared.
3. All pertinent research and reference materials are at hand.

A few words about each of these tasks:

1. *Familiarity with proposal requirements.* Review
   ■ All available material about the project and prospect, including marketing files

- Past proposals for the same prospect and in the same or related areas
    - All references cited in the RFP
    - Related technical and trade publications

2. *The proposal outline.* Losing proposals have poor organization in common. Organization is attained through outlining. Outlines allow you to
    - Organize thoughts logically
    - Identify and include useful information from previous proposals
    - See which areas require more research
    - Identify points requiring management or design decisions
    - Create checklists to ensure that the proposal includes all required information

3. *Research.* Researching the current literature, as a first step in proposal preparation, may save you from reinventing the wheel many times over. Time, naturally, is a limiting factor on how much research can be done for any given proposal. As a minimum effort, try to review the following:
    - Your own firm's brochures
    - Annual reports (if any) and other informational material from the prospective client organization
    - Prior proposals

And interview your own technical people who are knowledgeable in the subject areas.

Proposal Drafts   You should expect to write at least two drafts for any proposal—first and final. The detailed topical outline you develop will serve as the proposal's skeleton, to which you apply the meat and muscle. Make the first draft as complete as possible; don't use the fact that at least one more draft will be done as an excuse for inattention and sloppiness the first time around.

At the same time, don't be overly concerned about polished grammar and impeccable syntax, spelling, or punctuation in the first draft. Many writers believe such concerns block their creativity. At any rate, little of the first draft is apt to survive the rewriting and editing processes.

When the first draft is finished, move around the table (figuratively, if not literally). Read the draft proposal from the viewpoint of the client, making necessary changes as you spot errors and problem phrases. Most clients live and operate in a particular environment. The proposer must somehow put himself or herself in the prospect's shoes; figure out how to make it easy for the prospect to award the project to your firm.

First Draft Checklist   Still seated in the client's seat, ask yourself

1. Does the proposal get across the message you want to convey?

2. Is the organization of the material logical? (Logic is important as a support to your sales arguments, but logic doesn't sell the prospect. Benefits offered—what your offer of services will do for the client—are what sells. And never rely on a prospect reader of your proposal to read between any lines. Make your points crystal clear through your expositional skills.)

3. Is the proposal responsive to all requirements of the RFP?

4. (Being as objective as possible) If you were the evaluator, would your proposal go into the "second look" pile or the "out of the running" pile?

Appearance and Format   Your proposal should set your firm above all other proposers in

Clarity
Graphics
Attention to detail
Organization
Responsiveness to the RFP

Some of the appearance elements of a good proposal:

Clean paper
Clear, clean, and even typing—in a contemporary typeface
Adequate and correctly proportioned margins and spacing between
   paragraphs
Meaningful (helpful) titles and subheads, uniformly positioned on the
   page
Sharp illustrations, carefully reproduced
Care in binding and collating; no out-of-sequence or upside-down
   pages

If you do many proposals, it can be helpful to index the proposals done to date in your firm in order to make retrieval of the information easier. At least one copy of every proposal produced by your firm (including those from branch offices) should be in the files of the marketing department. These copies should be carefully controlled; insist that they be used *only* in the marketing department. It is extremely difficult to reconstitute a lost or misplaced proposal several years after the fact.

PROPOSALS AS SALES TOOLS

If you agree that proposals are sales tools—written sales tools, as it were—then it must follow that a proposal's effectiveness as a sales tool is based on how well it gets the sales message across. The basic sales message, should there be any question about it, is

> Our firm will perform exactly to the client's specifications, and our services are backed by an experienced organization of professionals—all of whom are anxious to serve and please the client.

In his book, *Architectural and Engineering Salesmanship*, David Cooper sets out a general theme for professional service marketing of all types, with particular application to proposal writing.

> When asked to . . . state in positive terms what they want from an architect or engineer, the owner's first requirement was service throughout the project, combined with the ability to anticipate needs and the initiative to meet them. They wanted a firm with good experience in building types they were considering and with a qualified in-house staff with specialized technical and professional expertise in all aspects of building technology. An in-house engineering staff was looked on as a great advantage. Owners have a predisposition toward local firms, but do not regard this as important as experience and service records. They looked for the firms who could produce a list of truly satisfied clients from past jobs.[9]

There, in a nutshell, is the message all proposals should get over to the prospective client.

THE EVALUATION PROCESS

In early review stages, evaluators look for any reason—however small or technical—to eliminate proposals. Jack Robertson, in his earlier referenced *Selling to the Federal Government*, points out some of the evaluation booby traps than can snare unwary proposers.[10] Many of them are simple errors or omissions, such as failing to sign a proposal in the proper places. Others include:

1. Failure to answer all mandatory questions in the RFP
2. Failure to supply the required number of copies of the proposal
3. Imposing extra contract terms or conditions in the proposal (optional extra terms may be offered, *subject to later negotiations*, but don't make agency acceptance of a proposal subject to such demands)
4. Failure to emphasize particular technical approaches or management control programs known to be in current fashion in the client

agency or company—value engineering, life cycle costing, construction management, and the like

5. In cost proposals, failure to document cost estimates adequately

Government evaluators are not very complimentary about the vast bulk of proposals submitted. One procurement manager estimates that up to 75 percent of all proposals received can quickly be eliminated as inadequate or nonresponsive or both. Perhaps another 15 percent of the original group are judged to be barely adequate and only somewhat responsive. If this manager's experience is representative, he is saying that only one in ten of all proposals received are good enough to get any serious attention. The other 90 percent—discarded in early evaluation rounds—probably cost no less to prepare and submit; they just aren't going anywhere.

PROPOSAL SELF-EVALUATION CHECKLIST

You will be better served in developing your own checklists, but here are some of the more important items to consider:

1. Is the proposal responsive to the RFP?
2. Does it reflect your understanding of the project requirements in a clear and convincing manner?
3. Did you identify potential problems apparent in the RFP?
4. Are there specific examples given of your related, successful past projects?
5. Is your technical expertise clearly established?
6. Do all staff résumés spell out all related experience? Is it evident that a well-qualified staff team has been named to handle the project?
7. Is the prospect assured that his or her occupancy schedules will be met—or if not, why not?
8. Is your firm's ability to handle the project (complexity, cost, scope, time) clearly demonstrated by the proposal's contents?
9. Are recommended support policies, procedures, and staff fully detailed?
10. Is the proposal logical in its presentation and also clear, accurate, and complete?
11. Are numbering and format consistent throughout?
12. Is the proposal easy to read?
13. Is the proposal professional looking?
14. Would you be happy to have the prospect accept the total proposal package as an example of your own professionalism and of your firm's attention to detail in design and execution?

15. Does the proposal demonstrate and document your confidence that the project will work out satisfactorily for the client?

PROPOSAL SUBMISSION

After pouring blood, sweat, tears, and dollars into doing a proposal, don't let down in your planning at the last, crucial stage. Make certain the proposal gets to the client—and on time. The final step before any proposal leaves your office is to run a last check of all copies to ensure that

1. The transmittal letter address is accurate in all respects.
2. All pages are bound in rightside up, with text sides facing the front.
3. All pages and sections are in the proper order.
4. All illustrations, charts, and appendixes are in the right places.
5. The cover is clean, and all type is readable.

One person on the proposal team should be assigned to make the final check—and be held accountable if anything less than cosmetic perfection leaves your office. Sloppiness of any kind is unprofessional and, therefore, unworthy to represent your firm.

Sometimes the expense and trouble of personal delivery are warranted, especially if you can get a few minutes with one of the evaluators or a member of the selection committee. Personal delivery also gives you the opportunity to eyeball the competition's proposals.

SUMMARY

In summary, here is a brief list of food-for-thought items about proposals, from personal observation and experience and as collected from other proposal consultants:

1. Your goal is to submit proposals that are not only understandable, but cannot possibly be misunderstood by the severest critic or the most carping quibbler.

2. Never omit significant information on the assumption it is known to evaluators and clients. Even if they do know it, they may make the collateral assumption that you *don't* know it if it isn't in the proposal.

3. Good proposals are not guaranteed winners; bad proposals are guaranteed losers.

4. Most proposals look like technical reports. Technical reports are not selling presentations; ergo, proposals should not look like technical documents.

5. The primary duties of a proposal manager:

■ Organizing the proposal so it quickly can be seen to be clearly responsive to all requirements of the RFP.

■ Screening out nonpertinent, irrelative material and less-than-meaningful claims.

■ Editing for a readable, smooth style.

■ Reviewing all sections (especially résumés) for uniform format and the relevance of information throughout.

6. Proposal submission is but one step in the marketing process, and if the submission was not preceded by all (or most) of the usual marketing steps and procedures—intelligence gathering, courting, marketing communications, and the like—long before the RFP was received, then everyone involved is kidding himself or herself and each other.

REFERENCES

[1]Jack Robertson, *Selling to the Federal Government*, McGraw-Hill Book Company, New York, 1979, pp. 62–66.

[2]Jill Ammon-Wexler and Catherine Carmel, *How to Create a Winning Proposal*, Mercury Communications Corporation, Santa Cruz, Calif., 1976, pp. 2–5. (Out of print.)

[3]Charles B. Thomsen, *CM: Developing, Marketing & Delivering Construction Management Services*, McGraw-Hill Book Company, New York, 1982, pp. 35–36.

[4]Ibid., p. 37

[5]Jack Robertson, op. cit., p. 74.

[6]Herman Holtz and Terry Schmidt, *The Winning Proposal: How to Write It*, McGraw-Hill Book Company, New York, 1981, pp. 177–178.

[7]Albert Shapero, "How to Write a Successful Proposal," Workshop given at the American Consulting Engineers Council Annual Conference, May 15, 1980, Atlanta.

[8]Diane Creel, *Proposal Preparation: Marketing Information Report #2*, Society for Marketing Professional Services, Alexandria, Va., 1978, p. 1.

[9]David Cooper, *Architectural and Engineering Salesmanship*, John Wiley & Sons, New York, 1978, p. 11.

[10]Jack Robertson, op cit., p. 71.

Chapter 9
THE PRESENTATION: PROLOGUE

The obvious goal of all direct marketing efforts is to get the job. Important subgoals along the marketing route include being among those firms to receive a request for proposal and, on the basis of your proposal submission, to become a short-list finalist. Achieving the latter subgoal usually means you are expected to appear for an interview before a committee representing (or constituting) the client group.

In today's world of professional design services marketing, project awards increasingly depend on a selection committee's reactions to formal presentations by the short-listed firms. Outstanding design credentials; a skilled, imaginative, and caring staff; and a textbook job of marketing matter not at all without a face-to-face session with the prospect—and the opportunity for you to give final, emphatic assurance that they are in the best of hands with your nominated project team.

Unbelievably, some principals adopt a Scrooge-like marketing mentality upon notification that their firm is to make a presentation to a prospective client. They try to squeak through the selection interviews on the cheap, when anyone with an IQ in excess of 20 should know that this is the time to pull out all stops; to go as first class as possible—and as the project's potential return justifies.

In this and the next chapter we will be concerned with surviving the selection process and with strategic and tactical considerations leading up to the formal interview—sometimes more properly termed a "formal confrontation"—with the prospect.

TRIM = EFFECTIVE COMMUNICATIONS

Effective communications are persuasive; persuasive communications sell. One writer reduced the basic ingredients of the process to the acronym TRIM:

T—the communication target at which you are shooting
R—the receiver to whom your communication is targeted
I—the impact required to influence the receiver properly
M—methods which can be used to accomplish the job[1]

The first two TRIM elements, target and receiver, usually are essentially self-defined for an architectural or engineering presentation. The impact (I) needed—how the presentation must affect receivers (prospects) if you are to hit the target and influence them as required—has been the underlying subject of most of the preceding chapters. This chapter and the next are concerned primarily with methods (M), the presentation payoff. On this point TRIM inventor George Vardaman recommends that presenters outline ideas at the outset of their presentation planning; specify presentation targets, receivers, and the degree of impact sought; and be clear about methods and devices to be used.

The ideal presentation, according to many marketers and principals, would

1. Be the last interview scheduled
2. Have your firm as one of no more than three presenting firms
3. Be held in the design professional's office
4. Consist of an informal, but structured, presentation, followed by a brief tour of the office, drafting rooms, and key support areas
5. Include lunch or dinner with the prospect in an unhurried, low-key atmosphere
6. Conclude with a tour of several of the firm's completed projects that are directly related to the prospect's job

One marketer not so jokingly adds a seventh element of the ideal interview; that the selection committee consist solely of members of the principal's immediate family.

WHY PRESENTATIONS?

Giving presentations is one of the most effective tools of communications (and selling) there is. In short, you do not have the luxury or option of *not* communicating to the best of your ability in today's business world. Not everyone reads brochures, reports, or proposals. Of those who do read the material you supply, a certain percentage will not understand it; others will forget all or most of what they read.

But a well-structured and expertly staged presentation is difficult to forget. Misunderstandings should be minimal owing to the opportunity to ask questions and get answers. The act of combining the senses of sight and hearing, as in a presentation, usually improves retention and understanding by several times over sight alone.

Productive presentation preparation requires that you first define three key elements; audience, purpose, and approach. According to consultant Donna Pond, the three basic forms of audience appeal, or approach, are ethos, pathos, and logos.

> *Ethos* is audience reaction because of who they think you are and how you act. For example, you look and act like a professional, you sound like a competent expert.
>
> *Pathos* is audience reaction because you hit a responsive emotional chord. While going for the sympathy vote may not often be good strategy, there are key words in every organization that appeal to pathos. "Benefit" and "loss," for example, are words more emotionally charged than most for the management listener.
>
> *Logos* is audience reaction because of the unrelenting power of logic. This applies when you are able to build a nearly irrefutable case after identifying a need, developing a well thought out plan, and defining the resulting advantages of your plan in meeting that need.[2]

THE PSYCHOLOGY OF SELLING

A quick review of the sections entitled "The Communication Process" and "Different Levels of Selling" in Chapter 2 should be helpful at this point, expecially the material on techniques of jam-joint selling.

As a reminder, marketing is the process of influencing people individually and in groups to select a firm, a service, or a product or some combination of the three. Selling is the method of finalizing the selection process; of making the individual or group buying decision irreversible. Selling may be viewed as the moral, psychological, and legal capstone of the marketing process.

Selling usually takes the form of a personal, oral presentation of services or products to prospective clients or customers for the purpose of making sales. Selling has become a highly developed technique, based on psychological analysis and application. Today's well-schooled salespeople base presentations on their understanding of customer buying motives and habits as related to a particular product or service. By subtle stimulation and manipulation the client is led to want the service or product.

The effective salesperson understands that he or she must first win the confidence and regard of a prospective client on a personal level; clients must feel that they can believe in the salesperson before they will put trust in the service being sold and the firm that offers the service. When the self-selling job is complete—and only then—can the sales agent begin transferring the residual buyer trust and confidence back through himself or herself to the firm.

Consequently, a knowledge of behavioral science—the study of how and why people act as they do—plus the acquisition of skills in applying the concepts of behavioral science are (or should be) fundamental requisites of all those involved in business development for their firm.

Positive self-image systems can be quite effective in selling. They attack fear of success (sometimes a real problem), reduce inhibitions, and encourage most people to perform up to, if not beyond, reasonable expectations. In the 1920s and 1930s psychologists established through clinical research that people will do no more and no less than they believe they can do. There is almost perfect consistency in human behavior; people invariably live up (or down) to their self-images. "People have a tendency to live up to their own labels once they have declared themselves. Labels always limit our options."[3]

The potency of a positive self-image can be demonstrated with a reverse example. Imagine yourself entering a business or social situation with the absolute conviction that you look like a bum, are going to act like an idiot, and are destined to fail miserably, no matter what you do. It would take a miracle for you *not* to fail. The opposite attitude—one of supreme self-confidence and positivism—doesn't guarantee success (your competitors may be even more self-confident and positive in their self-image), but it's an obvious precondition for doing your best.

Empathize   A productive interview must be a session for establishing and reinforcing *empathy*. The dictionary defines empathy as the projection of one's own personality into the personality of another in order to understand the other person better—intellectual identification of oneself with another.

When you can begin identifying intellectually with clients, you should gain a better understanding of *their* stresses and concerns about the selection process. For most selection committees it is no simple matter to commit the spending of from several hundred thousand to several million dollars of someone else's money to the principals of a design firm they probably didn't even know of a few months ago. Client difficulties and stresses obviously are compounded if this selection is their maiden effort. Have at least a little compassion for the position of selection committee members. Consider that the consulting firm and the potential client are contemplating entering into a close relationship that may continue up to five years or longer. If we believe some of the statistics of divorce, that's longer than most real marriages survive.

And try to think of a formal presentation as a momentary intensification or focusing of the selling process. Liken an interview to adjusting a garden hose nozzle from fine spray to a heavy stream—or the effect obtained from pouring a liquid into a funnel (Figure 9-1).

PLANNING AND STRUCTURING PRESENTATIONS

Proper presentation planning involves at least these seven steps:

1. Doing your homework (intelligence gathering on project, prospect, and probable competition)
2. Making an in-depth audience analysis
3. Organizing material and planning the presentation
4. Preparing yourself to present
5. Testing and revising the presentation
6. Giving it
7. Evaluating it

There are just two basic criteria for deciding what to include in a presentation. Everything said, shown, or done must relate to

1. The project
2. Improving the selection committee's understanding of your project team and its individual and collective qualifications for doing the job

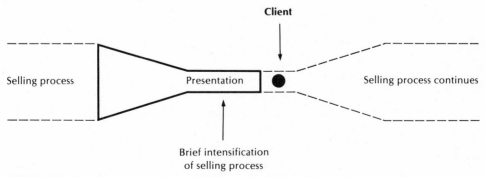

Figure 9-1 *The selling process intensifies during a formal presentation, similar to the way liquid pouring through a funnel speeds up in the neck of the funnel.*

Still another important checklist for presentation preparation: In structuring an effective presentation, these five questions must be answered:

1. What do we have to cover to fulfill the formal selection criteria as we understand and interpret them?
2. How should the members of our team (especially the nominated project manager) project themselves during the interview?
3. Which member or members of our team will the interviewers' personalities and interests relate to best (to help decide about individual positioning and time allotments)?
4. Which media are best for reinforcement and clarification of our primary message—and for projecting our style in *this* presentation?
5. What are the three main points about our firm, our experience, and our nominated project team that we want the prospect to remember twenty-four hours after the presentation is finished?

Recycle Proposal Outlines   If a proposal submission was part of the process for short-list selection and if a detailed outline was written for your proposal (as should be the case always), it should be safe to assume that the proposal submission adequately covered the prospect's main points of interest and concerns. Get out the proposal outline, and use it as the foundation for your presentation.

In the previously cited *Successful Marketing of Architectural Services* is a combined proposal-presentation flowchart (Figure 9-2). Observe how the planning moves logically and smoothly from the first RFP review meeting through the final organization checklist for the presentation.[4]

Content and Style   To become a successful presenter (success being equated with one's percentage of wins), a contemporary design professional must have more than a nodding acquaintance with

1. Audience psychology
2. Visual esthetics
3. Basic communication theories
4. Such show business principles and techniques as "grabber" openings, presence, pacing, timing, working the audience, and "leave 'em gasping" closes

"Hold it right there!" comes a cry from an architect in the first row. "I'm a design professional, not a top banana."

"That does it!" cries an engineer in the back of the house. "I design bridges, not production numbers. Leave all that show business foolishness to the likes of Johnny Carson and Raquel Welch."

The point here is that whether or not you realize it—and regardless of whether you like it or not—more and more job awards are made by selection committees on the basis of a presenting team's style. And the leader of the presenting group in increasingly known as the head presenter or the MC.

None of what has been said means that content is unimportant; obviously it is. But if a short list consists of firms deemed essentially equal by the prospect, then each of the firms in contention has convinced the prospect that they see the project and the design solutions in roughly the same ways. Another way of stating it: If you are astute enough to get included in the short list for an interview, you are smart enough to do your homework. Given that point, much of what is *said* in a presentation has a sameness to it—and effectively removes content as a primary basis for selection.

Figure 9-2 *Presentation flowchart.*

With content out of the picture, the prospective client is left with style on which to make a choice among finalist firms.

Charting for Style   An attention-grabbing opening for your presentation may hold a committee's interest and attention for several minutes in the beginning, but if the interest level isn't renewed periodically, that hard-won attention will quickly fade away. Charting a presentation from opening statement to closing remarks might produce the diagram in Figure 9-3.

The opening *must* take audience interest up to a high level—and quickly. This is one reason for the dictum that the first two minutes of a presentation are the most important 120 seconds of the entire time you are being interviewed. But the peaking of interest at the start is transitory; audience attention, unaided, soon drops back to or below the median line.

When you are aware of the process, you structure the thirty, forty-five, or sixty minutes of a presentation to ensure that the attention

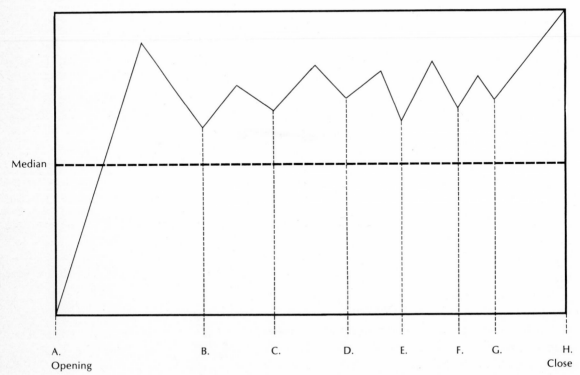

Figure 9-3 *Charting for presentation style; maintaining the interest level from opening to the close.*

factor is constantly renewed throughout the time your team has the floor. In Figure 9-3 these events, diversions, and pace-changers may be substituted for the letters marking attention-renewal points:

B. Brief introduction of the other members of the presenting team— bringing in new faces, new voices, new personalities, and some front-of-the-room action as introductions are acknowledged.

C. Use of a series of presentations aids; slides, photoboards, overhead projections, a model, and the like.

D and E. The other team members give their presentations.

F. The head presenter opens a question-and-answer session with se- lection committee members.

G. The close. Make it strong, memorable, and specific. Wind up with the phrase ''We want this job!''

Look at the two audience attention charts in Figure 9-4. Anyone can see that the presentation represented in the top chart was a dismal failure; the attention level never really got off the ground. Study the bottom chart for a moment. What kind of a presentation does it depict?

Someone new to presentations (and the rudiments of show business) might select it as a winner. Not so! It is no trick to take an audience up to the heights and hold it there for thirty or forty minutes, but no experienced playwright or presentation organizer would ever do it. In the vernacular, at around twenty minutes into the presentation you'd have the selection committee worn slick. An attentive, interested, par- ticipating selection committee is the goal—not a jaded, sated group of emotionally drained interviewers. If you carefully structure presenta- tions to keep interest peaking as shown in Figure 9-3, your win record should speak for itself.

Visit the Site   When the site of the project is known, a prepresentation visit should be arranged. Take a still camera along, and photograph the site from several vantage points and in several directions. Provide your- self with all available maps and reports that deal with the site—topo, utility, and political maps, boring test reports, environmental impact reports, and the like.

Site views and slides made from some of the maps may be used in the presentation. A different kind of site visit is chronicled with a tele- vision or movie camera when a staff planner records his or her com- ments as the site is walked out. A minute or so of the sound TV tape or movie film is then shown during the presentation as evidence of both your interest and attention to detail.

Some of the pictures made at the site may be similar to those on hand

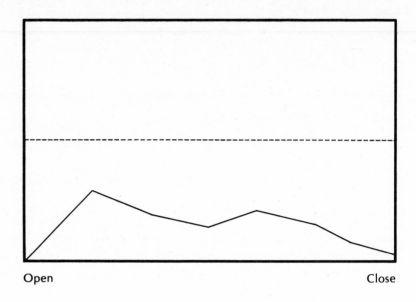

Open   Close

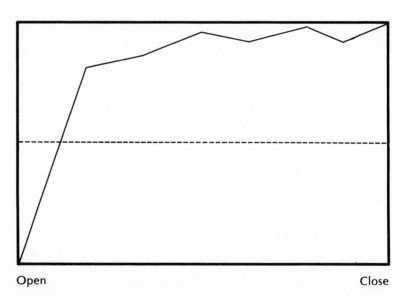

Open   Close

Figure 9-4 *The top chart is of an unquestionably poor presentation—but what about the presentation represented in the lower chart?*

of completed office projects. One firm made a photographic study of a long, narrow 105-acre site, bisected by a road, which was almost identical to a site for a corporate headquarters the design office had just completed a few miles away. The photographer knew what pictures he already had of the completed building, so he duplicated views and angles as closely as possible on the undeveloped site. A special brochure was then prepared, showing the similarity of sites and the design firm's related, completed project, which also spanned a roadway, as a possible solution. The corporate prospect was appreciative of this extra touch, and the architect eventually realized millions of dollars in work from the company. Many other factors in addition to the special brochure no doubt entered into the matter, but the little extra effort didn't hurt. As we all know, many marketing decisions are made on the basis of "if it can't hurt, it might help."

Within time and budget limitations, spare no effort to assemble information about the prospect and project. If the idea of this intensive intelligence gathering goes against one's ethical or moral grain, be assured that prospects run very thorough checks on every design firm they have under consideration.

It is, of course, possible to get carried away by this sort of thing. A few principals of larger firms have gone to a great deal of trouble to attract former employees of the Central Intelligence Agency to their business development staffs on the premise that CIA people are best qualified by training and experience to ferret out the necessary prospect information. Some of the exagents so recruited have become excellent marketers.

IN-HOUSE REHEARSALS

In some firms whether or not to do a dry run of presentations is still a point of controversy. Those in the firm who are the most resistant to the idea of rehearsals (often one or more of the founding principals) have some interesting, if unconvincing, rationalizations for their objections:

1. "Rehearsing would spoil my spontaneity."
2. "I've winged presentations for twenty-two years—and we've done O.K."
3. "I can't take a chance on sounding as if I've memorized my remarks."
4. "The selection committee people are old friends. They don't expect a Broadway production."
5. "The only way to do it is to ad lib it."

And there are other excuses. If you are a conscientious marketer and presenter, you've probably heard them all at least once. What do some of the marketing consultants say about rehearsing?

> Failure to prepare fully for the interview is a quick way to disaster. The interviewing process, as we know it today, is a complex psychological contest. Interviews are not won just on what you say, but on how you say it and how you react to the prospective client and his specific situation.[5]

> Professional people resist participating in "dry runs." They, like many others, feel that it is an artificial, unrewarding, and maybe even a humiliating experience. It is an interesting observation that a person's willingness to submit to "dry runs" is usually in direct proportion to his communication and presentation skills. Where do you find the golf pros before a round? In the practice sand trap or on the driving range. Where do you find the rank amateurs? In the bar.[6]

Our long-standing advice is to consider all interviews a special form of trial by ordeal.[7]

Presentation Case Histories   Over the last ten years a number of scenarios or case histories have been developed for presentation simulation and practice in the Marketing Management Workshop series. The case histories are all based on real jobs although locations and the names of individuals and client organizations have been changed in most cases.

The ten sets of mock presentation givens that follow are for you to use in practice sessions. Feel free to adapt, extend, and amend the information to meet specific in-house requirements.

PUTNAM CITY ELECTRIC AUTHORITY

The Putnam City Electric Authority, a municipal electric generating utility, has installed a total of eleven steam generating units and fourteen combustion turbines over the last thirty years. During the past eight years the utility has lacked sufficient maintenance funds for the equipment, with the result that the capacity of the units and their reliability have deteriorated.

The Putnam City Electric Authority proposes to retain a qualified consultant to (1) improve the capability of the generating units and (2) make recommendations about immediate maintenance requirements and implementation of a preventive maintenance program. George Stone, chairman of the PCEA planning committee, will represent the authority at the presentation. Stone is a registered professional engineer and is president of a local engineering firm.

Paula Havingsom, a former employee of your firm, is assistant general manager of the utility and will also attend the presentation. Havingsom, a professional engineer, is believed to have reservations about hiring your firm.

Considerations for the presentation:

1. Your firm has been responsible for the engineering design of all the units for the utility.

2. PCEA is concerned that they will not get an objective analysis and report if your firm is retained to do the work.
3. Should you propose the use of outside consultants?
4. What *relevant* experience does *your* firm have with this specific project type? Experience of your nominated project team?

GULF CITY INTERNATIONAL AIRPORT

Gulf City, Texas (population 1.5 million), plans to expand and modernize its airport—Gulf City International. The client anticipates that the following elements will be built in several phases:

1. A second 10,000-foot runway, parallel to the present one, to accept anticipated increases in air travel through 2000.
2. A continuum of four linear terminals (eventually six), designed to connect all forms of ground transport through passenger processing to the aircraft pavilions.
3. Four (eventually six) pavilions, each to accommodate a maximum of eleven large aircraft, including 747s and wide-bodies, or thirteen or more smaller aircraft; and to accommodate a total of 12 to 15 million passengers a year and the operation of ten or more airlines.
4. Interconnected four-level parking garages to hold 2000 cars.
5. An intraterminal transit system for the convenience of transfer passengers and parking patrons.

A master plan for Gulf City International (GCI) has been completed by the joint venture of RSI and Laydes and Lest, Inc. The client, Gulf City's Department of Aviation, is interviewing several design firms at this time. Representing the client is George Stone, director of the Department of Aviation. Stone is a retired U.S. Air Force major general and has been with GCI for eight years. Much of his time in the Air Force was spent in administrative positions with the Military Airlift Command (MAC). He is a graduate of the Harvard Business School and a proponent of management by objectives. Stone's son-in-law is a graduate of Notre Dame's school of architecture. Stone is open to all approaches, including construction management, value engineering, fast-track, design-build, and guaranteed price.

Considerations for the presentation:

1. Your firm has excellent airport experience, but the internal transit system in the last airport project has been plagued by mechanical breakdowns.
2. What approach or approaches of those listed in the last preceding paragraph will you propose to George Stone? Are there others you might suggest?
3. You've looked over the master plan and find you have several points of disagreement with the consultants who wrote it. Will you bring them up in the presentation? If not, when?

SANTA DISNICA SHOPPING CENTER

Developer Ford-Cabot & Hahn, Inc. (F-C&H), will retain a consultant for a proposed eighty-acre regional shopping center in Santa Disnica (population 465,000). The center will have a gross leasable area (GLA) of 850,000 sq. ft. and three-level parking facilities for 5000 automobiles. The developer wants full civil engineering and construction staking services, bid document preparation, and construction management. The consultant will also be expected to coordinate and interface with the architectural consultant, when selected.

Your firm did the survey work for a F-C&H housing development in a nearby county five years ago. There is some concern that one or more members of the F-C&H selection committee consider your firm to be surveyors only. George Stone, executive vice-president for Ford-Cabot & Hahn, is chairman of the interview committee. Stone served in the Army in World War II with the president of your firm (your president may or may not be at the presentation).

Considerations for the presentation:

1. How much area will the anchors probably require?
2. How can you sell the client on the total services offered by your firm?

NOTE: If desired, the presenting team may consider this as a project for

A feasibility study
An EIS
Planning only
Or for complete services, from initial studies through complete supervision

CANTRELL SOUP COMPANY ENERGY STUDY

The Cantrell Soup Company, located in Marshfield, New Jersey, is embarking on a program of energy evaluation and retrofit for seven of its major production facilities in the United States. Studies already completed for Cantrell have convinced its management that energy use will have to be cut back throughout its operation to keep retail prices of its products in line with those of its competition.

Cantrell has some thirty high-energy-use facilities around the world, and this project with seven of the largest ones could lead to additional consulting work. Plants in the first group to be studied are located in Georgia, Florida, Texas, Arkansas, Tennessee, Virginia, and New Jersey.

George Stone, Cantrell vice president in charge of facilities, is the selection committee member to be sold. The other two committee members are from the president's office, and their input for the final selection will be minimal. At this point Stone is looking for all possible ways to cut back on energy use. Some progress has been made through operational procedures (turning off every other light, cleaning offices during the day, and the like), but Stone believes any real savings must now come through hardware modification. He is open to discussion of the advantages of a computerized system. Stone has been with Cantrell for twenty-five years, rising through company ranks from assistant manager of the Prescott, Texas, plant. He holds an engineering degree from the University of Texas and is considered an expert in process engineering.

Considerations for the presentation:

1. Should you be able to demonstrate process engineering experience, as well as experience in energy conservation procedures?
2. If selected, is your firm large enough, with enough branch locations, to try to do the first seven plants (and eventually all thirty)—or will you suggest that your best role is as an advisor-consultant to the Cantrell

Company: helping them to select—and then supervising—local firms in each location?

3. Will you discuss additional possible operational procedures in the interview? (Or is it best to assume that Cantrell has covered the area completely?)

Putnam County Bridge Replacement

The board of Putnam County, Alabama, is selecting a consultant to design a replacement for a sixty-year-old, single-span bridge over the Holden River. The old steel bridge is eighteen feet wide and seventy-five feet long. A new county recreation area is under development on the north side of the river. (Putnam City is on the south bank of the river, across from the recreation area.)

The board chairman is William O'Donnell, owner of O'Donnell Mortuary in Putnam City (county board positions are part-time in Putnam County). O'Donnell's sister-in-law, Emily O'Donnell, represents Putnam County in the U.S. House of Representatives. George Stone, county public works director, has held his job for twenty-two years. He is a graduate of the University of Illinois school of engineering. Stone keeps up with most technological developments in structural and civil engineering, and he has shown some interest in a concrete precast segmental box girder bridge replacement. Federal funds will pay for 90 percent of the cost of the new bridge.

Considerations for the presentation:

1. Much of the design work for the new recreation center is still to be awarded.
2. For obvious reasons, Putnam County officials prefer to have as much local involvement as possible in the project.
3. Since this will be the first time the county has applied for funds under P.L. 80-017 (a bridge replacement act), the board is concerned that all of the correct procedures be followed.
4. Would it be smart to direct the presentation entirely to precast segmental concrete bridges, or should other types be discussed? (Initial *and* maintenance costs are important to the client.)
5. Will you look into the availability of utilities on the north side of the river before you go into the presentation?
6. What are some audiovisual aids that could strengthen your presentation?

Gas Pipeline

The Northwestern Gas Company (NGC) of Walnut Creek, California, will build a thirty-six-inch gas pipeline from the Canadian border to northern Oregon, crossing the states of Idaho and Washington. George Stone, NGC's senior engineer, expects the pipeline to be under construction in three years, with completion in three more years. No new engineering or construction applications or complications are expected; construction will be along an existing right-of-way for another pipeline.

Stone has shown some interest in your firm. In a preliminary meeting he asked if your firm could handle the moving target type of construction represented by the pipeline—as opposed to the more usual fixed-site project. You received an RFP from NGC and submitted a technical proposal about four weeks ago. This is a presentation to Stone, following up the proposal.

Considerations for the presentation:

1. How many construction teams will you recommend?
2. Can Stone's schedule be shaved? If so, how much sooner can the pipeline be in use? What, if any, additional profits to NGC would the earlier completion date represent?
3. Would the showing of a few minutes of TV tape or motion picture film, shot from a low-flying helicopter along the pipeline route, be helpful evidence of your attention to detail?

ACCELERATOR FOR DEPARTMENT OF ENERGY

The Department of Energy will build a 200–500 BeV circular proton accelerator near Batavia, Illinois. In line with current federal directives, the department is reviewing the qualifications of several firms with experience in the project type. The major facility is the $35 million main accelerator, approximately 1.25 miles in diameter, consuming some 60 megawatts of power. Also included is an 8 BeV booster accelerator (500 feet in diameter); air conditioned equipment galleries; a heavily shielded 500-foot linear accelerator; various work areas, pipe tunnels, and cableways. Support facilities include a sixteen-story central laboratory, central utility plant, and an industrial complex. Estimated value of all construction is $495 million, and a rigid time schedule of sixty months must be observed.

Construction management is anticipated to be operated on the basis of fast track, concurrent design-construct, through a multitude of separate contracts (approximately ninety-four major construction, sixty minor construction, and forty-five material contracts). The project owner will be the Department of Energy National Accelerator Laboratories, Batavia, Illinois; Dr. Robert Stone is the director. NOTE: Dr. Stone is a graduate and former director of Cal Tech at Pasadena, California. He also served as deputy director of the Argonne National Laboratories High Energy Physics Research Center.

Of primary interest to the client will be

Management plans for design and construction
Adherence to schedules and maximum costs
Value management services
Safety programs
Labor relations
Energy conservation and environmental protection
Job site facilities
Equal employment opportunities
Handling of disputes
Full utilization of construction management control system
Priced proposals
Examination of records

VOCATIONAL-TECHNICAL SCHOOL

The Botsford School District is interviewing design firms for a planned vocational-technical school in Bevwyn, Wisconsin. A bond issue of $15 million will be submitted to school district patrons in about three months. The site has been selected. Since this will be the first voc-tech school in the area, the school district's selection committee is understandably concerned about their design firm's capabilities and related experience. Other than a stipulation that the project be designed locally (through a branch production office or in the office of a local associate), the committee appears to be completely open at this point.

The assistant superintendent of schools for facilities, Dr. George Stone, was formerly with the Chicago School Board, where he supervised some $160 million in new school construction. Dr. Stone's son-in-law is a professional engineer with a large structural engineering firm in New York City.

Nadine O'Connor is president of the school board and is on the selection committee with Dr. Stone. O'Connor had some initial reservations about the need for a voc-tech school, but she now seems to be for the project. She is not convinced they need to go outside the Bevwyn area to find a qualified design firm. Your firm's headquarters is located in a major city about 500 miles from Bevwyn.

Considerations for the presentation:

1. The point about using a local associate must be dealt with.
2. Can your firm be of any help in promoting the bond issue? (Time is short.) What form would your assistance take?
3. What other help can you suggest to the Botsford School Board at this stage? (Have board members considered asking for contributions of equipment and money from local manufacturers and unions?)

NEW AT&T CORPORATE HEADQUARTERS

The presentation you are making is to a corporate client for whom you have not previously worked. The potential client is Algamated Trucks and Transport Corporation (AT&T), with headquarters near Jersey City, New Jersey. AT&T has an option on a twenty-acre site south of Saint Louis, on which the company plans to locate a new headquarters building. Firms being interviewed have been told the site's location.

About four years ago your firm designed an office and warehouse facility near Cleveland for International Bus Manufacturing (IBM), a wholly owned subsidiary of AT&T. The project was considered a successful one, and the president of IBM has recommended your firm to his boss at AT&T.

Approximately 500 executives and office staff will be housed in the new headquarters. Some computer space will be required, along with record storage, underground parking for 200 cars, a cafeteria, and perhaps some recreational facilities—tennis courts, a ball diamond, and the like. AT&T is probably talking about 200,000 square feet or so. The AT&T executives you've interviewed appear to have no preconceived ideas about the structure's design, siting, or size. Potential fallout work from the headquarters building could be a small (forty to sixty units) housing project in one corner of the site. Housing in the area has been tight, and while AT&T is not particularly known as a paternalistic employer, its top management are realists, and they understand the importance of available, desirable housing for middle and lower levels of management.

This will be the first nonindustrial building for the parent company in almost twenty years. The selection committee has indicated it is completely open on the A-E firm. Three firms have been interviewed and visited by AT&T representatives before today's interview. One is a large New York City-based firm, with heavy experience in corporate headquarters design. Another is your primary competition in the St. Louis area. The third firm, from Chicago, is about the same size as your firm and is known for its aggressive marketing techniques.

The committee from AT&T to whom you'll present is chaired by George Stone, executive vice president. Leo King, director of corporate engineering, may also be on the committee. Stone is a director of both AT&T and IBM—and an avid collector of antique guns. He has a daughter in Missouri University's School of Veterinary Medicine. King has been in his position for some twelve years and is known for his no-nonsense dealings with consultants. A native of Tulsa, Oklahoma, he holds a degree in mechanical engineering from the University of Colorado.

Considerations for the presentation:

1. Have you visited the St. Louis site? And the present AT&T headquarters located in New Jersey?
2. What arguments can you use to convince the selection committee that using a local firm is to AT&T's advantage?
3. Try to work some of the intelligence information about committee members in the last paragraph into your presentation remarks.
4. Does AT&T really need to include staff housing on the site?
5. Are there potential zoning problems about the site?

NEW PRINTING PLANT

The XYZ Press is considering a new plant for its printing activities. The proposed plant's location is a closely guarded secret because of ongoing site acquisition activities and expected union problems when the move is officially announced. Your intelligence-gathering efforts have confirmed the following points about the scope of the structure:

1. A total space requirement of 475,000 square feet, including 50,000 square feet of office space.
2. All support utilities are to be included—central ink piping system, central steam plant, central chiller plant, and the like.
3. The main structure will house high-speed printing presses, bindery equipment, storage spaces, and a large shipping area.

XYZ's construction engineering department in Indianapolis is headed by George Stone. Stone has been with XYZ since his graduation as a mechanical engineer thirty years ago from Notre Dame. Among those who may also represent XYZ at the interview are Burton ("Ink Face") Latouren, assistant vice president for corporate development; Wadsworth Cash, head of finance; and the proposed manager of the new plant, Adeline Blueline.

Considerations for the presentation:

1. XYZ is an old, family-owned company, steeped in tradition.
2. In spite of item (1), it is evident that nothing but the most up-to-date, state-of-the-art plant will be acceptable. George Stone is a vice president of the International Printing Association, the industry's trade group.
3. The firm wants all possible energy conservation techniques and systems designed into the new plant.

4. Project cost will be between $26 and $30 million. Printing equipment will be ordered by XYZ, and they will do the hookup.
5. Because the presses require heavy foundations, you must be able to offer expertise in press foundation design.

Use of Closed-Circuit TV   One of the best training aids for presenters, as several firms have discovered, is closed-circuit television (CCTV). All of the effects and tricks—stop action, split screen, superimposed images, quick cuts, and instant replay—that make commercial television interesting to viewers can be used to record, evaluate, and improve professional presentations. CCTV offers a close, even microscopic look at individual presenters and their interaction with others on the team and with interview groups.

Psychiatrists, some of whom use CCTV extensively in treating patients, point out that people can see how they really come across on videotape. "The behavior is there," one psychiatrist points out. "It's real." The initial confrontation with one's own image—in living color and reasonably high fidelity sound—can be a painful process, but it should invariably lead to more interesting and productive presentations. Videotape gives back a truer version of the original lighting and color than does film. And film images are often kinder to people.

College professors, in reviewing videotapes of their lectures, discover that they appear haughty and defensive, seem to look down on and talk down to their students, behave like stuffed shirts, and even appear to be frightened to death. Design professionals find that they speak with eyes averted from the interview group (or staring at the ceiling), mumble, swallow words, appear defensive, come through as stuffy (or cowardly), and appear to be frightened to death.

In conducting many in-house workshops on presentations, I've discovered that the first run-throughs are inherently hazardous. Participants go through a mock interview, which is videotaped, then adjourn to another room for the playback while the next presentation team is being taped. This is a continuing process for two full eight-hour workshop days.

In most cases, the playback of a group's initial presentation effort is the first opportunity any of them have had to watch and listen to themselves in an interview situation. All sorts of individual eccentricities, tics, and other front-of-the-room problems and mannerisms become glaringly apparent for the first time. Veteran presenters are confronted with incontrovertible evidence that they take from three to ten minutes to get the presentation underway—to get up to speed before an audience. They shuffle aimlessly back and forth of the room or appear to be trying to hide behind the table and their colleagues. Sentences and phrases come out choppy, unconnected, and laced with bad grammar and poorer syntax.

Every type of overt sign of nervousness parades across the playback screen: rolling eyes; wrung hands; jingling coins and keys in pockets; awkward hand and arm movements; playing with pens, pencils, pointers, rings, and eyeglasses; incessant throat clearing and lip wetting; ear, beard, and nose tugging; knuckle-cracking, and more. Any attempt at serious criticism during the first videotape playback can practically destroy an individual's further usefulness as a presenter. It's all there in vivid color and sound for him or her to see. In early viewings, therefore, the role of a workshop leader is to reassure participants and to reinforce the acceptable parts of the presentations. By the second or third playback some of the sensitivity is muted, and serious criticism can get underway.

Similar to the skill developed by novelists, politicians, and artists, videotapes has the potential to develop in most people a new perception of themselves and of others; to see the complex nature of human relationships and interaction. Some psychiatrists believe that 90 percent of any message's impact comes from facial expression and tone of voice. Evaluation by CCTV playbacks is an obvious assist to anyone interested in assessing this impact.

CCTV Costs   The costs of getting into CCTV are not negligible, but in view of the medium's potential for good, it is not a particularly expensive aid. Since the introduction of home-type ½-inch videotape recorders (VTRs) in late 1977, there has been increasingly good news on costs, simplicity of operation, and smaller total weight and bulk of the system. VTRs sell under a variety of trade names, including Sony, Sanyo, Toshiba, Panasonic, RCA, Sears, Magnavox, Sylvania, Quasar, and JVC. These VTRs traditionally use a ½-inch tape cassette, with recording and playback times of up to eight hours per cassette. Recorded tapes are played back through channel 3 or 4 (whichever one is not used by a commericial station in your area) on a standard color television receiver.

The real news, as of this writing, is the ¼-inch CCTV system from Technicolor Audio-Visual, introduced in late 1980. Technicolor's VCR is ten inches square by three inches high and weighs only seven pounds. List price for the VCR package, including power adapter, battery, switch box, tape, cables, and connectors, is $995.

The companion Technicolor cameras (model 412), with built-in mike, electronic viewfinder, and a 6 to 1 zoom lens, weighs 4.8 pounds and retails for $950. Other, lower-priced cameras can be used with the Technicolor system. The ¼-inch video cassettes, which are slightly larger than standard audio cassettes, sell for around $9 each.

Prototype combination camera-VCRs have been shown by several Japanese manufacturers. Combining all of the talking and recording elements into one unit should cut the total weight even more, and —if the history of CCTV is any guide—reduce the price of the system. My recommendation is to take the plunge into CCTV for your in-house training programs as soon as possible. Those who insist on waiting for the ultimate state of the art in miniaturization, for the lowest price, or for CCTV to meet some other criterion may still be waiting around in 1999.

Plan for the Unexpected   Nowhere does Murphy's law (if anything can go wrong, it will) govern events more than in formal presentations. Checklists of various types are helpful in avoiding room and audiovisual equipment foul-ups, but no checklist will be of any earthly good when members of your presenting team draw complete mental blanks as they step to the front of the room.

Even the best checklists and preplanning will not solve the problem of a team member's becoming too ill to stand on the day of the presentation. There is no easy solution to the problem of your presence in the right city while your projectors, slides, and change of clothes are 1000 miles away in an airport baggage room in Austin, Texas.

Not long ago, in an in-house workshop on presentations, a team was given this problem: The firm's experienced, thoroughly rehearsed presentation team was killed in a tragic airplane accident while on the way to an interview. You, as an individual and knowing next to nothing about the client or the project, have been dispatched to explain the situation to the prospective client, who intended to make the selection final right after your team (now deceased) had made the presentation. Your firm has in-depth experience with the project type and deserves consideration for the job. Not only must you explain the sad circumstances, but your primary mission is also to convince the client to postpone a decision for at least a week—until your substitute project team, now being assembled and briefed about the project, has been interviewed by this client.

It is an interesting and challenging assignment for even the most veteran marketer.

CLIENT EXPECTATIONS AND INTERESTS

Knowing what prospective clients expect (or believe they expect) from design consultants can be a considerable aid in developing strategies and tactics for marketing and sales efforts, especially in structuring presentations. You should always attempt to determine client expectations on an individual basis, but some general discussion of the subject may help you to focus on future specific situations.

Over the past few years several studies have been made about the criteria used by clients in making designer selections. Table 9-1 compares the answers given in four such client polls. Striking some sort of mean or average is difficult owing to variations in the questions asked, but the single most important consideration is without question the past direct experience of a firm with the present project type. This not very surprising result should convince even the most stubborn principal of the advisability of hitting the point hard in most presentations and avoiding a boring recital of the name, location, and cost of every project done by the firm, illustrated all too often by several hundred irrelevant slides.

The list of questions that follow should be of additional help in keeping your presentation on track. All of the questions have been asked in

Table 9-1   Client Selection Criteria Ranked by Importance

	Survey 1	Survey 2	Survey 3	Survey 4
Total service capability	1		9	
Engineering know-how	2	2	7	
Design creativity (excellence)	3	3	10	4
Similar project experience	4	1	1	1
Postconstruction follow-through	5		6	
Proximity of firm to project	6	8	4	
National prestige of firm	7		11	
Staff availability		4	2	
Ability to meet schedules		5		
Project size		6		
Cost control		7	5	3
Project management		9		
General attitude		10		6
Staff background			3	2
Satisfaction of past and present clients			8	8
Ability to deal with a principal				5
Effective selling techniques				7
Interior design reputation				9
Price				10

actual interviews by real clients. They can be used in internal practice presentation drills to keep presenters on their toes and thinking.

PRESENTATION DRILL QUESTIONS

1. What size firm do you have?
2. What experience does your firm have with this type of project?
3. What happens if the project manager leaves before our job is finished?
4. What consultants would you plan to use for our project?
5. How do you control your consultants?
6. How much will our project cost?
7. When can we start construction?
8. When can we occupy the building?
9. What type of construction do you favor?
10. What mechanical systems do you recommend?
11. How would you handle energy conservation on our project?
12. Your fees seem high. How do you account for that?
13. We really favor using a local firm. Could you do a good job for us from 500 miles away from the project?
14. How long have you been in business?
15. What kind of contract do you prefer? Why?
16. Do your roofs leak?
17. Have you visited our site?
18. What do you consider to be your firm's present worst constraint?
19. What is your current work load?
20. When could you begin design?
21. How many design awards has your firm won?
22. What kind of a postconstruction follow-up plan do you have for your projects?
23. To what extent do you use computer techniques for project control and design functions?
24. What functions should the client's project team perform so as to be of the most assistance to your team?
25. What cost control techniques would you use on our job?
26. Has your firm been sued for any reason in the last three years? If so, briefly describe the circumstances.
27. How can you justify a 2 percent higher fee than the last firm we interviewed? You both tell us you'll perform the same service.
28. Can your twenty-person firm really perform as well as firm ABC, which has 200 people?
29. Our city has paid for a lot of plans, and they all sit on a shelf. I think this one will end up on that same shelf, don't you?
30. Your firm appears to have more work than it can handle right now. Are you sure you can meet our tight time requirements?
31. You've said several times that you want to help us. Would you be willing to share your ideas about our project by making some drawings for us?
32. Why should we hire an East Coast firm to design our West Coast project?
33. Your firm doesn't offer construction management, yet we've heard there are many advantages. Could you comment briefly on that point?
34. Which of your past and current jobs would you recommend that we visit before we decide on a design firm? Why those in particular?

35. What are the three reasons you'd want us to take back to our board to justify our selecting your firm over your four competitors, all of whom appear to enjoy good reputations among their clients and other professionals?

PRESENTATION DOs AND DON'Ts

Most of the points in the following list of dos and don'ts were covered in this chapter. The remainder will be discussed in detail in Chapter 10.

DO

1. Plan, structure, have a dry run, and analyze presentations before inflicting them on potential clients.

2. Research clients and their projects thoroughly before outlining your presentation.

3. Determine early who the decision makers are.

4. Use your sponsors before and during the presentation.

5. Select the presentation team carefully. No one should be on it without a good reason or if he or she cannot make a significant and positive contribution to the presentation.

6. Relate everything possible in the presentation to the client's interests and the specific project.

7. Try to come up with at least one "competitive differential" or "unique selling proposition" (USP) for your firm.

8. Thoroughly prepare all audiovisuals and other presentation aids.

9. Check out the presentation room in advance of the interview.

10. Find out the composition of the interview committee.

11. Research the members of the interview committee and of the selection committee as well if they are different.

12. Learn who your competition is.

13. Dress appropriately.

14. Begin by distributing a printed, one-page agenda for your presentation.

15. Ensure a good introduction to the interview committee by writing it yourself and handing it to the chairperson.

16. Avoid obvious theatrics; strive for sincerity.

17. Assume a confident manner from the outset.

18. Be as brief as possible.

19. Be aware of time constraints. Make all of your important points within the time allotted.

20. Encourage discussion and participation by all present.

21. Anticipate questions, and have answers.

22. Have a plan for answering questions.

23. Have one member of your team act as a recorder during the presentation to note both important points and questions raised by the interviewers and an approximation of your answers.

24. Use examples and case histories.

25. Prepare for contingencies and emergencies—in everything.

26. Stay flexible throughout the presentation.

27. Remember that clients have every reason to relate the way you handle the interview to how you'd handle their project.

28. Write a follow-up letter to the selection committee immediately following your presentation.

DON'T

1. Check presentation materials and notes through if flying to the interview. Keep them in your possession.

2. Show up late for any reason.

3. Let your presentation team outnumber the interview group.

4. Lose control of the presentation.

5. Ever debate or argue a point brought up by a member of the presenting team in front of the selection committee.

6. Use overly complicated audiovisual materials or setups.

7. Talk down to your audience.

8. Let the interview drag out or wind down to a close. Have a plan for an upbeat finish.

9. Forget to have some type of relevant leave-behind material.

10. Forget to ask for the job.

11. Assume anything.

REFERENCES

[1]George T. Vardaman, *Effective Communication of Ideas*, Van Nostrand Reinhold Company, New York, 1970, p. 89.

[2]Donna Pond, "How to Prepare a Management Presentation," paper presented at the 1981 Conference of IEEE Professional Communications Society, Arlington, Va., September 16–18, 1981.

[3]Dr. Ernst G. Beier and Evans G. Valens, *People-Reading*, Stein and Day/Publishers, Briarcliff Manor, N.Y., 1975, p. 77.

[4]Robert B. Darling, *Successful Marketing of Architectural Services* (Unit I), MGI Management Institute, Larchmont, N.Y., 1980, p. 4–14.

[5]David G. Cooper, *Architectural and Engineering Salesmanship*, John Wiley & Sons, Inc., New York, 1978, p. 106.

[6]Robert B. Darling, op. cit., p. 4–13.

[7]Gerre Jones, "Client Presentations as Job Interviews," *Professional Marketing Report*, December 1981, p. 1.

Chapter 10
THE PRESENTATION: FORMAL INTERVIEWS

The presentation's content was fully outlined and then analyzed, modified, and polished. The presenting team was carefully and thoughtfully selected, thoroughly rehearsed, and expertly critiqued. Relevant, attention-getting presentation aids (props and scenery) were designed, produced, and inserted into the presentation outline at appropriate spots. In effect, a minidrama with the working title of "Get the Job" was written, cast, staged, and put through several "out-of-town" openings or dress rehearsals. Now, in theory at least, you are ready for the marketing equivalent of a Broadway opening—the client interview.

If theory lives up to reality, the similarities between formal presentations by design firms and show biz productions end here. Rarely does a playwright or a producer deliberately go to the trouble of staging a one-performance show. But if your efforts prove fruitful, one performance is all that's required. As a matter of fact, one performance is all you are usually allowed. For the next prospect and project a completely different show, possibly with an all-new-cast, must be put together. For marketers of design services, every presentation is "another opening, another show."

SETTING THE STAGE

Rule number one for presenters: Check out *everything* in advance. The corollary to rule number one: Nothing worthwhile ever happens by accident; only with a lot of help, from the right people at the right times, can you have any reason to expect that the desired result will occur. Even with all of the help and backup you can muster, nothing is guaranteed; without maximum attention to detail, failure is fairly certain.

Every marketer has his or her own ideas about what should go into formal presentations to prospective clients. It might seem obvious that no firm has yet come up with the perfect formula for successful interviews. Had anyone discovered a foolproof presentation process, then that firm would get every project it chose to pursue. The perfect presentation, like the Holy Grail, seems destined to be eternally sought for—but always to just elude the seeker.

Nevertheless, one must try. As I pointed out in the first edition of *How to Market Professional Design Services*, "No matter where or how information about a prospective job is turned up, or how outstanding a professional's qualifications are to design it, if he doesn't get an interview and an opportunity to present his credentials, there is just no possibility that he will get the job."

More often than not, the key to truly successful presentations is in the selection of the team leader. Regardless of what in-house title is used—team leader, MC, head presenter—the person put in charge should be given the authority to control every controllable aspect of the presentation. Once the team is in front of the interviewing committee there literally are dozens of stress factors than can come into play, over which one has little or no control. It is particularly important, therefore, to control everything possible before going through the door to the interview.

If the lead presenter has *any* reason for concern about any of the members of the presentation team, then that person or those people do not go. Period. If the leader is uncomfortable with any of the firm's promotional materials, they are left behind in the office. It makes no difference if the firm has just spent ten months and thousands of dollars to prepare a new brochure; when the presentation leader doesn't want it, that decision governs. The leader should also be completely satisfied with the total structure of the presentation and with any presentation aids that might be planned for use. The leader is the one who decides how many dry runs of a presentation are necessary. He or she must be fully and unquestionably in charge of the entire operation. It's a form of one-point responsibility for the design firm in that, if the presentation goes badly, the blame is more easily assigned. By the same token, if the presentation is a smashing success (based primarily on getting the job), then the credit goes where it is due.

Prepresentation Checklist   It is an unfortunate fact of life that few design professionals have an opportunity to watch other firms present.

Several years ago, as a member of a city selection committee, Phoenix architect Milan Srnka had such an opportunity. In his year on the committee, Srnka saw more than 100 presentations. He later wrote up his observations in the form of a four-phase checklist. Parts of the following are based on Srnka's list.

1. Do your homework. Find out everything possible about the project, client, and members of the interview committee. Try to determine goals and personal and special interests of each member.

2. Visit and photograph the site. Talk to the user. This helps to demonstrate your knowledge of the situation and underscores your genuine interest in the project. (See the remarks on this point in Chapter 12, "Selling to the Government.") It is surprising how many interview panel members will not have seen the site.

3. Visit similar facilities to observe operational and design problems.

4. Investigate legal and infrastructure conditions of the site (zoning, traffic, density, availability of utilities, and the like).

5. Always check out the room where the interview will be held. These points should be checked and double-checked:

- Dimensions of the room: length, width, height, and general shape (square, rectangular, L-shaped).
- Electrical outlets: location, type of plug required.
- Location of light switches and *what* they control. (Do any power outlets go dead when lights are turned off?)
- Location and operation of temperature controls. Try to start with the room cool. It will warm up according to the number of people involved in the interview.
- Location of all entrances: direction of door swings.
- Arrangement of furnishings: tables, chairs, coat racks.
- Shape of the setup; U, T, E, V, theater, classroom, horseshoe, modified herringbone—what? Make up a rough diagram showing the setup.
- Availability of the presentation room. When can equipment be set up? Will staff help be available?
- If you are driving to the presentation, where is the nearest parking?
- Acoustics. Check floor coverings, wall hangings, ceiling treatment. Clap your hands sharply; listen for echoes. Talk in loud and medium tones as you move around the room. Listen for echoes and dead spots.
- Equipment. Plug everything in and test it. If you are using projection equipment, is a table or regular projection stand available?

■ Is the screen distance O.K.? Is the screen large enough and in good repair? If you are using an overhead projector, does the screen have a keystone eliminator arm?

■ Seating and screen throw. Check this from the audience's viewpoint. Front row of viewers should be no closer than the equivalent of two screen widths; most distant viewers, no more than six screen widths back. Keystoning? Brightness?

■ Do you have enough extension cords, plug adapters (three-pin to two-pin; two-pin to three-pin), remote control cords, spare fuses, and extra projection lamps?

■ Availability of blackboard, flip chart and easel, cork board wall surface? Also, chalk, erasers, felt-tip pens, and a pointer?

■ If you plan to use a lectern, is it in the room and set to the right height? Is the reading lamp on it working? (Always carry a pocket flashlight for emergencies.)

■ *All* audiovisual materials. Inspect everything you plan to use for proper sequence, orientation, and cleanliness.

6. Just before you enter the presentation room, check out everything one more time.

All of the preparatory work finally boils down to one point; you will either control, or be controlled by, the physical environment of the room. It is up to you to make the physical aspects work *for* you and your message. Otherwise, they will certainly work against you.

Some of the environmental factors (most of which you can control) that can have a definite effect on your comfort and the eventual success of the presentation:

1. Lighting; quality, intensity, placement
2. Your location and visibility to the audience
3. The seating arrangement for the selection committee
4. Ambient noise; internal speaker systems, background music systems, HVAC systems, outside traffic noises
5. Air quality and temperature
6. Room decor (visual distractions)—too-bright or clashing colors; mirrors; sun or bright lights in your or committee's eyes
7. Acoustic and auditory distractions; noisy ventilating systems; squealing or static in the speaker system; a ringing telephone; noise from hallways or nearby rooms; and audience noise (papers rustling, private conservations, and the like)
8. Your dress
9. Your voice

10. Condition of the audience—thirsty, tired, hungry, need to make a phone call or go to the bathroom.

Milan Srnka's checklist points covering the interview itself are these:

1. Among other things, an interview is an opportunity for the prospect to watch applicant design firms under pressure. Go in relaxed and informal, and stay that way throughout the presentation. Let those from the firm who are most comfortable in front of the group carry the bulk of the presenting job.

2. Match the number and capabilities of the presenting team with the size of the project and the number of those on the interview team. As a rule of thumb, the presenting group should not outnumber the interviewers. When the project is small and yours is a large firm, it is good strategy to use younger project architects and engineers on your presenting team.

3. Let your spokesperson (head presenter or MC) do most of the talking, receive all questions, and generally run the show. This gives interviewers a single source to focus on. But avoid monotonous monologues.

4. Identify the primary continuing contact in your firm early in the presentation. Make certain the prospect knows who will follow the project all the way through. The selection and identification of this contact to the prospect is, in a sense, similar to the naming of an account executive in an advertising or public relations firm.

5. Show interest in and enthusiasm for the project at all times.

6. Develop the presentation into a discussion among presenters and interviewers—involve the client committee. Make it a seminar, not a lecture.

7. Interviewers often have a set list of questions to ask each presentation group. Anticipate such questions, and try to answer them before they are asked. Try, also, to anticipate the answers given by other firms, and couch your answers in different language and form.

8. Be clear, concise, and patient. Repeat important points. Don't assume anything.

9. Sell continuity of responsibility from start to completion, in-house capacity, project management capabilities, and your experience with the type of project under discussion. Refer to your firm's ability to handle special problems—zoning, environmental, contractors, and the like.

10. Explain your approach to designing the project. Take the client briefly through a typical planning process.

11. But don't go to the interview with the project mentally designed. Leave any preconceived ideas about design, systems, consultants, ma-

terials, schedules, and the like in your office. Make it clear to the selection committee members that their input is important and that their ideas will be sought out throughout the design process. (But don't go overboard on this point.)

12. While making the prospect's role and importance clear, as in number 11, give assurances that a senior person from your firm will give full attention to the project. Here again be careful not to oversell. Most clients know that a senior principal will not be checking shop drawings or chasing down change orders.

13. Keep the presentation relevant at all times. Answer questions directly and concisely; unnecessary elaboration can confuse the issue and take you into hot water. Don't go off—or be drawn off—on tangents. Don't give your life story or inflict your personal design philosophy on the interviewers. Talk about the project. Avoid the overuse of "I," "my," "we," "ours," "mine," and "us." Emphasize "you" and "your."

14. Don't get hung up on a sticky point. It's an interview; the contract will be negotiated later and under entirely different circumstances. Be flexible—things have a way of working themselves out.

15. Respect the interview schedule. The client sets the rules. If you were told you have thirty minutes in which to present, structure your material to fit well within that time. Many firms save five minutes or so at the end for covering questions and to summarize. If the prospect violates the time limits, fine—all bars are down. (Some lead presenters have developed techniques to force interviewers to cause the presentation to go into overtime.) Stay as long as the discussion seems profitable. If nothing else, your being held overtime by the prospect will induce nervousness and uncertainty among those firms waiting outside the room.

16. Related to number 15, friendly, time-killing, idle chatter may work to your disadvantage. Maintain control of the interview at all times. Don't let it lag.

17. Be aware of all subtleties such as body language and other forms of nonverbal communication. The mild-appearing old gentleman who says nothing may be the strongest member of the interview committee.

18. Don't oversell. No one can be all things to all people. If you have areas of inexperience, suggest the use of qualified consultants to fill such voids. But be careful about naming consultants unless asked. The prospect may have some definite ideas about the consultants he or she wants to use.

19. Use terminology understandable to the interviewers. Avoid technical terms and jargon, but don't ever get caught talking down to a group.

20. Expect the prospect to be interested in how your firm meets time and budget constraints. Today's clients rarely issue blank checks to design consultants. Try to develop a unique response to questions about these points.

21. Make certain that all material taken to the interview is pertinent, reasonably brief, and related to the prospect's job. Be able to relate all presentation materials (including leave-behinds) directly to the subject of the interview.

22. Hold leave-behind items for distribution *after* the presentation. Keep all such potential distractions under your control.

23. Ask for the job. Tell the interview group you want it.[1]

SPEAKING

As responsible and experienced marketers and principals, we know that there are large gaps between the ideal and reality in most presentations. It is an irony of modern day living that successful people—from the arts, from business, from the professions, in sports, and in most other forms of human endeavor—regularly are asked to speak before all types of public and private groups. A measure of success in operating a professional design firm is somehow equated with an in-born ability to speak brilliantly, entertainingly, and at length about practically any subject to almost any audience.

A superior knowledge of a subject and the ability to communicate that knowledge with skill and in relative comfort *should* be perceived as different and distinct qualitites. Many successful executives, including architects and engineers, are only effective at communicating on a one-to-one basis. Unfortunately, few significant interviews, particularly formal ones, are done one-to-one.

Every group has its own dynamic, and if a presenter cannot immediately relate to or tune in to the group, he or she has a problem. The ability to influence, motivate, and move others through one's speaking skills is a rewarding talent. Yet at some point in their career most design professionals would rank public speaking—in any form—at about the same level as their desire to participate in skydiving exhibition, scale the Matterhorn single-handedly, or enter a cage of hungry lions alone and unarmed.

The point, of course, is that no human is born to the platform. Rather, public speaking is a craft or skill gradually acquired through practice, determination, and repetition—just as is any learnable skill. One learns to speak well—and thereby to motivate—only by doing it; again and again and again. The budding concert violinist, an embryonic painter, or the aspiring public speaker who gives up too soon is condemned to live with the knowledge that, with practice, he or she might have succeeded beyond his or her wildest dreams.

A Fate Worse than Death? Making lists has become big business lately. David Wallechinsky, assisted by others in the Wallace family writing factory, turned out a best-selling *The Book of Lists* a few years ago. One of the many lists in the book has been around quite a while: the list of "Ten Worst Human Fears." If they are unfamiliar to you, here is the standard list, in descending order of their ability to inspire terror:

> Speaking before a group
> Heights
> Insects and bugs
> Financial problems
> Deep water
> Sickness
> Death
> Flying
> Loneliness
> Dogs

Note that speaking to a group is ranked far above such terrors as an attack by vicious dogs, going down in an airplane crash, going bankrupt—even death. The findings were replicated in 1979, when respondents to a survey from the London *Sunday Times* rated public speaking as their "most terrifying experience."

The fear of speaking, as are our fears of many things in today's world, is a "What if . . . ?" fear. In reality, we borrow trouble and generate phobias and stresses by worrying too much about future possibilities, many of which will never come to pass.

1. What if I forgot my opening statement?
2. What if I'm sick on the day of the presentation?
3. What if the projector breaks down?
4. What if the selection committee asks me a question I can't answer?
5. What if the committee doesn't like me?
6. What if I can't get them interested in our presentation?
7. What if I can't win them over in the first five minutes?
8. What if Joe forgets what he's supposed to say?

And so on. *Some* concern about appearance, content, and style is healthy, but many of us reach the point where we worry if we're *not* worried about how we'll go over in a public appearance.

Risk Assessment   Dr. Robert DuPont, president of the Institute for Behavior and Health and a practicing psychiatrist, labels such concerns as "the public psychology of fear." In a narrower context, a communications consultant calls the condition "speech anxiety."

According to Dr. DuPont, among others, three irrational principles govern risk assessment in a given situation.[2] The principles are

1. Your feelings about who or what controls the risk—you or some outside agency. External control of significant risks is an untenable situation, and that is why the case is made here for extensive preplanning, use of checklists, in-house rehearsals, and the like.

2. Whether or not the perceived risk involves a single, major event (a crash, an explosion, forgetting your entire presentation) or a series of smaller, separate events. One big event can generate excessive fears whereas most people can handle, or at least accommodate, stresses from lesser occurrences when they are strung out over a reasonable period of time.

3. The third principle is the degree of one's familiarity with a situation. We usually welcome the known—and resist the unknown. "Supported exposure" techniques are used successfully in treating certain phobias. Dr. DuPont suggests that such phobias as the fear of flying and riding on elevators can be tamed—even eliminated—by supported exposure. Going by the list of human fears, public speaking appearances might be an even better example of stress-inducing, phobia-arousing situations for most of us. Worrying in advance about how we will do helps not at all. Speaking for slowly lengthening periods before gradually larger groups on increasingly more difficult subjects is the supported exposure route to becoming an effective speaker and presenter. Using proven training aids such as closed-circuit television speeds up the process and reinforces confidence. There is no way to become an instant success in anything considered worthwhile or socially desirable.

Learn by Doing   In the beginning there is little reason to add to the normal stresses of speaking by worrying about such advanced subjects as perfect diction, gestures and upper body movements, gaze aversion analysis, platform presence, phonetics, and proxemics. All of these points can be dealt with later, when the basic learning stages are behind you—and under some control.

As was suggested a few pages back, it can be highly destructive to put a beginning speaker under the microscope of closed-circuit television unless an experienced instructor is standing by in a supportive role. Even an audio-only feedback, by means of a tape recorder, is shattering to many the first time it is experienced.

Most people have little idea of what they sound like to others, let alone any comprehension of how they *look* when speaking. Your stage voice can be approximated by cupping your right hand over your mouth, with thumb along the right side of your nose and the fingers directed upward toward your left ear. Cup your left hand over your left ear, fingers pointing upward. Rest the little finger of your right hand on the outside of your left palm, forming a passageway—a kind of horn—from mouth to left ear. Begin speaking and adjust your cupped hands until your voice comes through clearly. The sound you hear is very close to how you sound to an audience.

Your Voice   Force out all of the air in your lungs; then take a deep breath, and try to talk as you inhale. You've just demonstrated that intelligible speech comes only as you exhale.

Dorothy Sarnoff describes the process this way: "To produce speech [the chest and upper abdominal muscles] start a current of air up your windpipe from your lungs. The air passes through your voice box, along your throat, into your nasal passages and sinuses, back to your mouth, and finally, out into the open as spoken words.[3]

Most male voices are deeper (pitched lower) than most female voices because men's vocal cords are slightly longer; longer cords vibrate slower and give out deeper tones. Resonance (vibration) gives tonal *quality*. Nose resonators have a decided twang to their speech. With the right physical equipment, chest resonators can rattle dishes as they increase their volume. Articulation is added to the speech package by lips, tongue, cheeks—everything in or near your mouth gets into the articulation act.

Controlled animation, in both your voice and physical presence, is also important to the twin goals of holding audience attention and getting your message across. As I pointed out in Chapter 5, animation is from a Latin word meaning "to fill with breath"—you literally breathe life into presentations.

Stress—Enemy or Ally?   Take some comfort from the fact that even the most experienced speakers suffer from apprehension and tenseness until they are standing before the group to be presented to. Veteran stage performers, experienced politicians, and professional athletes are all subject to exactly the same nervous tensions as the rest of us. The difference between the experienced and inexperienced speaker, between the professional and the amateur, is that experienced speakers have learned to conceal, control, and redirect their tensions. Their outward air of calm confidence and of platform ease assures their audiences that they are in control of the situation and of their subject.

There are at least three ways in which you can build an inner confidence and, at the same time, present a poised, relaxed, in-charge appearance to your audience. First, by having a genuine enthusiasm for your subject matter; second, by having your thoughts thoroughly organized; and third, by studiously avoiding mannerisms which reveal inner tenseness and insecurity. Psychologist William James pointed out that action begets and increases emotion. A person may run because he is afraid, but the act of running increases the fear.

Certainly stress is not bad, per se. Stress produces nervousness; nervousness is one type of energy—extra energy, as it were. Trying to cover up or sublimate that energy will only compound the problem. Nervousness cannot be eliminated from the human condition. But understood, controlled, and channeled into the presentation, the stress-producing energy can become a productive, rather than destructive, force.

Direct most of that self-induced nervous energy into

Your voice (projection, timbre, animation)
Gestures (making them broader, more emphatic)
Enthusiasm (let it come through—for your firm, for the prospective client, and for the project)
Eye contact (aim for a minimum of 40 percent of the time you are speaking)

The Eyes Have It   Looking at another person signals interest in what is being said. Researchers have found that people *look* at one another during conversations between 25 and 75 percent of the time. Making *eye contact*—as when both parties to a conversation gaze into each other's eyes—happens much less frequently than mere looking. Depending on the distance between people, true eye contact occurs between 20 and 50 percent of the time. The farther apart you are, the more you sustain eye contact. Some profess to believe that breaking eye contact signals disinterest, guilt, and other negative attitudes, but the fact is that sustaining direct eye gaze over too long a time is uncomfortable and distracting—and unnatural.

Eye contact does give the audience an indication of the relationship desired by the speaker. Many listeners will associate eye contact and shifts in eye contact with directness on the part of the speaker and other such positive attributes as honesty, competence, and trustworthiness. As we normally present at some remove from those we are speaking to, the presenter's apparent eye contact should be in the upper range of 40 to 50 percent of the time.

An older school of speech training insisted on continuous, brief eye contacts with all members of the audience. Some speakers carried those instructions to such an extreme that it appeared they had lost control over their eye movements. And the quick, jerky movements involved made for tired eyeballs.

The contemporary technique is usually called eye control or gaze control, wherein a speaker maintains eye contact with an individual—or a small section of the audience—for four or five seconds. That's enough time to deliver a short sentence—or at least a complete thought—and makes eye contact a much more meaningful and dignified activity.

If you have a problem in maintaining sufficient eye contact while speaking to a group, here is an in-house exercise that should help you. Invite a group of six to ten coworkers to a presentation rehearsal. As you begin the mock presentation, ask them to raise their hands and lower them only after you have given them good eye contact. Hands should be raised again anytime someone feels he or she has not had positive eye contact for 30 or 40 seconds. This eyeball exercise will help you to stop staring past a group of anonymous faces as you talk and to become aware of brief, individual eye contacts. You should also notice that your words flow more easily and smoothly as positive eye contact increases and is brought fully under control.

Nervous Mannerisms, Awkward Gestures, and Other Tics   As I pointed out in Chapter 7, we communicate with one another in a variety of ways—orally, in writing, graphically, and kinesthetically. While all of these media have their specific applications (and certain advantages and disadvantages), in a formal talk or presentation they usually all are called into play.

Among the major forms of nonverbal communications are gestures, posture, facial expressions, sounds (nonfluencies), and silences. Practically all of these are attitude communicators—for better or for worse.

Hands are involved in most gestures, and may represent an asset or a liability to the presenter. Many gestures become liabilities when overdone or overused, and some should be avoided entirely. Here are some examples of both types:

1. Hands locked below the waist in the basic figleaf position. Looks awkward and ridiculous.

2. Hands in pockets. The most distracting manifestation of this position is the loose-change-and-key rattler. If you must occasionally put your hands in your pockets (and most of us do) and have a problem

with change and keys, simply make sure that all pockets are empty before a presentation.

3. Arms folded across stomach (the low arm fold).

4. Arms folded across chest (the high arm fold). To ensure audience intimidation, maintain a high arm fold, and stand very close to the interview committee.

5. Arms held behind back. This usually causes a speaker to lean forward; some interviewers may be concerned that the presenter will fall on them. If your goal is audience distraction, try rocking back and forth at the same time. This combination is practically guaranteed to cause any audience to miss the message.

6. Air chopping and slicing. The old Harry Truman "give 'em hell!" hand gesture. Avoid overuse; avoid entirely, if possible.

7. Clasping and wringing hands. Eliminate both of these distractions from your vocabularly of gestures.

8. Knuckle-cracking. Don't.

9. The propellor effect. It often starts out innocently enough as a small circling movement with one hand. When it is used to bridge idea transitions, the propellor can pick up speed and increase circumference. This gesture becomes particularly distracting when done with both hands (the twin-engine runaway).

10. Clenched fists. They are usually inappropriate for friendly presentations. If you must pound the table or a lectern, O.K., but don't overdo it. If you must clench something, try toes; they don't show.

11. Head scratching, beard combing, ear pulling, and face touching. These are not regarded as signs of a self-assured speaker. Perhaps a couple of head scratches per presentation is acceptable, but avoid checking ears, nose, mouth, chin, and beard with your fingers. None of these facial features has ever been known to move or disappear during a presentation.

12. Button twisting. Distracting; unnecessary—and where do you put the button after you've twisted it off?

13. Adjusting collars and neckties. Finish dressing *before* you step to the front of the room. The nervous necktie roller is to be shunned.

14. Removing, waving, cleaning, replacing glasses. O.K. in moderation; otherwise, it is very distracting. I have a personal aversion to seeing glasses pushed onto the top of the head, but that is technically not a gesture.

Any of these actions that speakers often make or do unconsciously may be distracting in various degrees to most audiences. By revealing inner uncertainties and tensions, they diminish the vigor and conviction of a speaker's delivery. Of equal importance is the fact that they may subconsciously make the speaker nervous.

Other Distractions   There are other tics, mannerisms, and habits that have similar distracting effects on audiences. Falling into awkward postures and restless shifting of the feet are two of them. Others have to do with the voice.

Audible pauses—what psychologists call "nonfluencies"—usually are evidence of nervousness, inner tension, and lack of preparation. Nonfluencies are those breaks in delivery or substitutions of sounds for words which interrupt the normal oral communication flow—tongue slips, repeated words or phrases when not done deliberately for effect, and the "ers," "ahs," and "ums" that plague most of us at least some of the time.

When pauses are deliberate—and inaudible—they can be used to gain or regain attention and for dramatic emphasis. Winston Churchill, among others, was a master of the dramatic pause. Audiences have no way of knowing whether a pause was intended to produce an effect, but inexperienced speakers seemingly are so terrified by silence that they must rush in to fill the voids with sounds (nonfluencies) or physical action or both.

Every individual has three basic tools for communicating orally: visual, vocal, and verbal. Visual covers general appearance—such items as dress, neatness, and posture. Vocal tools are concerned with the mechanics of delivery, voice timbre, volume, rate of delivery, and the like. And verbal considerations include vocabulary, grammar, and syntax. Use all three tools to achieve naturalness, conviction, confidence, and enthusiasm in a presentation. You are—or should be—your own best presentation aid.

Pacing and Timing   A consistently fast pace tires receivers, while a noticeably slow tempo quickly becomes dull and uninteresting. Constantly vary and adjust the pace of a presentation by mixing up slow and fast speakers, by cutting to a visual to illustrate, reinforce, or emphasize, and the like. Adjustments in pacing help to maintain receiver interest and give an audience an opportunity to process information already received.

Consider the average thirty-second network television commercial. You will rarely see a shot (image) held for longer than four seconds. That is because a group of television viewers were tested with an oculometer a few years ago. (The oculometer was originally developed to monitor eye movements of astronauts in space.) The subsequent, more down-to-earth study showed that TV viewers' attention spans are shorter than scientists had believed—about four seconds per image.

Never forget that most of our audiences today were raised on commercial television. On the average they will spend at least eight years of their adult life exposed to network and local station TV programming and the offerings of advertising agencies. Their expectations of presentations by design professionals consequently are much higher than those of interview committees of just a dozen years ago. If you assume that a selection committee will pay attention to your presentation simply because *you* believe it has value and imparts important information, you're in big trouble.

Handling Questions   An important element of every interview is your strategy for generating and answering questions from the selection committee. Some presenters prefer to have all questions held until the end; others are more at ease with what amounts to a continuing discussion throughout the time allotted for the interview. My preference is for the latter approach, but head presenters should use the format they are the most comfortable with.

If you use a printed agenda (see Figure 10-1), be sure to indicate in it if questions are welcome throughout or if you want the committee to observe a formal question-and-answer period at the end of your presentation. Once you have established the procedure, stay with it. Too many deviations from the announced agenda will give the impression that you are not entirely in control.

When you are ready for questions, avoid beginning the segment with "Any questions?" or "Now we're ready to take your questions." If no one responds, the silence will soon become embarrassing and overpowering. Worse yet, the pacing will suffer, and the head presenter will appear to have lost some of his or her hard-won control.

A better lead-in is this: "You may have some questions for us now." After a few seconds, if no questions surface, you can take it back and move into your close. You haven't dead-ended yourself into a formal question-and-answer period that didn't develop.

Some presenters make good use of sponsors on the selection committee by planting a couple of questions with them—to be asked if it appears that no one else has a question. As a rule, one seemingly spontaneous inquiry is enough to get the process moving; occasionally, it takes two or three of the planted variety to loosen up the rest of the group.

ABC Architects & Engineers, Ltd.

1472 Crystal Avenue
Central City, Indiana 46000

Presentation to

XYZ Manufacturing Co.

Briston, New York

Design of New Warehouse Center

<u>Agenda</u>

Introduction and opening remarks...................James Assento

Overview of ABC Ltd..............................George Bulfink

Project team.....................................James Assento

Project approach.................................Dorothy Caldo

Project schedule.................................George Bulfink

Applicable warehouse design experience............Dorothy Caldo

Questions and answers............................James Assento

Summary..James Assento

Representing ABC Architects & Engineers Ltd.:

       James Assento, AIA, Supervising Principal

       George Bulfink, P.E., Project Manager

       Dorothy Caldo, AIA, Assistant Project Manager

Figure 10-1 *Example of a printed agenda for a formal presentation. Copies are distributed to selection committee members in advance of the presentation.*

Presenters can generate questions on their own, of course. [To a member of the selection committee] "John, I recall one of your early concerns was about our ability to staff your project with our most experienced people. I'm sure you'll agree, after having heard from our nominated project manager, Peggy Martin, that you will get top experience. But since you raised the question, let me talk about some of the others on your project team." [Talks briefly about two others on the team.] "O.K., next question."

Actually, there never was a first question, of course, but the lead presenter leaves the impression that he or she was answering a question from the floor. This scenario might have to be repeated once more, but by the end of your second "answer," the real questions will begin.

The most satisfactory results are achieved when the head presenter fields all questions, answering them or passing them off to another presenter for the answer. All long questions (taking up to ten or twelve seconds or more to ask) should be received and restated (paraphrased) by the head presenter. This method ensures that everyone hears and understands the question. It also gives the presenter a few additional seconds to come up with an answer.

Try to avoid such obvious stalls as "That's an excellent question" and "I'm really glad you brought up that point." If you are desperate to gain some time to think, repeat and restate the question several times. In restatements it is usually possible to take some of the sting out of a troublesome query by changing a word or two in each restatement, but success with this technique requires practice.

Never argue with hostile or aggressive questioners. Part of the reason for exposing yourself to the extra pressures of a question-and-answer session is to demonstrate your coolness, knowledge, and control of the situation to the interview committee. Here is a sampling of some of the other types of questioners you may have to deal with:

The speechmaker
The provoker
The show-off
The loaded questioner
The faulty-logic questioner
The filibusterer
The drifter

If you are truly in control, it makes no difference what your audience does or asks. Your primary objective is to help the selection committee achieve understanding and gain confidence in your firm, not to debate or engage in shouting contests.

Never end a presentation with an answer to a question from the audience; always wind up with a statement or two to reinforce or summarize your main theme. And make your final sentence "We want this job!"

All It Takes Is Confidence   Before you read further, take out a sheet of paper, and list four or five methods you've observed by which other people demonstrate their confidence in themselves. Just below that list jot down some of the clues that tip you off to someone else's *lack* of confidence.

Confidence, psychologists tell us, is a state of mind. When you have it, it cannot be masked or hidden—and people, perceiving you as a confident person, are drawn to you (and to many of the things you represent). If you project too much confidence, it can slip across the line into cockiness and conceit, thus becoming a negative trait. Too little—or no—confidence invites others to use you as a doormat or ignore you altogether.

Because confidence is a state of mind and varies from individual to individual, it is difficult to define precisely. One psychologist suggests that confidence must come from the self-conviction that you are competent and effective in a variety of life situations. The confident person is perceived as a winner. Most people want to be associated with winners.

Confidence is developed, not inherited, and usually is the result of experience and interaction with others. Age helps. And so does wealth in that money buys travel and education and other opportunities for exposure to experiences that develop confidence.

As the Roman philosopher Lucius Annaeus Seneca put it, "Lack of confidence is not the result of difficulty; the difficulty comes from lack of confidence."

PRESENTATION AIDS

In connection with this section you may want to review the material in Chapter 7 under "Interview Preparation"—especially the information on customized presentation aids and the use of overhead projectors and flip charts.

Because it is somewhat misleading to refer to *audiovisual aids*, we'll use the more descriptive term *presentation aids*. The latter may appeal to any of the five senses and are not restricted to those of sight and hearing. Passing around a model or a swatch of cloth or a sample of brick or marble in a presentation would be an appeal to the sense of touch. Getting taste and smell into a presentation by a design professional is somewhat more difficult, but aids catering to those two senses no doubt have been used at some time or another.

David Cooper has this to say about presentation aids:

> Action aids are vital to your success as a public speaker. Action aids are flip charts, chalkboards, or any other surface on which you can write or draw to illustrate or emphasize particular points in your discussion as they occur. Ask any teacher how to keep the attention of a class, and they will always tell you, "Don't lecture." Then they will tell you to use a blackboard to write or draw what you are discussing. You are now moving, thinking on your feet, and holding the attention of the audience as you talk. The audience remembers things they see better than things they hear.[4]

In addition to the list of eight primary functions given in Chapter 7, presentation aids can also

1. Be great assets in holding an audience's attention. Statistical information can be made interesting and easily understood, for example, through visuals. But never forget that today's audiences are accustomed to seeing well-prepared visual presentations through years of watching television programs and commercials. Any presentation that does not meet or exceed this arbitrary standard will probably miss the mark.

2. Help to clarify major points and concepts. Differences of vocabulary, experience, and cultural backgrounds among members of the audience can be overcome. At the same time, areas of agreement and common experience can be reinforced.

3. Overcome limitations of time and space, providing experiences otherwise impossible or impractical. Time's passage can be speeded or slowed or stopped completely. One can visit London, the Taj Mahal, or even the moon, through the time and space compression potential of visuals.

4. Help to establish the same starting point for presenter and audience. It might be difficult to describe the aesthetic effect of a well-designed and sited structure to an audience that has never seen it. With a visual, everyone has at least seen and talked about the same thing. (Consider the difficulty of giving a words-only description of Pisa's leaning bell tower or the Piazza San Marco.)

Too many presentations are designed backwards; presenters begin with a handful of presentation aids, from which they develop themes and objectives—even strategy. The *idea* should generate or direct its own support, not vice versa.

And all too many presenters use slides or overhead projector transparencies as little more than enlarged 3 × 5 cards for their speaking outlines. The audience sees a topic sentence per slide; the presenter reads it to the audience, perhaps elaborating a bit on the theme, and then projects the next sentence to be read. The technique is boring, silly, and a gross misuse of presentation aids.

As you accumulate ideas for presentation aids, ask yourself these questions about each one:

1. Are there more ways than one to get your idea across (visual aids, demonstration, models, audience participation, audio effects such as sound effects, taped commentaries, and the like)?

2. Is support, reinforcement, or proof really needed at this point in the presentation?

3. Of the methods and techniques available, which is the best for *this* aid? (Essentially, which medium or media should be used?)

4. Will the presentation aid or device selected arouse your audience's interest or have a positive emotional influence?

5. Does every support element contribute to the basic message of the presentation? Does each aid add to the total effect?

Keep visual aids simple. Let the eye reinforce—not direct—what the ear hears. Usually, the less copy, the better the visual. If the point you are making really should be in the form of a four-page handout, don't try to cram it all on one slide. The limit is one idea to most visual aids, particularly to slides, flip charts, and overhead projection transparencies.

Visuals, like words, can be difficult or easy to understand, abstract or concrete in their effect. Use visual aids to present condensed information—not for full texts; for reinforcement, not as primary information sources. Visuals should support, reinforce, or restate the words.

Owing to growing client resistance and a desire to make their presentation aids more dynamic, speakers are increasingly deserting the 35-mm slide show for such visual aids as flip charts, overhead projectors, and large photo boards. One reason for this is that the ideal visual aid is created on the spot (during the presentation) by the presenter. This technique is dynamic, a crowd pleaser, and a clear signal to the selection group that your presentation is custom-made for *them*.

When you create flip charts as you speak, you can put key words or sketch outlines on the sheets in advance with a light blue pencil. The pencil markings are invisible to all but the presenter. Some speakers find they require no other notes for their talks. The ability to do similar advance preparation is also open to you when creating on-the-spot overhead transparencies; just make your notes on the cardboard frame of the transparency. If you opt for unframed transparencies, put your notes on 3 × 5 cards, and place them next to the projector.

Use of Flip Charts   Here are some thirty tips for the successful use of flip charts in presentations as discussed and illustrated in Marketing Management Workshops on formal presentations:

1. For the best visibility use as large a flip chart pad as can be obtained locally or comfortably carried on a plane.

2. Make sure the easel is steady and sturdy and the writing pad is securely attached. If the easel collapses or the pad falls off during the presentation, the pace you've established will suffer, to say the least.

3. Start with a new pad whenever possible. It is embarrassing to run out of blank sheets in the middle of a presentation.

4. (Related to number 3) If you are using a blank pad, make sure it *is* blank. In a recent presentation to a major corporation, the first four sheets were blank; the fifth had a four-letter obscenity scrawled across it in 6-inch high letters.

5. Use markers with broad-tipped points for lettering legibility.

6. Use at least two colors of marking pens—as a minimum, black with red or blue.

7. Test all markers before the presentation. Don't get caught with a dry one.

8. Ink in marking pens flows better when you cap the pens between uses.

9. Remember the rules for legible letter sizes. Most lettering on a flip chart should be at least 1½ inches high to be read from the back of the room. Two to three inches in height is better.

10. Carry a supply of drafting or masking tape so that single sheets may be torn off as they are completed and posted on walls for continuing reference.

11. It is considered bad psychology to make prospects stare at a blank pad until you are ready to use it. As soon as you set up the easel and attach the pad write a greeting—"Good Afternoon," "Good Evening"— and the name of your firm on the first sheet.

12. But during the presentation, after an illustration has served its purpose, flip the sheet over, or tear it off. Don't leave inactive illustrations in view; they are a distraction.

13. Consider photostatting up the cover of your proposal to flip chart size and using it as the first sheet of the flip chart when presenting to the prospect for whom you prepared the proposal.

14. Another idea for a flip chart cover: list the five or six or eight main reasons why the prospect should hire your firm on the top sheet. This information will face interviewers until you are ready to use the chart. Repeat the cover sheet information on the last sheet—to use during your summary.

15. Write and print legibly. *Practice.*

16. Be certain that all words on a flip chart are spelled correctly. Mistakes at that scale are glaringly apparent. In a recent interview a presenter put *correctly* on a sheet (in two-inch high letters) as *corectly.*

17. Write large enough for everyone to see.

18. Avoid lettering vertically or on an acute angle. It is difficult to read and is, therefore, distracting.

19. Make every flip chart presentation appear as customized as possible for a particular interview committee. Many prospective clients feel that most visual aids employed by design firms are too generalized and that the same props are used for all types of clients and projects. Avoid the implication that yours is a stock traveling road show by personalizing presentation aids.

20. For starters, neatly letter the prospect's name across the top or along the bottom of each sheet you will use. This can be done in advance.

21. Practice using a flip chart until you are completely comfortable with the medium. A flip chart has the disadvantage of causing presenters to turn their backs periodically. Get used to lettering and drawing quickly and to using the chart from the side.

22. Don't get so involved with your creating that you fall silent or keep your back to the audience too long while looking at what you've put on the chart.

23. Work quickly.

24. The flip chart can be a trap for speakers. Do NOT talk to the flip chart!

25. If all or part of a list, an illustration, or a chart must be predrawn in black ink, use colored marking pens to add arrows, to underline or circle words or phrases, and to check off points as they are covered. This technique helps to create interest and action in an otherwise static presentation and is another signal to prospects that the flip chart material is only for them. (Create the chart in the presentation; then destroy it as proof positive that yours is a customized presentation.)

26. Marking pens are attractive toys to play with between trips to the flip chart. Put them on a table or in your pocket when they are not in use. Put *all* such temptations out of sight or out of reach while speaking.

27. *Never* apologize for not being a commercial artist at the flip chart. That is not what the prospect is hiring.

28. Avoid excessive shading, shadowing, and other techniques of indicating dimension or depth. Keep it simple.

29. Try to keep the principles of good graphics and layout in mind as you sketch or letter on a flip chart. Use white space as a design

element on the page. Keep an imaginary layout grid in mind, or draw one lightly on the sheets in blue pencil in advance. Flip charts are available with preprinted blue or gray grid lines.

30. If you use a pointer when working with flip charts, keep its movements broad and pertinent. Don't use the pointer to gesture with, and don't point it at the interview committee; it is too threatening. Hand gestures usually are best for pointing to things on the chart; avoid spastic, choppy hand motions.

31. Because it is quite distracting, don't use the flip chart as a giant doodling pad while you present.

32. Some presenters develop sheets in a preplanned sequence and tape them in order to the walls of the presenting room so that the entire presentation is visible in outline form when the presenter is finished.

33. One marketer leaves the flip chart pad intact and gives it to the interview committee as a jumbo leave-behind and a record of the presentation.

EVALUATION AND DEBRIEFING

When the job goes to someone else, which will be between 50 and 90 percent of the time, try to find out why, particularly if you survived several cuts before the final interview. Your goal is not to have clients defend their choice (they won't do that anyway), but to get the prospect to give you suggestions and ideas for improving your own performance for the next presentation.

Unbelievable as it sounds, many offices drop all further contacts with potential clients as soon as they learn they were passed over for a particular project. It is only simple courtesy to thank clients for their consideration, and it is good basic public relations for future consideration by those same clients. Assure the prospect that he or she made an excellent choice, preferably in writing with a copy to the principal of the firm that was selected. Such a gesture costs nothing; is a sign of professionalism, shows the prospective client that you are a good sport—for whatever that might be worth when another job comes along in the same organization—and is bound to leave a lasting, favorable impression on the winning design firm.

Any client who has just made a decision to entrust X thousand or million dollars of someone else's money to a design firm is understandably nervous, no matter how many times he or she has been through the process. A little encouragement from another design professional about the choice can be an important psychological boost, and the client is not apt to forget where the needed encouragement came from.

Far too many design professionals are loathe to go back to clients for debriefings, believing it is somehow unprofessional or a possible imposition on the client. Neither supposition is true. It is unprofessional *not* to attempt to improve your marketing efforts and the image of your firm that is projected to prospects and others outside the firm. As for the client, debriefing research is justified on the basis of the investment made by the design firm in presenting to a client. The client *owes* you the information.

Sample Interview Evaluation Forms   The form shown in Figure 10-2 has been updated and revised over the years; it may well undergo more changes in the future. This form is intended for use both in in-house rehearsals and for actual presentations. It can also be used for rating performance in practice presentations by those interested in perfecting their overall presentation skills. Note that ratings are made by putting checks in the appropriate columns on the right. Narrative comments and criticisms can be written in the spaces provided or on the back of the sheet.

Figure 10-3 is for postpresentation internal use and is intended to supplement Figure 10-2. Form 10-3 helps a head presenter or a principal get all of the essential performance information together. The form then becomes part of the permanent prospect file.

135 WAYS TO IMPROVE PRESENTATIONS

Use this list as a planning guide, a checklist, or a debriefing outline.

Controlling Fears

1. Prepare thoroughly; know your material well. If you *are* an expert, you'll talk like an expert.
2. Give special attention to preparing the first two or three minutes (superpresentation).
3. Imagine yourself as a good speaker; exude confidence (the self-fulfilling prophecy).
4. Allow plenty of time for psyching yourself up. Force yourself to relax—breathe deeply, meditate, talk, or yell to yourself.
5. Establish your credibility early.
6. Take a course in public speaking or join a local chapter of the Toastmasters Club or both.
7. Get plenty of rest the night before a presentation, so you are physically and psychologically alert.

Presentation Evaluator

Name of presenter _____

	Excellent	Good	Fair	Poor
1. Eye contact/control Remarks_____				
2. Voice				
A. Animation				
B. Projection				
C. Timbre				
D. Rate of delivery				
E. Positivism				
F. Forcefulness				
G. Believablility				
H. Non-fluencies				
Remarks_____				
3. Presence				
A. Posture				
B. Professionalism				
C. Control of self				
D. Control of presentation				
E. Enthusiasm				
Remarks_____				
4. Physical appearance				
A. Dress, general neatness				
B. Use of gestures				
C. Mannerisms				
D. Other signs of nervousness				
Remarks_____				
5. Content				
A. If first, introduction of presentation and group				
B. Lack of jargon				
C. Grammar and diction				
D. Generated client participation				
E. Use of visuals				
F. If last, asked for job?				
Remarks_____				
6. General				
A. Handling distractions				
B. Quality of printed handouts (if any)				
C. Observance of time allocation				
D. Billboarded (introduced) next presenter				
Remarks_____				

Figure 10-2 *Presentation evaluator, for in-house rehearsals and formal presentations.*

```
┌─────────────────────────────────────────────────────────────────────┐
│                    INTERVIEW EVALUATION (Internal)                    │
├─────────────────────────────────────────────────────────────────────┤
│                                                                       │
│  Prospect name _____       │
│  Prospect address _____       │
│         _____      │
│  Did we get the job?   Yes ☐   No ☐                                   │
│  Our proposal/project number _____                  │
│  Type of project and brief description _____        │
│         _____      │
│         _____      │
│  Estimated fee _____        Project manager _____    │
│  Presentation team members                                            │
│         _____           _____         │
│         _____           _____         │
│         _____           _____         │
│  Selection committee members                                          │
│         _____           _____         │
│         _____           _____         │
│         _____           _____         │
│                                                                       │
│  INTERVIEW                                                            │
│         Date _____  Time _____  Length _____     │
│         Position _____  Location _____        │
│         Equipment/visuals used (if any) _____        │
│              _____        │
│         Problems (if any) with equipment _____         │
│              _____        │
│              _____        │
│  Handouts used at the interview _____        │
│  _____       │
│  Correspondence and/or documents sent to prospect after interview     │
│  _____       │
│  _____       │
│  Name of prospect debriefing representative _____        │
│  Why we (did) (didn't) get the job                                    │
│         Per prospective client _____        │
│              _____        │
│              _____        │
│         Per leader of presentation team _____         │
│              _____        │
│              _____        │
│  Feedback from prospect on interview _____        │
│  _____       │
│  _____       │
│  Feedback from prospect on proposal _____        │
│  _____       │
│  _____       │
│  Type and date for next contact _____        │
│  _____       │
│                                                                       │
│        Attach copies of all interview follow-up correspondence        │
└─────────────────────────────────────────────────────────────────────┘
```

Figure 10-3 *Interview evaluation form for postpresentation critiques.*

8. Begin speaking slowly, deliberately.

9. Focus on your ideas, not your fears.

10. Look directly at the members of the selection committee.

11. Pause frequently to relax yourself and to focus attention.

12. Manage your appearance. Dress comfortably and appropriately.

13. Obtain information about the audience in advance (through observation, by questioning its members, or by a questionnaire).

14. Identify your fears; categorize them as controllable or uncontrollable. Confront the latter.

15. Accept *some* fears as desirable—energizing stresses versus destructive stresses. Make the energy generated by stress work *for* you.

16. Anticipate questions; prepare answers.

17. Prepare and practice responses to potentially tough situations.

18. Assume the audience is on your side. They aren't *necessarily* antagonistic, hostile, or indifferent.

19. Introduce yourself to the group in advance—in social, professional, or other contexts.

20. Create an informal setting for yourself. Sit on a table or the front edge of a stage; lean against a bar stool.

21. For the two or three days before your appearance, live with a tape recorder. Use it to check timing, emphasis, volume, timbre, animation, and the like.

22. Don't look and act like a corpse. Be a little loose; let down some of your defenses; drop a few of your inhibitions; lighten up.

23. Don't be afraid to express personal opinions.

Beginning the Presentation

24. If someone else is to introduce you, write out the introduction you want, and give it to the person in charge.

25. Hand out an outline agenda for the presentation.

26. Put yourself in your audience's shoes. They are asking themselves, "What's in this for me?"

27. Provide an overview of the presentation; lead off with your educational or end objectives.

28. Create curosity.

29. Appeal to the audience's self-interests.

30. Ask a key question.

31. Ask a series of rhetorical questions.

32. Make a personal reference.

33. Open with a strong, relevant quotation.

34. Move immediately to your main topic.

35. Refer to the date, occasion, or place—or all three.
36. Show a model or other type of exhibit. (Remember that most people are fascinated with all types of miniatures.)
37. State the purpose of your presentation.
38. Tell a story, or make a humorous reference, but be certain any humor you use is appropriate.
39. Throw out a challenge. Dare the group to do something.
40. Use good illustrations.
41. Make a startling statement.
42. Create a mood; use suspense.
43. Open with a sincere expression of pleasure at being there.

Staging the Presentation

44. Don't use a script; don't memorize your presentation.
45. Put together your strongest presenting team.
46. Be enthusiastic.
47. Be gentle with people's feelings.
48. Cut out unnecessary words.
49. Define your terms as you go.
50. Use your own words. Draw on your personal speaking vocabulary, not a dictionary.
51. Keep your eye contact strong. Use eye control (an advanced form of eye contact) to establish rapport and to maintain audience interest and attention.
52. Make sure people can see and hear you.
53. Avoid jargon and technical terms.
54. Make the ideas personal and specific.
55. Prepare an outline for the presentation, and follow it. Plan the talk—talk the plan.
56. Use gestures spontaneously and easily.
57. Use a variety of involvement techniques. Encourage audience participation early and often—physically as well as mentally.
58. Learn participants' names, and use them during the presentation.
59. Use "power" words—*leaped* for jumped; *babbled* for talked; *smacked* for hit.
60. Use the outward-directed pronouns "you" and "yours" much more than the inward-directed "me," "my," "I," "we," "us," and "our."
61. Remember that the common denominator of all good talks and presentations is *brevity;* most nonprofessional speakers begin to lose an audience after twenty minutes.
62. Always build your speech or presentation around an identifiable

theme, and divide it into three parts; give it a beginning, a middle, and an end. When it ends, the end should be obvious to all, especially the audience.

63. Avoid clichés. The only fate worse than having to listen to a tiresome, boring speaker is *being* one.

Using Gestures to Dramatize

64. Keep all gestures broad and unself-conscious.

65. Vary your facial expressions to show feeling.

66. Cautioning (pointing index finger, head shakes, frowning, and the like).

67. Clenching the fist.

68. Counting and dividing with fingers.

69. Impersonation.

70. Pantomime.

71. Showing rejection.

Selling an Audience

72. Use your own style (never try to imitate another's style).

73. Appeal to people's dominant motives.

74. Present your ideas in terms that people already agree with and approve of.

75. Be specific, not vague. Use concrete examples—from your own experience when possible.

76. Use vivid illustrations.

77. Use the "this-or-nothing" approach; show how they *must* accept this response.

78. Use the yes response; begin with ideas they'll accept most easily.

79. Use third-party endorsements.

80. Use the rule of numbers (sometimes called "sign posts").

81. Watch for body language and other nonverbal forms of communication.

82. Repeat key points.

83. Never argue.

84. Don't oversell.

85. Be sensitive to audience reactions.

Dramatizing with Presentation Aids

86. Overhead projector. .

87. Flip chart.

88. Slides.

89. Photo boards.

90. Charts and graphs.
91. Blackboard.
92. Felt board.
93. Film strip.
94. Models.
95. Motion pictures.
96. Exhibits.
97. Magnetic board.
98. Opaque projector.
99. Tape recordings.
100. Television.
101. Representative contract documents.
102. Demonstration.
103. Diagrams.
104. Graphics and signs.
105. Magazines and catalogs.
106. Mock-ups.
107. Reprints (same size or blowups).
108. Phonograph records.
109. Pamphlets, booklets, brochures.
110. Reports and memos.
111. Specimens, samples, swatches.
112. Telephone (amplified conversations).
113. Role playing and simulation.
114. Appropriate gimmicks of all types.

Ending the Presentation

115. Respect the time limits set by the client.
116. Plan and rehearse your closing.
117. Make one member of the presenting team the timekeeper. He or she signals the last speaker when one minute remains.
118. Appeal to people's emotions.
119. Refer again to the occasion.
120. Repeat attention-getting techniques used in your introduction.
121. Summarize the theme.
122. Use an appropriate quotation.
123. Use an illustration, story, or anecdote.
124. Visualize the future.
125. Restate your key points in the conclusion—but worded differently from those in the introduction.
126. Suggest definite action.
127. Ask for the job!

128. Distribute relevant leave-behind materials. Demonstrate advance preparation and attention to detail with handouts such as copies of significant visuals shown in the presentation, endorsements, awards, special brochures, and the like.

129. Thank the selection committee members for the opportunity to meet with them.

130. Say individual good-byes; shake hands; be friendly; exude confidence.

131. *Never* apologize for anything in your presentation.

After the Presentation

132. Write thank-you letters to the interviewers.

133. Debrief the presentation team.

134. Win or lose (especially lose), ask for a debriefing from the client on your performance.

135. Get ready for the next presentation.

REFERENCES

[1]"How to Structure and Give Effective Formal Presentations," *Professional Marketing Report*, August 1977, pp. 3–4.

[2]Robert L. DuPont, "PATCO and the Fear of Flying," *Washington Post*, August 11, 1981, p. A-19.

[3]Dorothy Sarnoff, *Speech Can Change Your Life*, Dell Publishing Company, New York, 1970, p. 32.

[4]David G. Cooper, *Architectural and Engineering Salesmanship*, John Wiley & Sons, Inc., New York, 1978, p. 127.

Chapter 11
POLITICAL ACTION

Like "propaganda," the words "lobby," "lobbying," and "lobbyist" have gained unfortunate and rather shabby connotations among English-speaking peoples. Many automatically (but wrongly) equate lobbying with the activities of certain shadowy influence peddlers in Washington, D.C., and in state capitals—and with other, equally antisocial freebooters who prey on society and its institutions. (You'll find more about the "clout for cash" operators—and reasons to avoid them—in the next chapter on selling to government agencies.)

As far as I know, this is the only book about professional design services marketing in which you will find a chapter devoted to political action. The several other books written about marketing over the past ten years or so have all ignored the subject. This is particularly surprising in the case of one author, who spends a large part of his working hours in lobbying activities for a professional association.

At any rate, it is my firm conviction, based both on personal experience and observation, that marketers must have more than passing knowledge of practical politics, lobbying included.

LOBBYING

Several years ago the AIA defined lobbying as "the attempt to influence legislation advantageous to a particular interest. It is the supplying of detailed professional information—or opinion—to legislators and their staff."

Webster's Third New International Dictionary says lobbyists are "the persons who frequent the lobbies of a legislative house to do business with the members; specifically, persons not members of a legislative body and not holding government office who attempt to influence legislators or other public officials through personal contact."[1]

Still another definition—this from a practicing lobbyist—has it as "trying to influence the passage of national or state legislation, positively, so that it will be beneficial to, or negatively, not detrimental to, the interests of the client or clients who pay the fees for such services."

Lobbying Activities   This particular legislative representative recently explained his activities over one thirteen-month period, all directed at getting *one word* deleted from legislation pending before congressional committees. The word, naturally, was an important one and, had it remained in the bill, would have had an extremely adverse effect on his client's business. His actions on behalf of his client included

1. Writing to the members of appropriate congressional committees—two in the House and one in the Senate—and providing them with a reasoned analysis of why the word should be removed from the bill under consideration. This activity was repeated several times as the political climate changed and necessity dictated.

2. Appearances at open hearings of two committees as an informed (expert) witness and repeating the story of why the word should be dropped from the bill.

3. Corresponding with committee counsel and committee chairpersons regarding the general ramifications and potential impact of the proposed legislation.

4. Preparing and distributing fact sheets and position papers to key people in the industry suggesting amendments to the pending legislation as opposed to trying to block it entirely.

5. Writing occasional key articles and making speeches to industry groups.

The result of these activities was a bill without the offending word, which was subsequently enacted into law. The lobbyist gives some additional pointers about influencing legislation and the minds of those who propose new laws:

How to Lobby

1. When not too pressed by the demands of constituents and the need for reelection, most state and national legislators have open minds and try to do their job well.

2. They will welcome and consider carefully any suggestions about

pending legislation which are not obviously destructive, supremely self-ish, or demonstrably ignorant of the public need.

3. They are human and don't want to do anything or take a stand which might later be considered to be foolish, shortsighted, or ignorant of true conditions.

4. They are more impressed by, and attach more credibility to, facts and figures from parties directly affected by legislation than from lobbyists who work for hire.

5. Generally, legislators are open-minded about amendments, but "stop-legislation" movements tend to arouse their ire, particularly if the legislation is popular with the public. "Stop-action" lobbying also sometimes carries with it an implication that legislators who favor the bill are stupid or venal or both—impressions which tend to make the lobbyist unpopular.

POLITICAL INVOLVEMENT

"Politics is everybody's business" is a trite but true axiom for our times. Those who have not only heard the admonition, but also heeded it, are mostly in better shape today, practicewise, than those who were too busy or just decided not to get involved in politics. All that was said above about lobbying has a direct relationship to individual political action on one's own behalf. Personal and political relations are difficult to divorce from each other; when you talk to your congressional representatives about your interest in a new federal building or a post office renovation in your hometown, your are inevitably engaged in a form of lobbying.

A currently popular "in" word is *involvement*. Individual involvement is exactly what is required to understand, contribute to, and benefit from the political process in America. Involvement, unfortunately, is also the element most often missing.

Write Your Representative   Individually, each reader of this book is a member of many publics. Some possibilities:

The 40- to 50-year-old age group
Parents
Architects (or engineers)
Homeowners (or renters)
Automobile owners
Art collectors
Scouting movement leaders
Member of one or more professional societies

Member of one or more civic associations
Church members
College graduate group

Public opinion, however expressed, is a powerful influence on legislators' thinking. Tell your neighbors, your barber, or your doctor how you feel about state and national issues if you wish; but if you want results, you must make yourself heard where things get done—in state capitals and in Washington, D.C. If you have gone to the trouble of helping get candidates elected to office, you owe it to them to let them know your thinking on matters that come before them.

Give your opinions, or ask your questions as succinctly as possible (state and national legislators *do* get a lot of mail). Avoid form letters or cards supplied by organizations; they are readily identified as such by the receiver. A short note on one subject is best; a postcard is better than no communication at all—and occasionally a telegram commands the most attention.

From *Public Relations for the Design Professional* here are fifteen more tips for getting the maximum effectiveness from your letters to Washington, D.C., and to state capitals:[2]

1. Keep letters as brief and to the point as possible. Confine them to a single issue. One page is best; never exceed two pages.

2. Letters should be an individual creation, *not* form letters signed by the sender or a letter whose style and wording were obviously directed or inspired by some other individual or special interest group.

3. Write on personal or business letterhead, typed if possible, with the sender's name and address shown on the letter itself as well as on the envelope. Sign the letter over your typed name at the end. Don't follow business letter usage of showing your initials, followed by the typist's initials (GLJ:cmr) at the end of the letter.

4. Be specific about the subject. Give the name and bill number of legislation if you can.

5. Be explicit about your reason for writing. Explain how the legislation or the issue would affect you, your family, your business, your profession, your community—whatever is applicable and can be supported by the facts. Give examples.

6. An effective letter is carefully reasoned, clearly stated, natural in its phrasing. It should not be stereotyped, stiff, tendentious, affected, argumentative, extravagant in its demands, or threatening in tone, nor should it suggest that it was written at the direction or urging of an organization. Most organized pressure campaigns have little impact on Congress.

7. Don't enclose petitions, copies of your letter, or reams of documentation of your position.

8. Avoid name-calling and innuendo.

9. If you have some personal connection with the member of Congress you are writing, mention it in the letter.

10. When you've made your point, ask your senators or representative to state their position on the issue when they reply. Include your telephone number, and invite them to call you when they are near your home.

11. Be careful of timing. Don't fire off a letter detailing your position on a bill six months after it was enacted into law. Try to write when the bill is in committee.

12. Don't always write on negative matters. Let legislators know when their vote pleased you or has helped you. And when you get a reply to a letter about pending legislation, write again to thank the elected official for his or her interest and for taking time from a busy schedule to answer you.

13. As a general rule, don't send copies of your letter to local media. It can put legislators on the spot and is not a recommended way to initiate or cultivate productive, long-term relationships.

14. Don't be discouraged when the reply is obviously a form letter. Too many writers give up when they receive the "Thank you for your comments" answer. If your letter asked specific questions which demand a definitive reply, write again and refer to the questions in your original letter. The various forms of stock replies will eventually be exhausted, and you will finally get a personal, individual answer.

15. Above all, never write in real anger—about something or someone. Such letters generally serve no useful purpose. Sometimes it helps to write a letter when you're angry, without mailing it. Write it again the next day after you've cooled off.

Address letters to senators:

The Honorable John P. Doe
United States Senate
Washington, DC 20510

Dear Senator Doe:

And to representatives:

The Honorable Jane F. Roe
House of Representatives
Washington, DC 20515

Dear Congresswoman Roe:

A suggested close is "Sincerely yours," but if you know the member of Congress or other elected official personally, he or she may be addressed by first name or nickname—and the close can be as warm as you feel is appropriate.

Recommended address forms for other public officials:

The President
The White House
Washington, DC 20500

Dear Mr. President:

Cabinet Secretary:

The Honorable John G. Doe
Secretary of Commerce
U.S. Department of Commerce
Washington, DC 20230

Dear Mr. Secretary:

State Governor:

The Honorable John V. Doe
Governor of New Jersey
State House (or State Capitol)
Trenton, NJ 00000

Dear Governor Doe:

State Legislator:

The Honorable Jane B. Doe
Missouri House of Representatives
State House (or State Capitol)
Jefferson City, MO 00000

Dear Representative Doe:

Mayor:

The Honorable Jane F. Roe
Mayor of Chicago
City Hall
Chicago, IL 00000

Dear Mayor Roe:

WHERE THE REAL ACTION IS

Many design professionals never advance beyond the letters-to-Congress level of political action. A large percentage don't even get that far into participatory politics. But a few opt to try for the headier atmosphere of actively backing and working for candidates. And a tiny percentage are found as elected members of state legislatures, as mayors, and on county governing boards and commissions. In recent history, President Hoover is the only engineer or architect to attain a national elective office.

Elected representatives—city, county, state, and national—always appreciate an individual's committed vote plus as many others as the individual can influence at election time. A much more welcome (and remembered) form of support is active participation in the campaign, beginning with the primaries if you really want to stand up and be counted. If you don't have the time or temperament to serve as a volunteer campaign worker, the next most appreciated type of involvement is money contributions. Liken a primary win to the importance of surviving a prospect's last cut and making it to the short list of firms to be interviewed. Then compare winning in the general election to being awarded the design commission.

If the vanguard is not your cup of tea, practically all of the associations for design professionals have established some kind of legislative alert system, with member volunteers committed to making contacts on Capitol Hill when key legislation is under consideration. Most of these watchdog groups have "Minutemen" in their title. State components of the professional societies usually have counterpart legislative contact groups, to be fielded in state legislatures upon call.

Talk is no longer cheap. This is nowhere so true as in modern political campaigns, where even a locally broadcast television commercial can cost a candidate thousands of dollars for production and air time. Campaigning requires vast inputs of volunteer hours and money; winning demands even more of both, and the name of the game in politics (as in marketing design services) is winning.

Be Your Own Candidate   Up to this point the discussion has centered around moral and financial support of candidates by design professionals. As must be evident, all adult citizens of the United States who have not been deprived of their franchise through conviction of certain serious crimes are free to toss their hats into any political ring that appeals to them. There are age minimums for some leglislative and executive posts, but these should be no bar to most architects, engineers, or planners who have been in practice for a few years.

Standard 8 of the AIA's ethical practice standards (as revised in May 1974) says, "An architect may make contributions of service or anything of value to those endeavors which he deems worthy. An architect has the right to participate in the political process and to contribute time and money to political campaigns."

A January 1974 special issue of the AIA *Memo* newsletter was devoted to architects as community leaders. From the introduction: "This report profiles some of the AIA components and individual architects who are attempting to fulfill [a political leadership] role. It is by no means an exhaustive report. It makes no mention of the hundreds of architects who are serving on public planning commissions, design review boards, civic improvement groups, and a myriad of other bodies that serve the public interest. Neither does it attempt to describe all of the many public-service programs being carried out by AIA components in all parts of the country. To give space to all these efforts would require a publication hundreds of pages in length."[3]

POLITICAL ACTION COMMITTEES

Former Representative Joe Waggoner of Louisiana (the state generally credited with inventing hardball, down-and-dirty politics) once advised, "Get into politics or get out of business." Apparently, many business people have decided that political action committees (PACs) represent the best method of getting into politics *and* staying in business.

Making your political contributions through one or more PACs offers a degree of anonymity, imposes little personal responsibility for choosing candidates to receive the PAC money, and is a relatively painless, completely legal method of participating in the political process. PAC givers may take tax credits of 50 percent of their total contributions, up to a maximum of $100 per federal income tax joint return. The same tax credit can be used to cover direct contributions to candidates and to their newsletter funds.

In most respects, the PAC method of giving is almost as easy and anonymous as checking the box for $1 contributions to the presidential election campaign fund on individual federal income tax returns. This is the source on which presidential candidates may elect to draw by foregoing other forms of campaign financing.

Public financing of federal election campaigns was espoused as far back as 1907, when Teddy Roosevelt came out in favor of it. (Roosevelt also wanted a ban on all private contributions.) The Corrupt Practices Act of 1925 attempted to impose a degree of reform on campaign financing through disclosure requirements. Because of the general fuzziness and inconclusiveness of the act's language it proved difficult to enforce.

The Federal Election Campaign Act adopted by Congress in 1972 was a more comprehensive disclosure law, requiring detailed reports from candidates and their committees. Public financing of presidential campaigns in general elections was also part of the 1972 legislation. Later amendments added public financing of presidential primaries, set limits on campaign contributions, and established an independent body (the Federal Election Commission) to oversee the growing body of campaign finance laws.

PACs have been set up by most professional and business groups involved in design and construction, including the American Institute of Architects, National Society of Professional Engineers, American Consulting Engineers Council, National Association of Home Builders, and Associated General Contractors. Local components of many of these groups have established state-level PACs.

According to the Federal Election Commission, 2901 PACs were active as of December 31, 1981. The majority of the committees (1327) were corporate-sponsored. A commission spokesperson estimated that PACs spent more than $50 million on congressional elections in 1979 and 1980.

Because political action committees tend to support incumbents, success rates of up to 87 percent in the 1980 general election were reported by some of the design and construction PACs. (A Washington rule of thumb holds that congressional incumbents have something like a 9 to 1 advantage over their challengers. Other conventional Capitol wisdom says that with the incumbent's automatic edge there is no acceptable excuse for being turned out of office against one's will. Congressional perks could be the subject of another book.)

Dirk Van Dongen, executive vice president of the National Association of Wholesaler-Distributors, points out that his group's PAC funds go mostly to challengers. The rationale: it is easier to get "friendlies" elected than to spend PAC money on incumbents in an effort to change their ideology (and votes) to a more conservative, business-oriented outlook.

PACs are not restricted to associations and professional societies, of course. Almost any group can set one up; two of the larger PACs in the 1980 elections were those of Owens-Illinois, Inc., and Morrison-Knudsen Company. Review the list of possible publics you belong to, given a few pages back; you should find several possibilities for PACs. And you can be as active as you wish in deciding which candidates to help.

PARTY ORGANIZATION

If your decision is to work for a political party rather than for a specific candidate or to contribute to a political action committee, you should be familiar with the basics of party organization. Both major parties are organized roughly along the same lines. They are made up of committees: precinct, county, state, and national. Committees are governed by state laws and by rules established in the respective national conventions. Some states organize by wards, election districts, towns, and cities, but for purposes of this discussion, the precinct-county-state-national designations will be used.

The precinct committee is headed by a committeeman or a committeewoman or both, elected by party members of the precinct at a precinct meeting, in a primary or general election, or as otherwise provided by the party's state rules. The precinct committee is responsible for seeing that all of its party's voters are registered and vote on election day. It is the political unit closest to the voter.

The county committee is elected by precinct committeemen and committeewomen, by the voters of the party in the county, or as otherwise provided by state law. It consists of committeemen and committeewomen and other necessary officers. County committees must see that candidates are selected for local offices and are responsible for the campaigns of these candidates as well as for the vote from the county. The county committee is also charged with seeing that every precinct has active leadership, that the leaders are supplied with information and instructions, and that on election day every polling place is covered by trained election officials.

The state committee is composed of members, usually a woman and a man, representing the counties or other political subdivisions in the state. State party heads are chosen by this committee, which has the responsibility for conducting statewide campaigns and for building the county organizations.

The national committee is made up of a man and a woman from each state and territory. The national group acts as the governing body of the party on the national level. This committee is responsible for organizing national conventions, directing the presidential campaign, and formulating national campaign programs to be carried out in the states. The national committee also is charged with encouraging and assisting the states to build their organizations.

The national convention, made up of delegates from all states and territories elected by state primary, state convention, or state committee, nominates candidates for president and vice president, adopts a party platform, and serves as the ruling and governing body of the party.

With that brief overview of how the national political parties organize and function, let's turn to the practical matter of political fund-raisers.

WE CORDIALLY INVITE YOU . . .

When a firm has been the recipient of state or federal work, many opportunities are afforded the firm's principals to attend political rallies, dinners, receptions, luncheons, and a wide variety of other social get-togethers, all aimed at filling party coffers. Tickets to the affairs range in cost from $10 to $1000 per person. The more expensive and exclusive the function, the greater the pressure is to take a table, which never has fewer than ten seats. Elementary arithmetic tells you that the table-for-ten gesture, at $1000 per plate, will set your principals back $10,000.

An invitation to the 1974 Republican Senate-House Dinner is shown in Figure 11-1. An accompanying "Fact Card" gave the starting times of the reception (7 P.M.) and dinner (8 P.M.), costs ($1,000 per ticket; $10,000 per table), and the helpful information that complete tables could be reserved.

You'll probably agree that $10,000 is pretty important money to spend for the privilege of eating lobster with the President and other high-ranking members of the executive and legislative branches. Very few design firms are given to making the full table gesture at those prices although many take one or two tickets.

When the dinner host is the President or an officer of cabinet rank, the managing partner or senior principal usually will be able to get away for the event. As the function prices range downward to the $25- and $10-a-plate city and county affairs, it becomes increasingly more difficult to round up volunteers.

It may be useful to know that as long as you buy a few tickets to these lesser events, the sponsoring party organization doesn't really care whether or not you show up for the "anniversary banquet" or "victory dinner." (Losers seldom throw celebration parties.)

One can make an extra political point or two, while simultaneously avoiding a noisy, boring evening, by buying two or four or eight tickets, then turning them back to party headquarters with the request they be given to deserving city, county, or state employees. While it is conceivable that such turned-back tickets are occasionally resold, they usually are distributed to employees of the sponsoring government unit who could not otherwise afford to attend and who will definitely enjoy the opportunity to rub elbows with their higher-salaried superiors.

A FEW WASHINGTON GOODIES FOR YOU

Would you like to have an American flag for your office or home, guaranteed to have flown over the U.S. Capitol? Or would such a flag—

Figure 11-1 *An invitation to a $1000-a-plate political dinner.*

accompanied by a certificate of its historic role—be an appropriate gift to a new school client or for presentation at the dedication of a new corporate headquarters?

Admittedly, the time spent by your Washington memento on a Capitol flag staff is only a few seconds, but the crew that raises and lowers dozens of flags every morning on a Capitol roof will keep your secret, as will the Congressional Supply Office that sells the flags to members of Congress. As of this writing a 3 × 5 foot flag costs $5.77; for a 5 × 8 foot flag plan to spend $12.14. If price is a consideration, check with the office of a senator or representative; the cost may have gone up.

While birthday greetings and wedding anniversary congratulations from the White House are not available to just anyone, upon request a card or letter will usually be sent to anyone celebrating at least his or her eightieth birthday. This obviously rules out much marketing significance for most of your clients. Cards may be sent to those observing fifty or more years of marriage. Red Cross volunteers and others staff the White House office responsible for sending out some 300,000 cards and letters each year.

Exceptions to these criteria are occasionally made. If you are a good friend of the incumbent first family or a blood relative or a business associate of the majority leader of the Senate, the rules might be bent.

A little-publicized research and information operation in Washington is an arm of the Library of Congress called the Congressional Research Service. CRS exists to supply members of Congress with general reference help, including studies, special reports, and bibliographies on almost any subject.

Technically, CRS materials are not available to the general public, but the service compiles "Infopacks" on 100 or so current subjects, which are available through congressional offices. Ask your representative or senators which topics are currently covered by Infopacks. As always, contact their local district and state offices first to see if they have a list of Infopacks.

In November 1981 these were some of the subjects covered by CRS Infopacks, together with the identifying numbers:

Abortion	IP0001
Block grants	IP0157
Davis-Bacon Act	IP0027
Gold	IP0049
Interest rates	IP0107
Jobs overseas	IP0065
Lobbying	IP0066

Prisons and prison reform	IP0080
Solar energy	IP0089
Speech writing and delivery	IP0139
Water supply issues	IP0155

Another congressional goody is the insertion of material in the *Congressional Record*, as discussed and illustrated in Chapter 6.

REFERENCES

[1]By permission, From *Webster's Third New International Dictionary* © 1971 by G. & C. Merriam Co., Publishers of the Merriam-Webster Dictionaries, p. 1326.

[2]Gerre Jones, *Public Relations for the Design Professional*, McGraw-Hill Book Company, New York, 1980, pp. 227–228.

[3]American Institute of Architects *Memo*, January 1974, Special Issue, p. 1.

Chapter 12
SELLING TO
THE GOVERNMENT

As many design firms already have discovered for themselves, working for government clients can be educational, frustrating, interesting—even challenging—and often all at the same time. A firm can lose a considerable amount of money on a federal project it should never have pursued and accepted owing to badly drawn contracts and many other reasons, or profits may be comparable to those from private work. It is perhaps this Dr. Jekyll and Mr. Hyde aspect of government work which attracts some firms and repels others.

PURSUING FEDERAL WORK

It seems logical to cover the pursuit and winning of federal projects through example. Most of the basics and many of the intricacies of the process can be illustrated by a discussion of selection procedures used by two federal clients, the Veterans Administration and the U.S. Postal Service. While these two agencies do not necessarily represent all of the possible extremes of federal selection policies, their organization, funding, and reporting requirements vary enough to furnish a reasonable cross section of government procurement approaches.

The VA's selection process is still highly centralized for all major (over $2 million) projects. The agency's annual construction plans and expenditures must be approved and funded by appropriate congressional committees, with all the delays, haggling, and political interaction that that can engender.

The USPS, on the other hand, has been a quasi-private entity since July 1971. Its construction plans and funding are financed by what is known in Washington, D.C., as "off budget" means; expenditures "count" as total federal spending but because the USPS, as a form of private corporation, generates or borrows most of its own funds, regular congressional review and approval are not now mandated. The only handle Congress presently has on the postal service is through the annual operating subsidy. In many ways, therefore, marketing to the USPS is similar to marketing to regular corporate clients.

Veterans Administration   The American tradition of providing for disabled war veterans had its origin in sixteenth-century England, where "An Acte for Relief of Souldiers" was passed by Parliament in 1593 and made retroactive to 1588 to cover veterans of battles with the Spanish Armada. This early legislation was basically a pension law; not until 1681 did the English enact laws to provide hospital care for war veterans. Under the 1681 act the first hospital complex for veterans, designed by Christopher Wren and sponsored by Charles II, came into being in 1692 as Chelsea Hospital. The word "hospital" was used in its older meaning of "shelter" rather than in the medical sense.

More than fifty years before Chelsea Hospital accepted the first English veteran, the first disabled veterans' law in North America was enacted in Plymouth Colony. The Plymouth law provided that "if any man shalbee sent forth as a souldier and shall return maimed, he shalbee maintained competently by the collonie during his life."

Other American colonies gradually followed Plymouth's lead, and by 1776 the concept of special benefits for veterans was well established. One of the initial steps taken by the first Congress was to pass a federal pension law. This again points up the fact that early veterans' legislation placed heavy emphasis on pensions. Whatever direct medical aid and hospital care veterans received in the early days of the Republic was provided by individual states and communities.

In 1811 the first domiciliary and medical facilities for veterans were provided by the federal government when Congress authorized the U.S. Naval Home in Philadelphia "as a permanent home for disabled and decrepit officers, seamen, and marines." More than a century was to pass before the United States Veterans Bureau was established by Congress on August 9, 1921, following recommendations of a presidential study commission. In 1930 the Seventy-first Congress authorized the creation of the Veterans Administration.

Facilities for U.S. veterans of all wars have grown from the establishment of the U.S. Naval Home into today's sprawling health empire of almost a thousand centers, including hospitals, domiciliaries, nursing home care units, outpatient clinics, and a major medical research program. The VA is also involved in funding construction of state-operated veterans' homes. Design and construction contracts for these projects are awarded by the states.

Annual spending by the Veterans Administration for construction has ranged from $100 million in the early 1970s to an expected $1.4 billion in fiscal year 1984. Assuming the U.S. economy enjoys reasonably good health, yearly VA construction outlays should remain in the $1.3 to $1.4 billion range for several years. Out of some 30 million living veterans, about half (13.1 million) came out of World War II and are now in an age bracket that will impose increasingly greater demands on the VA and its health care facilities through at least the year 2000.

VA Selection Process   Planning projects (design development through schematics) account for around 80 percent of current VA selections. As of September 1981, the VA selected design firms for projects to be funded for construction in the FY 1985 national budget—approximately a four-year lead time.

The full VA interview board is chaired by the director of the A-E Evaluation Staff (formerly known as the A-E Selection Board). Making up the remainder of the five-person board are a project (contract) officer, a health-care representative, an engineer, and an architect. The last two named board members usually are the directors of their design disciplines with the VA. Some two dozen interviews a month—an average of more than one every working day—are held in Washington. When the VA does its own preliminaries (now done on about 15 percent of all projects), a three-person selection board interviews prospective design firms to make working drawings for the project.

Roland Vaughan, as of this writing the director of the A-E Evaluation Staff, gives these highlights of the VA's selection process:

1. Unless the project is a smaller one at a remote site, VA policy is to hold interviews in its Washington, D.C., headquarters on Vermont Avenue. An important consideration is whether or not the potential fee justifies travel costs for design firms being interviewed.

2. For projects valued at up to $2 million, local VA hospital or station directors are responsible for conducting interviews and selecting design firms. The supply officer or contracting officer usually sits as head of the selection committee. Local stations have full authority for these "minor" projects; the director's office does not get involved unless a problem arises. Up to a $10,000 fee limit, local VA stations may make designer selections solely from Standard Form 254s on file. To be considered for these smaller projects, periodically contact nearby VA facilities to confirm your interest and availability.

3. For most formal interviews in Washington, D.C. (for projects val-

ued at more than $2 million), a firm has a maximum of one hour for its presentation. For more complex projects (replacement hospitals, major master planning efforts and the like) the time limit is 1½ hours.

4. A typical one-hour interview might be structured along these lines:

   ■ The first five minutes are for familiarization of the presenting group by the VA selection panel. The VA staff tries to set an informal tone for the session.

   ■ The next thirty to forty minutes are to be used by the presenting firm to cover five subject areas: (1) the team proposed for the project; (2) experience of the firm, both direct and related; (3) cost and schedule control procedures; (4) the project management plan; and (5) design approach.

   ■ The final fifteen to twenty-five minutes should be given over to open discussion among members of the presenting team and the interviewers.

In the VA's invitation to firms selected for interview, the firms are asked to notify the VA as to who will make up the presenting team—and the project assignment of each. If there could be any question about it, this should be a big clue to the design firm to include at least the nominated project manager among the presenters.

Evaluation Criteria and Scoring Sheet   At one time the VA furnished copies of its structured grading sheet (Figure 12-1) in advance of interviews to all firms invited to present. Note that, in addition to the five subject areas listed earlier, the scoring form includes (IV) Location and Facilities of Working Office(s); (VII) Present Examples of Recently Accomplished Similar Projects; (VIII) Experience and Capabilities in the Following Areas (eight specialized areas follow, including value engineering, fast-track construction, and environmental assessment); and (X) Have You Been Involved in Litigation in the Last Five Years?

Presumably, most of the information asked for in these five areas, except for litigation, is easily derived from the firm's Standard Form 255 on file. According to a VA official, advance access to the scoring sheet caused too many firms to follow the grading form slavishly, meticulously covering every item listed whether or not the VA interviewers had any real interest in the point. The VA now makes it clear in advance of presentations that the concentration should be on the five key points. The VA still follows its long-established policy of furnishing copies of the short list to all firms to be interviewed.

Once the interview is underway, if it appears that the team nominated in the firm's Standard Form 255 is not what the VA is getting, the head presenter can expect to be challenged on that point.

Many interviewers from federal agencies believe that a skilled, organized speaker can deliver an hour of canned presentation and look terrific, but that unrehearsed answers to the interviewers' questions provide a much better basis for judging how well a firm will perform on the project and how capable the nominated team really is. At the VA, firms can hurt their case when they insist on taking the entire hour for a structured presentation, especially when they really have nothing new to add toward the end of the period. The discussion time is important to VA interviewers.

For presentations that sell to the VA, Roland Vaughan has this advice:

1. DO know and analyze your competition, including all of the elements of joint ventures and associations and their consultants. (Since, as was pointed out earlier, the VA furnishes a list of all firms to be interviewed to those on the short list, there is no excuse for not knowing who the competition is.)

2. DON'T go overboard on "leave-behinds." Many of them are far too expensive in appearance; most interviewers automatically equate high-powered booklets and folders with high overhead rates. VA interviewers have been given thick (up to 4 inches), leather-covered volumes with selection committee names individually embossed on the covers. That is counterproductive.

3. DO, in job descriptions, make certain that project assignments are realistic for each person shown, especially for all those from the firm's top management.

4. DON'T, unless you are truly skilled in the technique, try to draw board members into gaming situations during an interview. Sometimes gaming can be effective, but when it is overly transparent, interviewers will be put off by such tactics.

5. DO relax, and remember the VA board prefers that you maintain an informal, give-and-take atmosphere during interviews.

6. DON'T bore interviewers to death with your presentation. Keep it crisp and snappy; don't let it drag. Don't wear out one communication medium; don't overemphasize one communication mode.

Design professionals have, almost without exception, found VA personnel in the office of the director of the A-E Evaluation Staff approachable, helpful, understanding, and cooperative. The VA, like most clients in and out of government, does not care to serve as a training institution for design firms without direct experience, regardless of their general reputation or size. If your firm has never worked on a VA project, be prepared to be tested on something less than a new multimillion dollar treatment and teaching center.

ARCHITECT/ENGINEER EVALUATION BOARD
EVALUATION CRITERIA AND SCORING

PROJECT DESCRIPTION						DATE	
PROJECT LOCATION						PROJECT NO.	

FACTORS	SCORES					WEIGHT	SCORE
	POOR	MARGINAL	ACCEPT-ABLE	GOOD	OUT-STANDING		
	0.5	0.7	0.8	0.9	1.0		

I - TEAM PROPOSED FOR THIS PROJECT
A. Background of the personnel
 	
  1. Project manager
  2. Other key personnel
  3. Consultant(s)							

II - PROPOSED MANAGEMENT PLAN
A. Team organization
 	
  1. Design phase
  2. Construction phase							

III - PREVIOUS EXPERIENCE OF TEAM PROPOSED FOR THIS PROJECT A. Describe projects							
IV - LOCATION AND FACILITIES OF WORKING OFFICE(S) *(Design and Construction)* A. Prime firm B. Consultant(s)							

V - PROJECT CONTROL
A. Schedule
 	
  1. What techniques are planned to assure that schedule will be met?
  2. Who will be responsible to assure that schedule will be met?
 	
B. Cost
 	
  1. What control techniques are planned?
  2. Review recent projects to demonstrate ability to meet project cost target.
  3. Who will be responsible for cost control?							

VI - PRESENT PROPOSED DESIGN APPROACH FOR THIS PROJECT A. Describe proposed design philosophy. B. What problems do you anticipate and how do you propose to solve them? C. Describe possible energy applications. D. Describe innovative approaches in production and design.							

VII - PRESENT EXAMPLES OF RECENTLY ACCOMPLISHED SIMILIAR PROJECTS
A. Describe the projects to demonstrate:
 	
  1. Schedule control
  2. Cost control
  3. Construction problems and means taken to solve them.
  4. Any additional construction costs caused by design deficiencies; not program changes.							

VIII - DESCRIBE YOUR EXPERIENCE AND CAPABILITIES IN THE FOLLOWING AREAS A. Value Engineering B. Life Cycle Cost Analysis (LCCA) C. Critical Path Method D. Fast-Track Construction E. Energy Conservation F. New Energy Resources G. Environmental Assessment H. Specialized experience							

VA FORM MAR 1976 08–3375   553007

Front   VA Form 08-3375

Figure 12-1 *Presentation scoring sheet used by the Veterans Administration.*

FACTORS	SCORES					WEIGHT	SCORE
	POOR	MARGINAL	ACCEPT-ABLE	GOOD	OUT-STANDING		
	0.5	0.7	0.8	0.9	1.0		
IX. DESCRIBE AWARDS YOU HAVE RECEIVED FOR DESIGN EXCELLENCE							
X. HAVE YOU BEEN INVOLVED IN LITIGATION IN THE LAST FIVE YEARS? A. If so, describe circumstance and outcome. B. What type and amount of liability insurance do you carry?							
SUB-TOTAL ▶							

POINT ADJUSTMENT

A. EVALUATION OF PAST VA PERFORMANCE

1. Poor . . . . - 10 points
2. Marginal . . . . - 5 points
3. Acceptable . . . . 0 points
4. Very good . . . . + 5 points
5. Outstanding . . . . + 10 points

(Firms with no previous VA project will receive 5 bonus points)

B. EVALUATION OF VA PROJECTS

1. Firm with an existing VA project . . . . . . - 10 points

2. Firm with a VA project completed in past 5 years . . . . - 5 points

C. PREPARATION FOR INTERVIEW . . . . + 5 points

TOTAL SCORE ▶

REMARKS

SIGNATURE OF CHAIRMAN

SIGNATURE OF PROJECT DIRECTOR

SIGNATURE OF MEMBER

SIGNATURE OF MEMBER

SIGNATURE OF MEMBER

Back

A booklet, *Opportunities for Private Architect-Engineer Firms,* is available from the A-E Evaluation Staff office. As of this writing, the 1976 edition was still in use. Parts of it are somewhat outdated, but it should still be helpful to those with no previous experience with the agency.

U.S. Postal Service (USPS) As is true of the Veterans Administration, the roots of USPS are planted firmly in the early history of America and in such historic figures as the first colonial postmaster general, Benjamin Franklin. The first official postal service in colonial America operated out of a Boston tavern. In 1639 the General Court of Massachusetts designated Dick Fairbank's tavern as the official repository for mail going to or arriving from overseas.

Among federal offices, departments, bureaus, and agencies, however, USPS is a relative newcomer as the successor to the U.S. Post Office Department. In July 1971, following years of negotiation, debate, and discussion, the U.S. Postal Service as an independent entity became a reality. The stated objective of the fledgling agency was to provide an efficient, prompt mail service to the public at the lowest possible cost. A massive modernization plan—in excess of $1.5 billion for each of the next five years—was announced. According to a U.S. General Accounting Office report (Federal Capital Budgeting: A Collection of Haphazard Practices, No. PAD-81-19), the actual annual capital outlays for the 1974–1978 period averaged $683 million.

The most active areas for new postal service construction are predictably in the South and West. As might be expected, demographic changes essentially dictate active construction locations for many federal agencies. However, the replacement program for many of the older postal facilities in the North and East continues to be pressed by USPS.

Many USPS projects are fairly large in scale, with a planned life of thirty years or more. That point, coupled with postal service policy of using local design firms whenever possible, does not make USPS a likely candidate for much repeat business. And while a firm is working on a major USPS project, the general policy is not to award another job to the same firm.

USPS Selection Process As with the Veterans Administration, USPS allows one hour for presentations. At variance with VA procedures, however, is the USPS policy of interviewing firms in their own offices. In the case of a joint venture or association, the interview normally is held in the office of the firm designated as lead or prime. USPS makes no attempt to structure the hour of interview time. Questions may be asked by selection committee members for clarification of a point.

The attitude at USPS is that if a firm can't tell what the postal service is looking for, after reviewing the *Commerce Business Daily* announcement and the information furnished by the selection committee in establishing the interview, then the design firm probably is not competent or astute enough to serve as a USPS designer.

There are no mysteries about what USPS looks for in its design consultants (and expects to have brought out in interviews):

1. Experience with USPS-type structures (basically, industrial buildings housing a process operation; ideally, with over-the-road trucking involved).

2. Design approach, especially a demonstrated ability to design for mechanization.

3. Makeup of the nominated team and how individual talents represented relate to the project.

4. Project control.

5. Minority business enterprise (MBE) participation.

6. Knowledge of local codes and conditions.

7. Adequacy of resources, including financial strength.

8. Energy efficient design.

9. Track records for accuracy of estimating and efficiency of cost control over the past year.

10. Quality of documentation (Organized? Well detailed?)

11. Construction expertise.

12. Adequacy of the designer's own physical facility; order, organization, and use of modern drafting techniques. (To be able to inspect the offices is one of the reasons USPS interviewers prefer to hold sessions on the design firm's home ground.)

Beyond those basics, the USPS selection committee considers several other factors:

1. Whether the firm has all required disciplines.

2. Whether the firm could sustain the loss of a key principal in the middle of a project without going under (to the point of adequate management depth).

3. Is the firm (or the branch under consideration) truly local? (USPS wants its projects locally run and supervised although consultants may be from elsewhere.)

4. Computer capability of the firm (an in-house computer is not required equipment, but its presence and use count extra.)

5. Specialized building design expertise, such as architectural and engineering abilities in seismic and energy conservation design.

As of this writing, Vincent Hennessy is the director of USPS's Office of Design and Construction Management. Hennessy observes that a firm makes a definite, positive impact on the selection committee when it is apparent that some thought has been given to the project for which a presentation is being made. The site, for example, is always known before the interview. Many firms visit the site; winners discuss the site during the interview. Some firms take the trouble to find out where similar USPS buildings have been completed recently. The buildings are visited; photographs are taken and notes made; and this, too, becomes part of the formal presentation.

Perhaps the best preinterview activity of all is to visit operating postal service facilities to observe the general mail flow throughout the structure. Talk to the postmaster and some of the people who work on receiving, sorting, and delivery. Such visits help to convince USPS interviewers that a firm cares enough about a project to find out something about its internal operation. All of this has obvious benefits for a design firm with no previous postal service experience.

There are also size-of-firm maximums and minimums. USPS prefers to use smaller firms for smaller projects. As is the case with many clients, USPS believes that small jobs can get lost and receive less top-level attention in a large office, while very large jobs can strain the resources of small offices, leading to completion delays and other problems.

USPS wants to know the number of registered people in a firm. Since this is difficult to tell from the information called for in Block 8 of Standard Form 254, or Block 4 of S.F. 255 ("Personnel by Discipline"), the recommendation is to set out in S.F. 255's Block 10 exactly how many are registered and in which disciplines. Registrations of the nominated team obviously are covered in the 255's Block 7f, but USPS prefers to have the total firm picture of registrations.

USPS Regional Office Role in Selection   Designer selection for postal projects up to $5 million in total costs (site, design, construction, and support) is handled by USPS regional and field offices.

Regional offices are located in New York City (northeast region), Philadelphia (eastern), Chicago (central), Memphis (southern), and San Bruno, California (western). Field office locations:

Northeast Region
- New York, N.Y.
- Lexington, Mass.

Eastern Region
- Bala Cynwyd (Philadelphia), Pa.

- Columbia, Md.
- Corapolis, Pa.

Central Region
- Chicago, Ill.
- Louisville, Ky.
- Mission, Kans.
- St. Paul, Minn.

Southern Region
- Atlanta, Ga.
- Dallas, Tex.
- Memphis, Tenn.
- Tampa, Fla.

Western Region
- Kent (Seattle), Wash.
- San Bruno (San Francisco), Calif.
- Inglewood (Los Angeles), Calif.
- Denver, Colo.

The selection role of regional directors and field office managers varies somewhat around the country. Although the process is essentially the same, the safest procedure is to visit the nearest regional office and ask how selection is handled in your area. Copies of your S.F. 254 should be filed with USPS offices in the field, as well as with the Office of Design and Construction Management in Washington, D.C. And get a copy of the booklet *USPS Facilities Design and Construction Program.* Published in April 1981, the pocket-sized guide contains a lot of information about the USPS and its selection procedures in its eighteen pages.

STANDARD FORMS 254 AND 255

An article about the U.S. Government Standard Forms 254 and 255 appeared in *Professional Marketing Report* several years ago.[1] Since the forms are unchanged and copies of the original article still are distributed by some federal agencies to firms with questions about the preparation and use of the important forms, this section is based on the newsletter article. Certain new material and updating have been added.

Standard Forms 254 and 255 have been in use by design professionals and government agencies for more than six years, as of this writing. Relative newcomers to the design profession may never have seen a copy of Standard Form 251, the predecessor of S.F. 254 and 255. Standard Form 251 was used during the fourteen-year period 1961–1975.

In November 1974, deciding the familiar S.F. 251 had outlived its usefulness, the General Services Administration (GSA) began circulating copies of a proposed Standard Form 254 and 255 among federal agencies for comment. The proposed S.F. 254 included a "Project Code List," and GSA had this explanation in its transmittal memo:

Considerable effort has gone into the development of the project code list utilized in Questions 10 and 11. A joint committee . . . considered more than 280 different types of services or projects for inclusion in such a listing. A decision was made to pare the number to 50 project codes. It was later recognized that this was inadequate and the list was set at 100. While the listing is limited, every effort has been made to cover the broad range of professional services normally handled by architects, engineers, planners, surveyors, etc. It is recognized that agencies and individuals may desire that some project types be excluded or added to the published list; but, hopefully reviewers will understand that incorporation of every possible A-E service or project type is impossible and could defeat the purpose of codifying such data.

The listing contained on the proposed S.F. 254 is the result of numerous compromises and debates by representatives of the participating federal agencies and the A-E professions. Addition of a category to the current 100 project codes may require elimination of some other project type which is strongly desired or needed by another agency. If there is a particular field of practice which an A-E feels must be on the list, line number 100 is provided as a blank for write-ins.

In the proposed S.F. 254, they were called "Project Code Numbers"; in the final version, they are "Experience Profile Code Numbers" (perhaps the original name didn't sound sufficiently bureaucratic). As indicated in the preceding paragraph, the proposed form had ninety-nine project code numbers and one blank. The version finally adopted contains 117 experience profile code numbers and five blanks (see Figure 12-2).

Block 9 in S.F. 254 underwent a considerable change, after some reviewers of the proposed form registered complaints about furnishing exact figures on total gross fees received for the last five years. Instead of the actual figures, one now inserts index numbers to show "Ranges of Professional Service Fees." Initial reactions to the proposed format seemed to indicate that practitioners feared a copy of their S.F. 254 would be forwarded to the Internal Revenue Service. (See Figure 12-3).

Other differences in the proposed and final versions were relatively insignificant. For example, in Block 11, "Project Examples," IE was added to the top of column 2. "IE" stands for "Individual Experience" and is supposed to give some break to firms in practice less than five years.

A key paragraph in the early informational release from GSA about the proposed forms: "A-Es and related professionals may also, if they desire, *tailor their S.F. 254 to different contracting agencies.* [Emphasis added.] For example, they may emphasize their abilities to handle design of airports, terminals and hangars to federal agencies specializing in Air Force projects, while listing work performed on television, microwave and telephone systems in forms submitted to other agencies with responsibilities in the communications fields."

Unfortunately, this advice was not made a part of the official instructions for filling in a S.F. 254. The implication, therefore, is that identical forms are to be filed with all agencies in which the submitting design firm has an interest in working for. Agency representatives agree on at least this one point: S.F. 254s should be customized as much as possible to each agency's interests and requirements. In other words, in a 254 for the VA, one should not list highways, hotels, high- and low-rise office buildings, or suspension bridges.

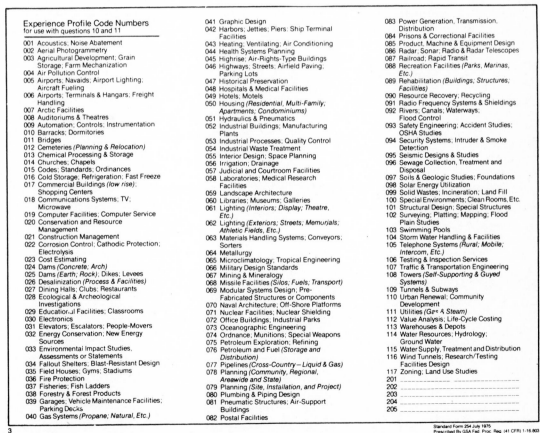

Experience Profile Code Numbers
for use with questions 10 and 11

001 Acoustics; Noise Abatement
002 Aerial Photogrammetry
003 Agricultural Development; Grain Storage; Farm Mechanization
004 Air Pollution Control
005 Airports; Navaids; Airport Lighting; Aircraft Fueling
006 Airports; Terminals & Hangars; Freight Handling
007 Arctic Facilities
008 Auditoriums & Theatres
009 Automation; Controls; Instrumentation
010 Barracks; Dormitories
011 Bridges
012 Cemeteries *(Planning & Relocation)*
013 Chemical Processing & Storage
014 Churches; Chapels
015 Codes; Standards; Ordinances
016 Cold Storage; Refrigeration; Fast Freeze
017 Commercial Buildings *(low rise);* Shopping Centers
018 Communications Systems; TV; Microwave
019 Computer Facilities; Computer Service
020 Conservation and Resource Management
021 Construction Management
022 Corrosion Control; Cathodic Protection; Electrolysis
023 Cost Estimating
024 Dams *(Concrete; Arch)*
025 Dams *(Earth; Rock);* Dikes; Levees
026 Desalinization *(Process & Facilities)*
027 Dining Halls; Clubs; Restaurants
028 Ecological & Archeological Investigations
029 Educational Facilities; Classrooms
030 Electronics
031 Elevators; Escalators; People-Movers
032 Energy Conservation; New Energy Sources
033 Environmental Impact Studies, Assessments or Statements
034 Fallout Shelters; Blast-Resistant Design
035 Field Houses; Gyms; Stadiums
036 Fire Protection
037 Fisheries; Fish Ladders
038 Forestry & Forest Products
039 Garages; Vehicle Maintenance Facilities; Parking Decks
040 Gas Systems *(Propane; Natural, Etc.)*

041 Graphic Design
042 Harbors; Jetties; Piers: Ship Terminal Facilities
043 Heating; Ventilating; Air Conditioning
044 Health Systems Planning
045 Highrise; Air-Rights-Type Buildings
046 Highways; Streets; Airfield Paving; Parking Lots
047 Historical Preservation
048 Hospitals & Medical Facilities
049 Hotels; Motels
050 Housing *(Residential, Multi-Family; Apartments; Condominiums)*
051 Hydraulics & Pneumatics
052 Industrial Buildings; Manufacturing Plants
053 Industrial Processes; Quality Control
054 Industrial Waste Treatment
055 Interior Design; Space Planning
056 Irrigation; Drainage
057 Judicial and Courtroom Facilities
058 Laboratories; Medical Research Facilities
059 Landscape Architecture
060 Libraries; Museums; Galleries
061 Lighting *(Interiors; Display; Theatre, Etc.)*
062 Lighting *(Exteriors; Streets; Memorials; Athletic Fields, Etc.)*
063 Materials Handling Systems; Conveyors; Sorters
064 Metallurgy
065 Microclimatology; Tropical Engineering
066 Military Design Standards
067 Mining & Mineralogy
068 Missile Facilities *(Silos; Fuels; Transport)*
069 Modular Systems Design; Pre-Fabricated Structures or Components
070 Naval Architecture; Off-Shore Platforms
071 Nuclear Facilities; Nuclear Shielding
072 Office Buildings; Industrial Parks
073 Oceanographic Engineering
074 Ordnance; Munitions; Special Weapons
075 Petroleum Exploration; Refining
076 Petroleum and Fuel *(Storage and Distribution)*
077 Pipelines *(Cross-Country — Liquid & Gas)*
078 Planning *(Community, Regional, Areawide and State)*
079 Planning *(Site, Installation, and Project)*
080 Plumbing & Piping Design
081 Pneumatic Structures; Air-Support Buildings
082 Postal Facilities

083 Power Generation, Transmission, Distribution
084 Prisons & Correctional Facilities
085 Product, Machine & Equipment Design
086 Radar; Sonar; Radio & Radar Telescopes
087 Railroad; Rapid Transit
088 Recreation Facilities *(Parks, Marinas, Etc.)*
089 Rehabilitation *(Buildings; Structures; Facilities)*
090 Resource Recovery; Recycling
091 Radio Frequency Systems & Shieldings
092 Rivers; Canals; Waterways; Flood Control
093 Safety Engineering; Accident Studies; OSHA Studies
094 Security Systems; Intruder & Smoke Detection
095 Seismic Designs & Studies
096 Sewage Collection, Treatment and Disposal
097 Soils & Geologic Studies; Foundations
098 Solar Energy Utilization
099 Solid Wastes; Incineration; Land Fill
100 Special Environments; Clean Rooms, Etc.
101 Structural Design; Special Structures
102 Surveying; Platting; Mapping; Flood Plain Studies
103 Swimming Pools
104 Storm Water Handling & Facilities
105 Telephone Systems *(Rural; Mobile; Intercom, Etc.)*
106 Testing & Inspection Services
107 Traffic & Transportation Engineering
108 Towers *(Self-Supporting & Guyed Systems)*
109 Tunnels & Subways
110 Urban Renewal; Community Development
111 Utilities *(Gas & Steam)*
112 Value Analysis; Life-Cycle Costing
113 Warehouses & Depots
114 Water Resources; Hydrology; Ground Water
115 Water Supply, Treatment and Distribution
116 Wind Tunnels; Research/Testing Facilities Design
117 Zoning; Land Use Studies
201 _____
202 _____
203 _____
204 _____
205 _____

Standard Form 254 July 1975
Prescribed By GSA Fed Proc Reg (41 CFR) 1-16.803

3

Figure 12-2 *Page 3 of Standard Form 254, with the complete list of 117 "Experience Profile Code Numbers."*

It is not as burdensome as it might sound—this customization—since few firms can justify sending a form to more than five or six agencies.

S.F. 255 survived the review process virtually intact. It is the project-oriented form—to be submitted in response to the announcement of a federal project.

In the some half-dozen years of their use, certain facts and not a little fiction have grown up around the most productive ways of preparing and filing S.F. 254s and 255s—and about the manner in which agencies use the information contained in the forms.

Covers   Some consultants have adopted the technique of adding covers to their S.F. 254s. There is no regulation specifically forbidding the graphic touch (Instruction number 13 says only, "Additional data, brochures, photos, etc. should not accompany this form unless specifically requested."), but after examining the filing systems now in use, I would recommend that you forego this expression of individuality. Most federal agencies staple the forms into a standard file folder, and any covers must first be removed. Occasionally, the form gets torn or dog-eared in this process. The best advice here, which applies to practically all federal agencies, is to skip the cover for S.F. 254, no matter how dull and drab the naked form may appear.

Highlighting   Some 254s have entries printed in a different ink color from black. Red, green, and dark blue inks have been used, and they

Figure 12-3 *Standard Form 254 instructions for completing Blocks 9 and 10 on the form.*

tend to snap the information out at the reader. One firm uses colored tint blocks to emphasize certain entries.

None of the agency representatives we've talked to had any strong feelings—pro or con—about this technique; no one said it would be counterproductive. One agency representative suggested the use of colored inks to highlight the main or important points.

In other words, the fact that a firm goes to the more expensive second color for all of the information supplied will not necessarily impress an agency representative one way or the other. There seem to be no objections to the use of broad-tipped felt lining pens to draw a reviewer's eyes to especially pertinent information about personnel and design experience. This type of highlighting seems desirable for both consultants and agency evaluators.

One other point to keep in mind about the S.F. 254; other than for small projects from the Corps of Engineers and the Veterans Administration, agencies do not normally select from the form, so a lot of glamorizing and jazzing up of the 254 is essentially wasted.

Problem Spots—S.F. 254   Many design firms take the S.F. 254 apart so that the information can be filled in by typewriter or by running the pages through an offset press. Just be certain that when the pages are reassembled, they are bound or stapled across the top (long) edge. An oft-voiced complaint in the agencies, from those who have to deal with the forms, is directed at firms who insist on binding or stapling the forms along the left side. This forces a reader to continually flip the form around to be able to read the even-numbered pages rightside up. One agency representative observed that such faulty reassembly of the forms does not fill him or his staff with great confidence in the submitting firm's attention to detail.

Some offices list the same job several times in Block 10 under different codes, which often confuses agency reviewers. To avoid misunderstandings, the VA recommends that in column 3 of Block 11, immediately following a project listing, you set out the featured service, as "HVAC" or whatever is appropriate.

Such further clarification about why a project is listed is even more important in Block 8 of S.F. 255. Confusion can occur among evaluators when a listed project's name sheds no light on what kind of a project it was.

For example, in submitting an S.F. 255 for a VA project, you list ten hospital jobs in Block 8. Unless you explain in Block 8 or Block 10 or both that the ten hospitals have a total of 160 geriatric nursing beds— or that seven of the ten are teaching hospitals—VA evaluators and the selection board probably won't know those details. Final selection could turn around such data.

Another early problem area on S.F. 254 was the "Cost of Work (in thousands)" column in Block 11. "In thousands" means to drop the last three numbers from all figures entered, of course. $1,000,000 thus becomes $1000. You know that and the agencies know it, but there were hundreds of firms out there somewhere who refused to recognize the confusion to be caused by a four-person firm apparently claiming annual billings of $500 million or so.

GSA and others use the profile code entries to get a feel for a firm's general capabilities and as a check on a firm's experience with a particular job type along with similarities in scope, costs, and complexity. If the project was done by a joint venture, the agency wants to know the submitting firm's true involvement.

Certain differences about "proper" submittals of S.F. 254 and 255 exist among federal agencies. Your best protection against being caught up in individual eccentricities is to review what is really wanted in the forms with each agency you want to work for.

"Be honest in filling out the 254," counsels one agency head, "and don't be overly modest." As for where to file a S.F. 254, the best advice seems to be everywhere it might do you some good. Send one to every regional and district office of the agencies you'd like to get work from. File one with the same agencies' Washington, D.C., headquarters. Send copies to your U.S. representatives and senators—to their district and state offices and to their offices in Washington, D.C. And always send an up-to-date S.F. 254 with each S.F. 255 submittal.

S.F. 255   Practically all of the foregoing dealt with S.F. 254. Let's now turn to S.F. 255, the project-oriented follow-up form to S.F. 254.

Vincent Hennessy, director of the USPS Office of Design and Construction Management, states:

> Standard Form 255 is designed to allow a firm to present its qualifications for a specific job. Anything in the form that doesn't pertain to the project is a waste of space and of everyone's time. When we see a lot of extraneous material in a 255, it tells us someone in that firm's management can't read instructions, and it usually works against them.

Roland Vaughan and his staff at the Veterans Administration place a lot of emphasis on the nominated team. As pointed out earlier in this chapter, the VA holds firms to the teams set out in their S.F. 255s.

All this is by way of pointing out one of S.F. 255's real problem areas for many firms—Block 7 (pages 5–8 in the form) for résumés of key people who will work on the project. Bannered across the top of Block 7, you'll see "Brief Resume of **Key** Persons, Specialists, and Individual Consultants Anticipated for this Project." Aside from exhibiting a bureaucratic tendency to capitalize just about every loose adjective and common noun in sight, that is a very clear statement.

Nevertheless, a lot of general, nonspecific, nonpertinent information shows up in Block 7, especially its section g. In the event someone missed the opening caution, Block 7(g) is headed "Other Experience and Qualifications relevant to the proposed project." It is difficult to understand how "relevant to the proposed project" can be misinterpreted, but it is. Constantly.

Representatives from every federal agency advise design professionals to be specific about the nominated project manager and all others listed. *Qualify* your team with pertinent, relevant references to the project and your direct and related past experience.

Most agency people recommend that top echelon executives of the firm be omitted in filling out Block 7; skepticism rears its ugly head when owners, principals, and other top management executives are shown as being in charge of a project in Block 7.

Give good coverage to every member of the team who will do the work. The fact that a member of the nominated project team was an infantry rifleman in World War II or is active in a local PTA or teaches a Sunday school class is not germane to the progression of most federal projects. Experience at a responsible level on projects at least as large and complex as the one under consideration, along with a description of design awards and other professional achievements, is important— and pertinent.

A few firms still list projects more than five years old in spite of specific instructions to the contrary on S.F. 255.

A final recommendation from the agencies is that all materials for a S.F. 255 submission—letters, brochures, photos, the form itself, and the like—be bound or packaged together in some manner. Otherwise, the review panels may accidentally separate or mislay loose elements during their deliberations, especially if 100 or so S.F. 255 submittals are under consideration.

A model S.F. 255 submission might have these elements:

1. Cover (covers are O.K. on S.F. 255s).
2. Letter of interest and transmittal.
3. A brief summary page, answering and highlighting the main points (criteria) called for in the *Commerce Business Daily* ad.
4. S.F. 255
5. Supportive materials:
   - Relevant project photos, with identification attached.
   - Copies of pertinent awards.

- Relevant news clippings and article reprints.
- Brochures.
- Your S.F. 254. If it is a joint venture, include a 254 for all elements of the joint venture.

In Summary: S.F. 254 and 255

1. Do not attempt to improve upon or glamorize S.F. 254. Send it in as you received it, without a cover or any other added elements.

2. Feel free to use ink colors other than black to highlight and snap out important information in the 254, but make certain the colors are dark enough to be easily read. The use of felt-tipped liner pens to call attention to important projects and personnel qualifications is recommended for both S.F. 254 and 255.

3. When reassembling S.F. 254 for submission, put it back together in the right order. Staple or bind it along the *top* edge so agency evaluators can read the form straight through.

4. In Block 11 of S.F. 254, following a project listing, refer to the profile code illustrated by the project—"computer systems," "dams," "HVAC," "office buildings," and the like.

5. Customize the contents of S.F. 254s to the receiving agency's interests and requirements. Don't tell the VA about flood control work or bulk mail postal facilities. And don't bother the postal service with information about hospitals and clinics.

6. Read the instructions for filling in S.F. 254 and 255. When you are told to list project costs in thousands (Block 11, second column from the right in S.F. 254, and Block 8, column e, in S.F. 255), drop the last three zeros. Pay attention to details.

7. If your participation in a project was as a member of an association or a joint venture, spell out the actual involvement.

8. File an S.F. 254 for every office of your firm. And in addition to the copy sent to an agency's headquarters, send a 254 to every regional or district office of any federal agency from which you might be selected for work. But be realistic with your distribution—a ten-person firm in Portland, Oregon, has little reason to file an S.F. 254 with the Corps of Engineers office in Huntsville, Alabama.

9. Send a well-written transmittal letter with each S.F. 255. Make it completely responsive to the *CBD* announcement, and don't be afraid to make it a sales tool. Ask for the job!

10. Don't oversell, especially in Block 10 of S.F. 255. If you need more space for Block 10, attach extra sheets, but don't be guilty of overkill.

11. Key person resumes in S.F. 255s should be factual and relevant to the project at hand.

12. Don't list projects more than five years old. Read the instructions. If you have a really important, related job completed more than five years ago, mention it in Block 10 or the letter of transmittal or both.

13. Work out some method of packaging thick S.F. 255 submittals. Even a couple of rubber bands around the material is better than sending in an envelope full of loose pages, forms, photographs, and brochures.

14. Realize that agencies—even regional and district offices within the same agency—may have certain variations in how they like to have S.F. 254s and 255s submitted.

15. Make it a point to stop in occasionally for a visit with selection people in agencies you want to work for. Such visits do not have to be in connection with a specific project (usually, it's better if they are not). While always difficult to quantify, the human factors in A-E selection are too important to ignore. With reference to number 14, use an early visit to learn about any quirks and differences in that office's requirements and wishes for S.F. 254 and 255.

CONTINGENCY FEE MARKETING

Chapter 4, "Where to Find Prospects," included some of the pros and cons about full-time representation of your firm in Washington, D.C. In this connection, the *modus operandi* of commission agents was covered, along with some of the reasons for ethical firms to avoid such consultants, who at least imply in their sales pitch that they have the only real lock on many federal jobs.

Not so long ago political clout was a definite marketing consideration in chasing federal work. I am not so naive—and I doubt that many practicing professionals are so naive—as to believe government work always goes to the best-qualified firm or that federal jobs are never sold. I *do* believe the incidence of blatant job peddling at the federal level is now at a very low level. And representatives of VA and USPS selection boards are quick to assure anyone who raises the question that influence-for-hire consultants are not welcome, are not encouraged, and do not influence job awards in their agencies.

In a *Professional Marketing Report* article on this subject, "The Seven Percent Non-Solution," was the advice to check all such promises—direct and implied—that a consultant can guarantee a job award back to the source. Some more advice about commission-agent consultants from that article:

> If you believe any of the consultant's pitch suggests or borders on something illegal, call the head of the selection committee or a contracting officer

in the federal agency involved. It will often be the Postal Service but one such consultant takes occasional flyers in "selling" VA and GSA projects. Ask the agency representative if the consultant is in a position to promise delivery of any projects from that agency. The answer will be no. If you'd really like to follow it up, drop a letter to your representative in Congress, detailing the promises made (oral and written), the agency involved, and the consultant's name. Suggest the situation seems to have a certain odor to it and ask your Washington representative to look into it.

It probably will take more than one or two letters from design professionals, but eventually some congressional committee will ask the Government Accounting Office to look into the matter. The VA, USPS, and GSA already have extensive files in-house on most of the commission sales people.[2]

One weapon federal contractors have against the fee-for-influence consultants is the "Covenant Against Contingency Fees," wherein a contractor "warrants that no person or selling agency has been employed or retained to solicit or secure this contract upon an agreement or understanding for a commission, percentage, brokerage, or contingent fee, excepting bona fide employees or bona fide established commercial or selling agencies maintained by the contractor for the purpose of securing business. For breach or violation of this warranty the Government shall have the right to annul this contract without liability or in its discretion to deduct from the contract price or consideration, or otherwise recover, the full amount of such commission, percentage, brokerage, or contingent fee."

Incorporated into most government contracts is a section requiring the supplier of services or products to certify whether or not an outside person or company was used to secure the contract. If such was the case, the supplier must then state whether or not payment of "any fee, commission, percentage, or brokerage fee" is "contingent upon or resulting from the award of this contract."

The contingency certification section does not prohibit such arrangements, but if you used a commission agent, you must say so. Some firms, who were less than truthful in answering the question (usually on the advice of the agent), have learned the hard way that false certification entries are taken seriously by some federal agencies, and some contracts have been voided as a result. Once a firm is caught in what amounts to lying under oath, it should be obvious that the federal agency involved will not be particularly interested in that firm's future expressions of interest in projects. And, while there is no formal interagency blacklist of which I am aware, procurement and contracting officials in Washington do communicate with their counterparts in other agencies about many things.

THE 6 PERCENT FEE LIMITATION

Many firms choose to forego federal work because of misunderstandings about the so-called 6 percent fee limit rule for government projects. The 6 percent cap exists, but it is possible to earn much higher fees on government jobs, depending upon the services required by the client.

Here is the official version of what the 6 percent fee limitation *really* covers, from the *Federal Register.*

(I) The 6 percent fee limitation on architect or engineer services set forth in section 304(b) of the Federal Property and Administrative Services Act of 1949, as amended, applies to those services generally required in preparing working drawings and specifications which form the basis for bidding and for the award of the construction contract. The fixed fee limitation does *not* apply to the following architect or engineer services:

(A) Investigative services including but not limited to:

(1) Determination of program requirements including schematic or preliminary plans and estimates.

(2) Determination of feasibility of proposed project.

(3) Preparation of measured drawings of existing facility.

(4) Subsurface investigation.

(5) Structural, electrical, and mechanical investigation of existing facility.

(6) Surveys, topographic, boundary, utilities, etc.

(B) Special consultant services not normally available in organizations of architects or engineers not specifically applied to the actual preparation of working drawings or specifications of the project for which the services are required.

(C) Other:

(1) Reproduction of approved designs through models, color rendering, photographs, or other presentation media.

(2) Travel and per diem allowances other than those required for the development and review of working drawings and specifications.

(3) Supervision or inspection of construction, review of shop drawings or samples, and other services performed during the construction phase.

(4) All other services that are not integrally a part of the production and delivery of plans, designs, and specifications.

(D) The cost of reproducing drawings and specifications for bidding and their distribution to prospective bidders and plan file rooms.

(II) The total cost of the architect or engineer services contracted for may not exceed 6 percent of the estimated cost of the construction project, plus the estimated cost of related services and activities such as those shown in paragraph (I) of this section.[3]

Having all of this information at hand won't guarantee the elimination of debates about fees in negotiations with federal project managers, but, armed with full knowledge of what the 6 percent fee limitation really covers, you may win more arguments—and higher fees.

WHO'S WHO IN
THE FEDERAL GOVERNMENT

At least one reference book of government agencies and officials should be in your marketing library. It seems that every year or so another, more expensive directory joins those already in the field.

The basic reference is that old standby, the *Congressional Directory*, published for each session of Congress. The Congressional Joint Committee on Printing is in charge of compiling the *Directory*, which is published and sold by the Superintendent of Documents, U.S. Government Printing Office, Washington, DC 20402. As further evidence of our not-so-creeping inflation, price of the paperback edition has risen from $3 to $10 in the years since the first edition of *How to Market Professional Design Services*.

Sometimes referred to as the bible of Congress, the *Congressional Directory* includes biographies, assignments, and names of office and committee staff members for all senators and representatives; district and state maps; the composition of federal bureaus, departments, and agencies; and the full membership of various press groups and galleries accredited to the House and Senate.

A private enterprise competitor of the *Congressional Directory* is the *Congressional Staff Directory*, published by a former member of Congress. Included in this directory are hundreds of biographies of key congressional staff members, along with the committee and subcommittee assignments of members of Congress and the names of key personnel of executive departments and agencies. It is available from Congressional Staff Directory, P.O. Box 62, Mount Vernon, VA 22121.

A sampling of some of the other references:

Congressional Yellow Book It contains essentially the same information as the two directories just described, but it is in loose-leaf format to allow for quarterly updating. It is available from *The Washington Monitor*, 499 National Press Building, Washington, DC 20045.

Federal Yellow Book From the same publisher as the *Congressional Yellow Book*, this one concentrates on the executive side. Names, titles, addresses, and phone numbers of some 27,000 upper-level federal employees are all here in a loose-leaf binder. It has the same update feature as the *Congressional* version.

U.S. Congress Handbook Of compact size (4 × 10½ inches) and featuring photographs of members of Congress, this one is a worthwhile supplement to the larger directories. It is published by U.S. Congress Handbook, P.O. Box 566, McLean, VA 22101.

Congressional Telephone Directory   If you'd like to have telephone listings for all members of the House of Representatives and the Senate, contact the Clerk of the House, H-105 Capitol Building, Washington, DC 20515. It is one of the few free directories around.

Washington Information Directory   It has about everything offered by the others, plus a rundown on quasi-official and unofficial (nongovernment) organizations located in Washington. It is obtainable from Congressional Quarterly, Inc., 1414 22nd Street, NW, Washington, DC 20037.

And a list such as this would not be complete without a mention of an organization called Washington Researchers, 918 16th Street, NW, Washington, DC 20006. Founded a few years ago by Matthew Lesko, Washington Researchers makes a tidy profit from knowing where to find information in the federal government, packaging it, and selling it to those who need it. Since the firm publishes so much, your best bet is to send in an inquiry based on a specific requirement. Their newsletter, *The Information Report,* is a helpful publication about sources of all kinds of information—mostly free.

REFERENCES

[1]Gerre Jones, "How to Prepare and Use Standard Forms 254 and 255," *Professional Marketing Report,* September 1977, pp. 3–8.

[2]"The Seven Percent Non-Solution," *Professional Marketing Report,* June 1979, p. 3.

[3]*Federal Register,* January 22, 1976, vol. 41, no. 15, p. 3293.

Chapter 13
A MARKETING POTPOURRI

In this chapter we will deal with three subjects that seemed to rate a full chapter each in the first edition:

Joint ventures and associations
Overseas client acquisition
Taking a piece of the action

It is not that these topics have declined in importance; they all have varying degrees of emphasis in most marketing programs. The deemphasis here is due largely to the fact that many design professionals have gained at least some measure of practical experience in the areas of greatest individual interest. Another reason is the publication of several specialized books in recent years, which go into greater detail than would be possible here.

On the establishment and administration of joint ventures, for example, one should refer to *Joint Ventures for Architects and Engineers*, the definitive book by David Dibner, FAIA (McGraw-Hill Book Company, New York, 1972).

For the most practical guidelines on all aspects of pursuing and winning work overseas, read *The International Consultant* by H. Peter Guttmann, P.E. (McGraw-Hill Book Company, New York, 1976).

Taking a piece of the action, as exemplified by a design firm's exchanging some or all of its normal design fee for part-ownership of the project, has not yet generated what I believe to be the definitive work. If you have not yet read it, I can recommend *The Architect as Developer* by John Portman and Jonathan Barnett. This work will be referenced a few pages farther along in the chapter.

What follows, then, is an addenda of sorts to the other sources of information available.

JOINT VENTURES AND ASSOCIATIONS

We need not concern ourselves at this point with whether the professional amalgamation is called an association, a joint venture, a consultancy, or a consortium. The differences are not that great in practice, and they turn primarily on legal definitions and considerations of liability insurance coverage.

In *Architectural & Engineering Law*, the difference between a partnership and a joint venture is explained:

> Two or more persons or firms may associate together to carry on a single specific enterprise, such as the performance of a contract with a third party to render architectural or engineering services for a single construction project. This type of association, closely akin to the partnership, is the joint venture. The only distinction between the two is that a joint venture is formed to carry on a single specified enterprise or transaction, whereas a partnership is formed for the transaction of a general and continuing business of a particular kind.[1]

Justin Sweet, in his book about legal considerations for the design and construction fields, gives several meanings for the term "association." This passage is pertinent to the present discussion:

> [One] use of "associate" relates to the arrangement that may be made between two architectural firms to perform certain work. For example, a New York firm might associate with a firm in Los Angeles, if the New York firm has agreed to design and administer a project in Los Angeles. There may be many reasons to "associate" with a local firm. Such an association could be a joint venture if the firms agree to share profits and losses in some manner. If the local firm merely agrees to perform certain designated functions, without any stake in the profits, the local firm is merely performing these services on a contracting, rather than an entrepreneurial basis.
>
> Similar to the "association" with a local firm is the arrangement under which an architect "associates" with another local architect or engineer. The purpose of this association may be to use the particular skill of the other architect or engineer. This is common in complex construction projects. Unless there is a true joint venture, this form of "association" is like hiring a local firm for an out-of-town project. Such "associations" are unlike the other associations discussed, since there is no element of joining together in an entrepreneurial sense.[2]

Either "adventure" or "joint adventure" are proper legalese, incidentally. This terminology dates back to early maritime law, when associating to ship goods to or bring cargoes back from overseas ports was literally an "adventure" for all concerned.

Why Joint Venture?   Make no mistake about the basic rationale behind joint venturing or associating with other design firms. Decisions about when to associate and with whom have to do with the successful marketing of your firm—and with little else. In the final analysis, there are only two reasons for entering into any kind of an association:

1. You can't do the project alone.
2. You can't win the project alone.

Number 2 often turns out to be the most important consideration.

As projects have become larger, more complex, and increasingly specialized, most small- to medium-sized firms (and many of the giants) have found association to be the quickest, easiest, and most logical way to mutually strengthen or supplement individual firm capabilities and marketing assets.

There is no mystery about how to conduct project pursuit when it is obvious that your firm lacks certain staff skills and specialties required to do the job (or to convince the prospect that you can do the job). The first option—and one that should be taken more often than it is—is to pass up the job after you've applied your own selectivity criteria (the go or no-go analysis).

When the analysis gives a negative answer, but you believe there are good and compelling reasons to go after the project anyway, these four alternatives present themselves:

1. Hire the necessary expertise for your own staff.
2. Buy or merge with other firms that you know have the required expertise in-house.
3. Rent the needed expertise by bringing in individuals or firms as consultants.
4. Go the route of associating or joint venturing.

I did come across a fifth possibility recently, but it is not a practical solution for most established firms. Soon after starting his practice, the owner of a small engineering firm decided he would use associations as the method for pursuing larger projects. Accordingly, he set up a plan to associate with practically all of the other design firms in the area on almost every project that came along.

Over a period of several years the engineer deliberately built up an impressive association experience record with local firms, so that when a prospect asked about previous work of the association, the answer could always be a positive one. Most clients want assurance that the several elements of an association have worked together on previous projects at least equal in size and scope to theirs; federal clients usually insist on it. Knowing this, the engineer positioned his firm so that his answer to the standard question could be in the affirmative.

Some Dangers of Associating   While there are a number of administrative pitfalls that seem to be endemic to associations, our main concern will be with those most apt to affect the marketing process.

Client Concern   If a majority of the responses received by a prospect are from large, multidisciplinary firms, all of which appear to have the required skills and specialties under one roof, your association may be perceived as a crazy-quilt kind of operation regardless of the experience and skills represented in its various elements.

It then behooves you in your marketing to present your group or team as both comfortable and productive in past associated efforts, offering a kind of synergistic bonus to clients in its approach to design and production.

Internal Conflict   An association of design firms must not only appear to be a team, it must act as a well-oiled mechanism in all its marketing efforts. Egos must be sublimated, and one person must be in charge. Unless a single leader (who may be self-elected) is allowed to call the important marketing shots, the association probably is doomed from the outset. And the group's leader need not come from the largest firm in the association.

Picking Up the Tab   To avoid later (and inevitable) misunderstandings, the associated firms should reach general agreement about how the costs of marketing will be shared during the first organizational meeting. It is not fair to expect the lead firm to carry the entire load, of course. Equitable arrangements are much easier to make in the beginning than after the project award, particularly if the job goes to someone else.

Division of Project Responsibility   While there is no point in trying to dot every i and cross every t before the job is won, some early thought should be given to how the design work will be done, by whom, where, and for how much of a share of the overall fee.

A few years ago a format for dividing design responsibilities was developed by Duncan Black for a talk given to the East Tennessee Chapter of the American Institute of Architects.[3] Black's approach is shown in Figure 13-1.

Black suggests that the complete joint venture agreement, which also spells out such things as the amount of insurance each firm will carry, publicity guidelines, and principals' responsibilities, can be used as a marketing tool. The agreement is shown to prospects, but not left with

Division of Responsibility for Architectural Service

Percent of Basic Fee	ARCHITECTURAL AND ENGINEERING SERVICES	Responsibility	
		Firm A	Firm B
15%	**Schematic Design Phase**		
	Conference with owner.................................	X	O
	Analysis of project requirements		
	A. Program analysis and concepts.....................	X	O
	B. Site analysis.....................................	X	X
	C. Space and cost analysis...........................	X	O
	D. Climatic studies..................................	X	O
	Building code information............................	X	O
	Diagram studies of space requirements................	X	O
	Assembling of utility and survey data................		X
	Schematic design studies and recommended solution......	X	O
	Schematic design plans...............................	X	
	Sketches and study model.............................	X	
	General project description..........................	X	X
	Engineering system concepts..........................	O	X
	Statement of construction cost based on area or volume.	X	X
	Presentation of schematic design documents to owner....	X	O
	Percent of fee	12	3
20%	**Design Development Phase**		
	Conference with owner.................................	X	O
	Refinement of project requirements......................	X	O
	Formulation of structural system.......................	O	X
	Formulation of mechanical and electrical system........	O	X
	Selection of major building materials..................	X	O
	Preparation of design development documents		
	A. Plans...	X	X
	B. Elevations..	X	
	C. Building profile sections.........................	X	
	D. Outline specifications............................	X	X
	E. Description of electrical, mechanical, and structural systems................................	O	X
	Perspective, sketches, or models.......................	X	
	Semi-detailed cost estimate............................	X	X
	Equipment schedule.....................................	X	O
	Reviewing plans with all applicable agencies...........	X	X
	Presentation of design development documents to owner..	X	X
	Percent of fee	11	9

Symbols:
X = major responsibility
O = minor responsibility
Blank = no responsibility

Figure 13-1 *A joint venture agreement on the division of project responsibilities and fees, developed by Duncan Black. The breakdown shown covers the first two phases only—schematic design and design development. Black's complete form covers all phases through supervision.*

them. In effect, the written agreement not only is evidence that the association or joint venture exists, but it is also proof that all parties have agreed to work together.

Giants in Joint-Venture Land   Enormous projects sometimes require gigantic joint ventures. In 1976 the Federal Railroad Administration selected a firm to serve as principal contractor and to provide engineering, design, and construction management services for the $1.75 billion rail passenger improvement program between Washington, D.C. and Boston.

Of the nineteen companies and joint ventures initially competing for the project, one individual company and three joint ventures made it to the client's short list. The joint venture of DeLeuw, Cather/Parsons Associates was selected from among the four finalists. This was the composition of the winning team:

1. Principals
   - DeLeuw, Cather & Company, Chicago
   - The Ralph M. Parsons Company, Pasadena, Calif.
2. Associates
   - Electrak Inc., Union, N.J.
   - McDonald and Williams, AIA, Washington, D.C.
   - Parametric, Inc., Philadelphia
   - Skidmore, Owings & Merrill, Washington, D.C.
   - Sverdrup & Parcel and Associates, Inc., St. Louis
3. Specialty Contractors
   - Automated Sciences Group, Inc., Silver Spring, Md.
   - Boone, Young & Associates, Inc., New York City
   - Commonwealth Research Corporation, Reston, Va.
   - Ensco, Springfield, Va.
   - General Research Corporation, McLean, Va.
   - Hudson, Leftwich & Davenport, Washington, D.C.
   - Louis T. Klauder and Associates, Philadelphia
   - Mueser, Rutledge, Wentworth & Johnson, New York City
   - Price, Williams & Associates, Inc., Silver Spring, Md.
   - Transportation and Distribution Associates, Inc., Media, Pa.
   - Unified Industries, Alexandria, Va.
   - Wilson, Ihrig & Associates, Inc., Oakland, Calif.

That nineteen-member group, if you need the reminder, represents a lot of experience, staff, and geography.

While the example just given deals with an authentic megaventure, such associations are relatively rare. Associations and joint ventures are really of more marketing value to smaller, newly begun design firms than they are to the giants of the profession. Associations allow young, untried offices to present themselves as part of a larger, experienced group—and thus become an important marketing tool for small firms.

Finding Associates   Assuming that you are familiar with the advantages of entering into an association to pursue a specific job, how do you know which firms to talk to in putting together a joint venture with the desired combination of strengths and local or regional contacts? If yours is a smaller firm, you will usually look for a larger, multidisciplinary office with significant experience in the project type and a past history of successful associations. This should not be much of a problem if you regularly follow the news sections in such publications as *Architectural Record*, the *AIA Journal,* and *Building Design & Construction.* From those and similar sources you should have a pretty accurate picture of which firms have been the most active in the project type in recent months. You might also make it a point to talk about your interest to some of the salespeople who call on you regularly; they may have some good suggestions.

For architectural firm listings, refer to the latest issue of *Profile,* published by Archimedia, Inc., Philadelphia. (More and more clients, incidentally, are using *Profile* to help them put together a list of firms to talk to.)

The lists of large design firms carried annually in *Engineering News-Record* and *Building Design & Construction* should also be helpful in your search for appropriate associates.

"Permanent" Associates   While most associations and joint ventures are entered into for the pursuit of a specific, single project, some associations have been established on a long-term or "permanent" basis. These usually are associations set up to go after a specific project type, such as airports, or to work in a certain area, such as Southeast Asia or the Middle East.

In a permanent airport joint venture you might find an architectural firm, an engineering office, a systems group, a research organization, and a specialist in the design of navigational aids. Members of the association may be free to pursue any other building or project type on their own or in other associations, but they are expected to return to the fold whenever a likely airport project turns up.

These so-called permanent associations are viewed by some practitioners as running counter to the main purpose of an association, which is to put together the best possible team of experts and specialists for the needs of a particular client and a specific job. Proponents of the permanent association point to the advantage of team members' gaining a greater degree of working comfort and coordination with each job, much as a professional football team must put in hours of practice together before they can expect a winning season. In my observation, permanent associations have not been very effective; my personal preference is for the traditional ad hoc approach of assembling a team to meet the requirements of each new project.

OVERSEAS CLIENT ACQUISITION

It may be the understatement of the decade (at least) to say that things have changed markedly in the overall foreign client market during the last ten years.

Capital spending by several of the thirteen oil-rich members of the Organization of Petroleum Exporting Countries (OPEC) played a major role in altering marketing plans and concentration of the world's design firms. Among the many interesting developments of the period was the emergence of the U.S. Army Corps of Engineers as the client rep for much of Saudi Arabia's multibillion-dollar capital program.

International political considerations caused a certain amount of U.S. foreign aid largesse to be shifted from some countries to certain other nations. Egypt, among others, benefited from the changing political climate.

If you have not yet explored the foreign prospect field, the early and mid-1980s may not be the most propitious time to begin. It's not for lack of potential work; even the most destitute of the world's under-developed and developing nations have lengthy shopping lists of projects, ranging from the mundane to the monumental, they'd like to get underway. The two main problems, as several U.S. firms learned during the Iranian unpleasantness of 1980–1981, arise from trying to keep track of prime clients and in getting paid. Government clients in particular have a way of disappearing at inappropriate times.

Lead Sources   Many firms have discovered firsthand the difficulties of getting established with overseas clients, both public and private. As in many other project areas, the lack of a track work in overseas work is difficult, if not impossible, to overcome. For this reason, design offices usually associate or enter into joint venture agreements in their early efforts to gain a foreign experience record and a foothold of sorts.

Commerce Business Daily (*CBD*) is one source of job listings. *CBD* notices are normally restricted to projects supervised by the Corps of Engineers and those funded by certain international lending agencies.

The best advice to any firm starting from the equivalent of ground zero in overseas business development is to check in with the nearest

Department of Commerce field office. In Washington, D.C., the International Trade Administration (ITA) is the place to begin your search for information. Within ITA, which is headed by an under secretary, is the Trade Development Area, successor to the old Bureau of International Commerce. (Federal image makers are trying to get rid of "bureau" titles, apparently in the belief that the pejorative "bureaucrat" will also pass out of common use.)

Other Commerce Department sources are Office of Export Marketing Assistance divisions dealing with major projects and country marketing. Major projects covers the world by project types and tracks projects valued at $5 million or more. Country marketing specialists, similar to those who staff the State Department's country "desks," concentrate on one or more countries.

The Export Reference Room, once known as the Foreign Projects Reference Room, contains a wide range of material on major foreign projects. In addition to project announcements from international agencies, copies of U.S. embassy target industry reports are kept in the reference room. These reports are compiled by Commerce Department employees who serve as commercial attachés in our embassies and consulates around the world.

You may want to add to the information available from Commerce Department sources by talking to trade representatives or commercial attachés in the embassies of foreign countries. International Chambers of Commerce, such as the German American Chamber of Commerce, can be helpful, as can the special national and regional industrial development agencies and economic missions. Examples of the latter:

The Federal Industrial Development Authority of Malaysia
The French Industrial Development Agency
Thailand Board of Investment

Other Information Sources   *The American Industrial Property Report (AIPR)*, a controlled circulation magazine, annually publishes a "World Wide Guide for Foreign Investment," with a good country-by-country review. Send a request to be added to the mailing list to

AIPR
P.O. Box 2060
Red Bank, NJ 07701

The Overseas Private Investment Corporation publishes a free newsletter you may find helpful (1129 20th Street, N.W., Washington, DC 20527).

Some of the major international lending and development groups to contact:

The Asian Development Bank
The Abu Dhabi Fund for Arab Economic Development
The Arab Fund for Economic Development in Africa
The World Bank
The Inter-American Development Bank (IDB)
The International Labor Organization
The Kuwait Fund for Arab Economic Development
The United Nations Development Programme (UNDP)
The United Nations Industrial Development Organization
The World Health Organization

Registration Form for International Work   In 1980 the ten organizations in the preceding list agreed to use a single consultant registration form. Information from the form is entered into a computer system known as DACON (DAta on CONsultants).

That's the good news. The bad news is that the "Consulting Firm Registration Form—No. 1600" is seventy-one pages in length and comes with a twenty-seven-page guide to completing the form, plus a seven-page letter to help you interpret the guide. The four-part form number 1600 covers

Firm description (fourteen pages)
Firm capabilities and fields of specialization (forty-two pages)
Firm experience (six pages)
Attachments (nine pages)

If you still want to participate in DACON, the form, guide, and explanatory letter may be obtained from

Consultant Services Officer
The World Bank
Washington, DC 20433

or

Office of Professional Service Firms
Inter-American Development Bank
808 17th Street, N.W.
Washington, DC 20577

Unfortunately, there is no central receiving office for the forms. If you want to register interest with the World Bank, two copies of the completed form and one set of "appropriate" brochures should go to

DACON Receiving Center
The World Bank
Washington, DC 20433

To get on IDB's list, one copy of the form goes to the World Bank and another copy, with brochures, goes to the Office of Professional Service Firms at the IDB (address given earlier).

If you want to register with the UNDP, that's another address—as are all of the other participating agencies. Their addresses are in the seven-page letter that accompanies the form and guide.

The United Nations publishes a twice-monthly international job tip sheet, *Development Forum Business Edition*, at $250 a year. Monthly operational summaries from the World Bank and the Inter-American Development Bank are included in the UN publication. Since much of the *Development Forum's* information is available elsewhere (see Figure 13-2), the subscription rate seems high.

A PIECE OF THE ACTION

Taking a piece of the action these days may range from a design firm's leaving all or part of the design fee on the table in exchange for a share of ownership in the project to assuming all of the responsibilities (and risks) of the developer. The latter role includes land acquisition, financing, project management through design and construction, and ownership and management of the completed structure.

The ultimate participation—financing, designing, building, and owning—means taking *all* the action rather than a piece. The number of design firms financially and psychologically able to take on the total-risk position is still relatively small. The number of individual practitioners who feel completely comfortable in the role of designer-developer is even smaller.

If asked for examples of successful designer-developers, most practitioners would respond with the names of Atlanta architect John Portman and Houston engineer Gerald Hines. In the book cited earlier in this chapter, *The Architect as Developer*, coauthor Jonathan Barnett limns John Portman:

> John Portman is an architect who can and does design the headquarters for a bank or nonprofit institution, but he found the usual professional role to be too passive and too uncertain. Instead he became a real estate entrepreneur, developing projects and then hiring himself to design them. By doing so, he has been able to change the practice of both architecture and real estate. Portman's vision as a designer has seen possibilities in situations that look unpromising to conventional investors. At the same time, he has demonstrated that large and splendid spaces, which are usually found only in heavily subsidized institutional buildings, can be practical commercial developments.[4]

And Portman on the development process:

> Portman defines seven aspects of the development process that architects must master to participate in all the critical decisions about a building:

World Bank

1818 H Street, N.W., Washington, D.C. 20433, U.S.A. • Telephone: (202) 477-1234

IDA NEWS RELEASE NO. 82/26
December 24, 1981

Contact: Sandaram Sankaran
(202) 477-3962

NEPAL WILL EXPAND MANPOWER
TRAINING WITH IDA ASSISTANCE

Nepal will establish a new training center for skilled craftsmen with the assistance of a SDR 12.5 million ($14.3 million) credit from the International Development Association (IDA). The credit will help reduce the shortage of skilled manpower.

At completion, the new training center at Pokhara will provide facilities for providing training to 160 craftsmen in basic engineering skills, and 90 technicians in civil, electrical, and mechanical engineering every year. Pokhara was selected to provide better access to this kind of training for candidates from the relatively less well served areas of the Western and Far Western Regions. Since available accommodations are scarce in Pokhara, boarding for 400 students (90% of full enrollment) and for all 45 teaching staff will be provided on campus.

This project will be the second educational credit made to Nepal by IDA, the World Bank's concessional lending affiliate. The first IDA-assisted project is strengthening the existing certificate level training program for electrical and civil engineers at Pulchowk campus of the Institute of Engineering, near Kathmandu. Its programs are also being upgraded to diploma level civil engineering. A similar program at the Dharan campus is being assisted by the Asian Development Bank. Forestry education is also being assisted by the IDA with cofinancing by the United States Agency for International Development, and the United Nations Development Programme.

The second educational project will also assist the establishment of national skills standards that will be applied to all training institutions.

Related staff training and specialist services will be partially financed by a grant from the United Nations Development Programme.

The IDA credit to Nepal is for 50 years including 10 years of grace; it is interest-free but carries a service charge of 3/4 of 1% a year to cover IDA administrative costs.

NOTE: IDA credits are denominated in SDRs (Special Drawing Rights), which are valued on the basis of a "basket" of currencies. The U.S. dollar equivalent of the SDR amount of the IDA credit reflects the exchange rates existing at the time of negotiation of the credit.

Figure 13-2   *IDA News Release No. 82/26 is typical of project announcements from the World Bank and its affiliate lending organizations.*

1. The structural organization of the city and its existing growth pattern.
2. The real estate market and the effect of design and cost on marketability.
3. The preparation of studies that measure feasibility: economic, social, and political.
4. Projections of total development cost, of which building cost is a substantial percentage but by no means the whole story.
5. Projections of income and expenses over a long period of time, usually called the "financial pro forma."
6. The financial market and the ways to put together the financing of a building.
7. The renting and operation of the completed building.[5]

Portman is perceived by many as having operated for many years on a grand—even swashbuckling—scale with a truly worldwide practice. With but one exception, all of the buildings he completed between 1953, when he opened his first office, and 1971 were in Georgia locations, mostly in the Atlanta area. The exception was a 1964 addition to the Pollack Paper Company in Birmingham. The year 1971 saw the opening of his Chicago Hyatt Hotel at O'Hare airport.

The other role model for designer-developers is Houston-based Gerald Hines. Hines has concentrated on developing projects in the Houston area, but, like Portman, in recent years he was wandered rather far afield in his speculative endeavors.

Hines, unlike Portman, doesn't pursue his professional registration. He is 100 percent entrepreneur, the reinsholder for all his developments. Hines regularly uses some of the country's top designers and knows every entry in the project's pro forma by heart. Like Portman, he understands that good design helps to fill his buildings. Both men are familiar with the value of good promotion for their projects; both seem to have an innate flair for the theatrical—in personal style as in their buildings.

Architect Philip Johnson, a Hines designer, has characterized Houston as "the last American city where free enterprise still works." Whatever else it may be, with its absence of zoning laws, overburdened utilities, and an ever-increasing auto-borne population, Houston certainly is a prime candidate to become the first major American city to be overtaken by permanent gridlock.

Taking Part of the Action   If a firm's principals are not yet ready to take the full plunge into the development game, is it possible to become a partial-Portman or a half-Hines? The answer, of course, is yes. There are all manner of degrees of stepping outside the traditional boundaries of architectural and engineering practices.

In March 1981 the Lexington, Kentucky, A-E firm of Chrisman, Miller, Wallace, Inc., became one-third of Community Development Associates. A securities group and a public relations consultant made up the remainder of the CDA joint venture, formed to offer comprehensive project development services. The services included

Research
Planning
Engineering
Architecture
Financing
Construction management
Communications
Marketing
Administration

A major activity of CDA is assembling development syndicates for projects to be carried out by the consortium. Helping clients qualify for state bond assistance and government grants is an allied role. An important side benefit from the venture is the prospect input from all three of the partners. The result is a much-expanded marketing group, which feeds leads to each of the elements, as well as to the CDA entity.

In some ways, the CDA concept is one approach to meeting the oft-voiced desire of a growing number of clients for one-stop, all-services-under-one-roof firms. Figure 13-4 shows how some practitioners (and at least one consultant) see the design profession evolving between now and the year 2000.

As a matter of fact, some signs of the organizational transition began showing up in the early 1970s; recent years have seen an intensification of the process. The right-hand diagonal in Figure 13-4 represents very large, generalist firms—the one-stop, all-services-under-one-roof approach. Eventually, most of these professional giants (giants from the standpoint of size) will offer everything from syndication, initial and long-term financing, and handling zoning and other regulatory matters at the front end—through design, construction management, and construction. The package will be completed with comprehensive management and maintenance services.

The other diagonal, angling off to the upper left, represents a number of smaller, highly specialized firms. These offices will mostly serve as consultants on specialized, high technology, and information transfer matters to the large firms on the right.

These firms of 30 to 100 people will exist because none of the giant enterprises will ever really be able to become a true one-stop operation.

For most projects the large firms—with staffs of 2000 to 10,000, or more—will be prime, bringing in specialist consultants from the left side as needed. Occasionally, clients will hire a specialist as the prime, with the smaller firm then aiding in the evaluation and selection of one of the giants to run the project.

These two groups will do most of the significant work in the future. They will finance, design, build, and operate the large projects.

Sort of floating in the middle of the V will be some small engineering

Figure 13-3 *An advertisement announcing the Community Development Associates joint venture.*

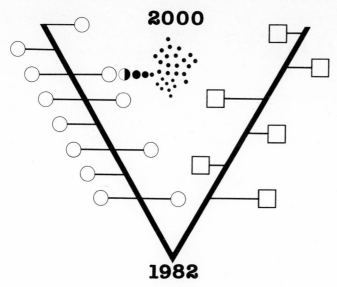

Figure 13-4 *One theory of where the design profession will be by the beginning of the twenty-first century.*

and architectural firms (you might call them mom and pop design stores) to serve clients with smaller projects and clients who still prefer a close relationship with their designer. These firms may win a disproportionate number of design awards, but none of them will make much money.

Note the activity in the left center of Figure 13-4. One of the mom-and-pop offices has had it and decided to move over into the specialist group. What you see is a small firm "going nova."

If there is validity to the theory, then marketers and principals should give serious thought to the operational mode they want their firm to follow for the remainder of this century—whether they want to act as one of the smaller specialist consultancies or become part of a one-stop, very large firm. Or one could opt for the middle of the V, staying small and unspecialized. The point is to not end up in the center by default.

REFERENCES

[1]Bernard Tomson and Norman Coplan, *Architectural & Engineering Law,* 2d ed., Reinhold Publishing Corporation, New York, 1967, p. 55.

[2]Justin Sweet, *Legal Aspects of Architecture, Engineering and the Construction Process,* West Publishing Co., St. Paul, MN, © 1970, p. 92, sec. 4.10.

[3]Duncan M. Black, AIA, "Joint Ventures—DOs and DON'Ts," talk given to the East Tennessee Chapter, AIA, April 21, 1978.

[4]John Portman and Jonathan Barnett, *The Architect as Developer,* McGraw-Hill Book Company, New York, 1976, p. 4.

[5]Ibid., p. 148.

Chapter 14
THE ROAD AHEAD

When the subject of writing a second edition of *How to Market Professional Design Services* was first broached by my editors at McGraw-Hill, an early question was raised about how much new material it would include. (There is an informal requirement that revisions consist of 70 to 75 percent new material.) After thinking about it a few days and rereading the first edition, my answer was that it easily could contain 90 to 100 percent new material; there has been that degree of change in marketing professional design services in less than ten years. Of at least equal importance, most of the people engaged in marketing today are well-trained professionals in all respects and have a sense of organizational place and self-worth unknown just a decade ago.

If you are familiar with the first edition of *How to Market Professional Design Services*, I hope you'll agree that this new edition does contain much new information and that it also reflects an awareness of the increased sophistication and appreciation for the craft of marketing that exists among those marketing professional design servics.

A BRIEF REVIEW

Those familiar with my basic communications philosophy—through previous exposure to my writing or by participation in one or more of the some 250 marketing workshops I've led since 1974—are aware of the importance I place on the old-time preacher's three-sentence outline for successful sermons:

1. Tell 'em what you're going to tell 'em.

2. Tell 'em.
3. Tell 'em what you told 'em.

In the interests of completeness and clarity, I recently revised the outline; it now has four sentences:

1. Tell 'em what you're going to tell 'em (the introduction).
2. Tell 'em (the body of your presentation).
3. Tell 'em what it means (to help an audience put number 1 and number 2 into perspective).
4. Tell 'em what you told 'em (the summation or close).

We are now ready for "Tell 'em what you told 'em."

Chapter 1 begins with some hard-hitting advice about the importance of marketing, specialization, and selectivity in prospect targeting. The same subjects were underscored in a 1981 news release announcing the formation of a new public relations firm (Capelin, Carton & Landreth):

> Competition among professional firms has intensified noticeably in recent years. When commissions slowed because of the economic downturn of the early and mid-70s, designers began business development activities in earnest, and often aggressively. This extraordinary change in practice, underscored by substantial revisions of professional codes of ethics, became inevitable because of the tight marketplace. Thus, in the 80s, it will no longer be a question of whether or not design firms rely on marketing and communications, but how extensively.

Some typical reader profiles are set out in the first chapter: students, principals of new firms, educators, and experienced executives of larger, established firms. The characterizations are to make the point that individual readers, because of uncommon fields of experience and varying frames of reference, will be looking for different kinds of guidance in a book such as this one. The book was written for all members of the design profession and for all categories of firm experience, professional disciplines, and staff size.

Chapter 2 concentrates on generally accepted marketing principles and the psychology of marketing. The related processes of communication and selling are covered in some detail. Without effective communication there can be no persuasion; lacking persuasion, no sale will be made.

The several levels of selling are investigated, with the nonprofessional level illustrated by jam-joint selling. Tested guidelines for productive selling are spelled out. Many of the principles and concepts covered in Chapter 2 are further illustrated and discussed in the chapters following.

In Chapter 3, "Getting Organized," the differences (and similarities) in marketing and selling products and services are outlined. Principals and marketers are advised to take a long, objective look at their firm's strengths, weaknesses, opportunities, and threats (the SWOT team inventory so necessary to have in hand before beginning a marketing plan). The most important elements of a marketing plan are presented, and the total effort is related to the critical role played by in-depth research. Several guidelines and rules of thumb for establishing and administering a marketing budget are given. Advice on staffing for marketing and performance measurement guides conclude the chapter.

Chapter 4 tells you where to find prospects; Chapter 5, how to qualify them. The importance of being selective in all marketing efforts is emphasized in Chapter 4 as is a simple record-keeping system for the marketing program. Chapter 5 concentrates on the use of the telephone (cold calls) to generate and qualify leads. Various checklists and exercises are included to help the uninitiated and the unsure develop comfortable, productive styles on the telephone.

Chapters 6 and 7 take up marketing communications, both direct and indirect. Under indirect communications are public relations, printed marketing tools, direct mail, and advertising. (The first edition of *How to Market Professional Design Services* had two chapters on public relations. Much of the updating of this earlier material—and a lot more— is contained in my 1980 McGraw-Hill book, *Public Relations for the Design Professional.*)

"Direct marketing communications" usually includes marketing correspondence, one-on-one interviews, qualifications submittals, proposals, and preparation for formal interviews. For the most effective correspondence, marketers are advised to write to the *MOM/Y²* ratio. Lists of words to avoid and other rules for good writing are also found in Chapter 7.

Following along the marketing process in logical steps, Chapter 8 is about proposal preparation. A thorough analysis of the request for proposal (RFP) should always precede any go or no-go decision. Twenty-two possible elements of a proposal are described and dissected, and suggestions are given for assembling a proposal-writing team and scheduling their efforts.

The formal presentation—the make-or-break marketing step and the goal of all marketing efforts thus far—is the subject of Chapters 9 and 10. It's a big subject, so Chapter 9 deals with prepresentation efforts; and Chapter 10, with the presentation itself and with postinterview activities. The psychology of selling, the importance of rehearsals, and the critical role of style in successful presentations are all discussed in detail. Ten case histories for use in practice presentations are found in

Chapter 9. A prepresentation checklist is presented in Chapter 10, along with a list of "135 Ways to Improve Presentations."

Lobbying at all levels and support of political candidates are two of the topics discussed in Chapter 11, "Political Action." The emergence of political action committees (PACs) as a force in U.S. politics is examined, as is the organization of the two major political parties. Practical advice about how to deal with political fund-raising events is offered.

Since public or government-sponsored work traditionally accounts for about a quarter of the annual construction dollars in the United States, Chapter 12, "Selling to the Government," deals with government as a client. The U.S. Postal Service and the Veterans Administration serve as models for design clients at the federal level. Advice on producing marketing-oriented Standard Forms 254 and 255 is also in Chapter 12.

While triskaidekaphobia seems to afflict those in charge of numbering the floors of hotels and other commercial structures, publishers apparently have no fear of the number 13 when numbering chapters in a book. This book's Chapter 13 is called "A Marketing Potpourri" and is primarily concerned with joint ventures and associations, marketing to foreign clients, and designer-developers (the takers of a piece of the action).

All this brings us to the present and concluding chapter. The final chapter in the first edition was called "A Mood of Change"; this time around I'm calling it "The Road Ahead." One tries to close out a book such as this with a certain amount of sound and fury, nicely combined with exhortation and prognostication. Publishers tell authors that readers expect a kind of look-into-the-future-where-do-we-go-from-here, wrap-up chapter.

One reviewer of the first edition characterized "A Mood of Change" as "eclectic, without much apparent relation to the rest of the book." Since I fully intend to include a few thoughts on marketing which did not seem to logically fit into any of the preceding chapters, readers may want to prepare themselves for a certain amount of eclecticism.

THE MISSING LINK

Archibald Rogers, FAIA, a founder of the Baltimore architectural firm now known as RTKL Associates, Inc., and one of the more articulate American designers, once described a design professional as "an artist surrounded by a professional wrapped in a businessman." (Today, no doubt, Rogers would have said ". . . wrapped in a businessperson.") To this restatement of the original Churchillian phrase, he added, "We are therefore a sort of missing link—a triphibian that must be understood and survive in three worlds."

Two of the qualities involved in Rogers' trinity, artistry and professionalism, are probably present in most designers through some combination of genes, training, and attitude. The third in the triplicity of traits, an entrepreneurial bent, is often forced upon the totally unprepared practitioner. Even today, little is required at the university level in the way of formal business training for engineers, architects, and others of the design profession.

As William Dudley Hunt, Jr., put it in *Total Design*, "The slightest attention to the history of architectural practice, even in its earliest eras, will reveal architects selling their services to pharaohs, kings, wealthy merchants and others. Yet the myth that architects need not sell their services persists even down to the present."[1] One could just as well substitute "engineers" for "architects" in Hunt's statement.

Little Preparation for the Real World   A handful of respectable courses in marketing are now offered in office practice courses in schools and colleges of architecture and engineering. A few professors have put together ambitious programs for their students, using outside lecturers to make the real world of practice more understandable.

In recent years I have had the pleasure of serving as a visiting lecturer on marketing subjects before several dozen classes of architectural and engineering students. (With but one or two exceptions, these have not been in the prestigious, Ivy League–type of schools.)

An example of the practical approach is Course #648, Professional Practice, given in the School of Architecture at Washington University in St. Louis. It is an elective, graduate-level course taught by architect Paul Henderson of the St. Louis firm of Henderson Gantz, Inc. Unfortunately, the class is offered only every other year.

Some excerpts from the 1982 course description (the class meets once a week):

Session I. Introduction
   Distribution of course outline, schedule, and recommended reading list. Overview of the course, stressing that PROFIT is not a dirty word and that good design, good management, and aggressive marketing are not mutually exclusive. Introduction of the concept that marketing and management can improve design by providing quality opportunities and the wherewithal for their accomplishment.
Session IV. The Marketing Plan
   Once financial goals have been established, the marketing plan must analyze and determine methods for achieving these objectives. Setting targets within realistic limits of capabilities and marketing budget. Market forecasting, goal setting, and implementation strategies will be discussed.

Session V. Pursuing the Elusive Client
   Description of the many marketing steps, from finding leads through prospect qualification, cold contacts, courtship, and closing; methods of playing the numbers game (and winning) while maintaining the personal touch. How to develop the ability to spot future leads before they are even projects, while avoiding standard lead sources used by everyone else.
Session VIII. Presentations
   How not to lose a project. Simple DOs and DON'Ts of effective presentations. Pre-presentation research and post-presentation debriefing, whether or not you get the job. "You've gotta have a gimmick" and other ideas on how to make the best impact.
Session XV. The Clients' Point of View
   Architecture and architects from the clients' point of view. Who's calling the shots, which way, and why? "Money talks" about design and, by inference, how you have just spent six years of your life. A healthy "case of the realities" from the people who pay your fee.

Another approach to preparing students to don comfortably Rogers's triple mantle of artist, professional, and entrepreneur is found in the visiting professional lecture series at Lawrence Institute of Technology's School of Architecture in Southfield, Michigan. Featured as guest speakers at the twice-monthly sessions are noted designers, design critics, writers, and consultants to the design profession on management and marketing subjects. The collegiate and professional audience for the LIT lectures is drawn from throughout Michigan and from cities in Ohio, Indiana, and Canada.

MANAGING YOUR MARKETING

Until the recent past, principals and owners of design firms traditionally learned the necessary management and marketing techniques through experience, with no real standards against which to measure successes and failures. *Poor Richard's Almanac* reminds us, "Experience keeps a dear school."

To make the schooling a little less dear, most professional organizations for engineers and architects regularly sponsor formal training courses for their members. The American Consulting Engineers Council (ACEC) is perhaps the most active group in offering a variety of courses in office and project management areas and on marketing subjects.

In addition to the association seminars and workshops, several universities hold periodic sessions on management and marketing, and a half-dozen experienced consultants lead regular workshop series on both subjects. Many local chapters of the Society for Marketing Professional Services combine short training courses with monthly membership meetings.

If you prefer to study on your own, several home-study courses have come on the market in the last three or four years. Two examples are the six-volume course from McGraw-Hill, *Marketing Professional Design Services,* and the two-unit, loose-leaf MGI Management Institute course, *Successful Marketing of Architectural Services.* The point is that a variety of continuing education training for running an office and marketing services is available to design professionals who want the help.

The Marketing Mortality Rate   A worrisome trend in professional services marketing is the tenurial impermanence of marketing executives and staffs in many firms. Management consultant John Simonds, in a thoughtful piece, "Why Marketing Directors Fail," set out six reasons for the revolving-door phenomenon:

1. The key decision makers do not accept the need for a strategic plan or the applicability of modern marketing techniques to the design profession.
2. The principals fail to communicate by word and deed to others in the firm that a marketing director is critical to the firm's continued success.
3. The principals fail to agree on the scope and authority of the marketing position.
4. The individual selected lacks the unique constellation of attributes and skills necessary in order to market "intangible" professional services as opposed to tangible products.
5. The principals assume they can delegate marketing to one person and thus free themselves from any substantial role in marketing the firm's services.
6. The marketing director is not included as an equal in the key group of top decision makers.[2]

From my own experience and observation, the last three reasons are of critical importance.

Marketing Maxims for the Eighties   Over the years I've come across a lot of advice—good and bad—for marketers. At least some of the eight maxims that follow might seem harsh, even cynical, but marketers deal with the world as it is—and with clients and competitors as they are.

1. Know that nothing worthwhile ever happens by accident. A lot of hard work by someone is always required.
2. Do anything short of self-immolation to avoid having your creative efforts directed by a committee. (Nothing worthwhile has ever resulted from a committee action.)
3. If you aren't the winner (and there is only one winner in every contest or competition), then you are a loser. Being ranked second or third or fourth brings no profit or honor to your firm.
4. (After Ed Macauley) "When you aren't practicing [your marketing

skills], remember that somewhere, someone *is* practicing. And when you meet him he will win."

5. Don't be one of the multitude who always asks, "How did they do that?" Be one of the ones who does it, and you'll never have to ask.

6. (After Bill Veeck) "There's nothing wrong with stealing other peoples' ideas. And anyone who doesn't is presumptuous, because there simply aren't that many new ideas. Just take something used somewhere else and adapt it for your own use."

7. The world of great ideas is populated by thieves stealing from other thieves.

8. For 99 percent of all marketers there probably is no such thing as a weakness; only underdeveloped or undeveloped skills.

CHANGING TIMES; CHANGING MARKETS

A few paragraphs ago I mentioned that final book chapters should include a certain amount of prognostication. The best long-range prognosticating is about events that come to pass, granting the forecaster the right to a few "I told you so's."

On advertising, from the first edition:

> . . . some veterans in the design profession expect most, if not all, of the strictures on advertising and self-promotion to be relaxed or voided completely in the next five to ten years.

The initial breakthrough for design professionals occurred less than four years following *How to Market Professional Design Services'* publication in December 1973. On October 1, 1977, the New York State Board of Regents authorized print media advertising of fees for specific, routine services by architects, engineers, and other professionals registered in the state. Radio and television commercials, without mention of fees, were also permitted.

Mounting pressures from the Justice Department, the Federal Trade Commission, and the U.S. Supreme Court succeeded in toppling most of the long-standing taboos against advertising by professionals. A growing number of design firms have tested the new promotional tool, but the jury is still out on the amount of marketing bang one can reasonably expect from an advertising buck.

On growth of the gross national product:

> In the first quarter of 1972 the United States began producing goods and services at an annual rate of more than $1 trillion, the first nation to pass this economic milestone. There are predictions that we will achieve a $2-trillion gross national product by 1980.

The 1980 GNP of $2.626 trillion easily exceeded predictions, of course, with the 1981 GNP almost reaching the magic $3 trillion level (it was $2.922 trillion). Some of our elation over the achievement must be tempered by the roughly 1 percent monthly increase in inflation rates over the past several years. Between 1974 and 1982 prices exactly doubled. The seventeen years between 1965 and 1982 saw prices triple. The GNP increase of 1981 over 1980 appears to be 11.3 percent, but, with inflation taken into account, the increase was less than 2 percent.

And the outcome of one other prediction in the first edition:

George Romney, then secretary of the Department of Housing and Urban Development, in the early days of Operation Breakthrough, forecast that "at least two-thirds of all housing production in the United States will be factory produced by the end of this decade." [*Does anyone remember* either *George Romney or Operation Breakthrough?*]

As of this writing, the National Association of Home Builders would probably be happy to settle for that one-third of non-factory-produced housing.

Future Markets   If you've done your market research homework there should be few, if any, surprises in this and the next section about future markets for the design profession. There can't be many secrets about where the work will come from in the foreseeable future.

The Bad News   The housing market, as of early 1982, could hardly be in worse shape, giving rise to the logical prediction that it will improve. From the present level, housing starts can only go up. Mortgage interest rates will have their usual influence on the degree of activity in new starts. Over the near term (the mid-1980s) housing *might* improve by as much as 25 to 30 percent. Most new units will be smaller; the amenities, fewer; local taxes, higher.

As for government work, with the important exception or defense and defense-related projects, little hope is offered for significant federal, state, and local work in the face of actual and predicted cutbacks in spending at all levels. The expected increase in federal block grant programs (with a net reduction in the overall funds involved) may make identification of clients more difficult for many marketers.

If your firm is located in the Sun Belt, schools may still be a viable project type. The only bright spot in the school market for northern design offices is in the four Rs—restoration, renovation, remodeling, and retrofitting. As schools are closed and come into the market for conversion to commercial, residential, or other institutional use, they will provide a certain amount of work for enterprising architects and engineers.

Since the end of World War II, the transportation market has been a lucrative one for many firms. Transportation was one of the country's postwar problem areas that politicians believed could best be handled by throwing great sums of money at it. But politicians are realists; they know it is difficult to make headlines by voting money to repave deteriorating roads and highways and to replace crumbling, unsafe bridges. The moratorium on new metropolitan subway systems is apt to be of long duration, and railroads will continue to get short shrift from Washington. Some airport work will continue, especially where it can be shown to have a national defense connection.

Environmental projects will not enjoy a very high priority. Air pollution, hazardous waste disposal, wastewater treatment, and related work can pretty well be written off for the time being. Some of the work underway may not be completed.

The Good News Commercial, industrial, defense, health care, and correctional facilities markets look like the near-term winners.

Commercial As was the case in the early 1970s, the office building boom appears to have peaked again in the early 1980s in many areas. Some activity will continue on suburban sites as companies look for ways to beat city center square-foot office rentals of up to $35 and more and to get away from increasingly onerous city taxes and regulations, paced by decreasingly effective city services.

Other than office buildings, the commercial classification includes retail stores, shopping centers, and hotels. The picture is a little brighter here, especially for hotels.

Practically all of the major hotel chains have embarked on major expansion programs; in many cases they are scheduled to extend through the 1980s. Most of the plans call for new structures in areas identified as active meeting and convention centers, but some hotel funds will go into buying existing properties for upgrading.

Smaller shopping centers are expected to show an increase over the next few years. Large regional centers are doing poorly in many locations; few are doing the business they did in the late 1970s.

Industrial Industrial clients—particularly those with outmoded, worn-out production facilities—have a great potential, always assuming they can find financing at interest rates they can live with. Many economists believe the 1981 tax-cut passage, with its revised depreciation schedules, will spur both industrial and commercial building. A few think the new tax structure could result in as much as 20 to 25 percent additional investment in plants and equipment. As of this writing, it is too early to tell whether a fifteen-year depreciation schedule will help generate the necessary new capital.

These industries show expansion potential for the 1980s:

Aircraft parts
Communications
Food
Printing
Fabricated metals
Semiconductors
Instruments
Specialty chemicals
All types of electronic equipment

Defense   In 1981, President Reagan called for outlays of some $1.5 trillion in defense spending by 1988. Much of that is committed for hardware items—ships, tanks, and missiles—but a respectable piece of the total will go for new construction and for renovation of existing structures.

Realistically, more of the defense construction funds will go to sunbelt locations than will be spent on building new installations in the north. But nothing ventured, nothing gained. Take a base engineer or post engineer from a nearby air base or army post to lunch; find out what is scheduled in your area. Some of the items on every general's and admiral's wish list will come to pass.

Health Care   The health care project type encompasses everything from large teaching hospitals to the smallest of physician's offices. If your firm is already in the field, you have a pretty good idea of the possibilities. If you don't have a solid experience base in hospital design, it can be a difficult field to crack.

An emerging subtype of prospect is the freestanding emergency clinic, a hospital emergency room without the hospital. This building specialty has grown up along with a new medical specialty, emergency medicine. Nursing homes and hospital renovation are two other major areas of health care work.

And one government agency, the Veterans Administration, may prove to be a worthwhile client between now and the end of the century. As was pointed out in Chapter 12, the great bulk of the 13 million-plus veterans of World War II have now reached the age of increased hospitalization and general health care requirements.

Correctional Facilities   I have written extensively about correctional facilities and the importance of this project type to marketers in past issues of *Professional Marketing Report*. Suffice it to say here that with crime rates increasing annually in the magnitude of 15 to 20 percent and more, the country will need more jail cells to hold even the relatively small number of criminals who are caught and sentenced. If we ever reach the point where crime is made *not* to pay (only about 3 percent of all reported crimes result in the perpetrator's being incarcerated), the demand for new prisons will be phenomenal.

Self-development Area   A project type not yet touched upon is the self-development (or find-it-yourself) area for design firms. It is the "find a need, find a site, find the financing, find the tenant, and design it" kind of project, which many firms undertook during the last fiscal unpleasantness in the mid-1970s. Ownership of your own buildings can be a comforting income source at any time, but it is particularly helpful when the new work pipeline takes on that undernourished look so common during recessions.

THE LAST WORD

Marketing is basically a game of ideas; selling a game of numbers. When both endeavors are predicated on a thoughtful, written plan, backed up by intelligent research and carried out by trained, resourceful people, success is practically assured.

The rules for selling professional design services revolve around the simple ratio set out in Chapter 3: 50:5:1. Fifty contacts with suspects or prospects should get you into the finals (usually in the form of a formal presentation to the prospect) for five projects, out of which you should net one job. The ratio is both conservative and uncomplicated; most firms regularly beat the numbers. The point here is that once you initiate the process by making a certain number of contacts, it is next to impossible to stop. You *will* average at least one job from every fifty contacts.

Marketing, to repeat, is based on ideas. Firms whose principals and marketing directors encourage creative thinking by example are mostly winners. Buck-passing, idea-killing, risk-avoiding environments breed losers. In conclusion, I give you the 111 steps to corporate stagnation. Listen to the responses to new ideas around your office. As you identify the idea killers on your staff, mark them for early retirement or replacement.

111 Reasons for Preserving the Status Quo
1. Our firm is different.
2. It's too much trouble.
3. The staff won't buy it.
4. The partners won't go for it.
5. It doesn't grab me.

6. I don't have the authority to O.K. it.
7. We tried that before and it didn't work.
8. It doesn't fit into our system.
9. O.K., but who's going to do it?
10. Why change it? It's working O.K.
11. It's been done to death.
12. The business office will bounce it.
13. It just doesn't sound professional to me.
14. It's not up to our standards.
15. Clients won't like it.
16. Are we really ready for this?
17. We've always done it the other way.
18. You don't really mean that!
19. It's not broken, so why fix it?
20. You can't argue with success.
21. We don't have enough help.
22. It costs too much.
23. Nobody will understand what you're talking about.
24. The computer can't handle it.
25. It sounds too simple.
26. It's too complicated.
27. It's not our style.
28. It isn't in the budget.
29. We're not ready for it.
30. It's not in our image.
31. It will cost a fortune.
32. We'll never find the time to do it.
33. I know a firm that tried that.
34. That's not our bag.
35. We're already overextended.
36. Put it all in writing first.
37. Let's give it a little more thought.
38. The last guy who came up with that idea isn't here anymore.
39. Sounds crazy to me.
40. Just wait until they run the numbers.
41. Has anyone ever done anything like that before?
42. You're right, of course, but . . .
43. Why fight City Hall?
44. So what else is new?
45. We've never done anything like that.
46. Don't you know there's a recession on?
47. You gotta be kidding.

48. Let's be realistic.
49. Basically, I don't like it.
50. Maybe we should test it first.
51. It's bound to run up our overhead.
52. That's not my department.
53. Why rock the boat?
54. It's just not feasible.
55. It turns me off.
56. I hate it.
57. I'd rather not get involved.
58. Shelve it for right now.
59. The timing just isn't right.
60. Come on . . . get serious.
61. Great idea—but not for us.
62. Good idea, but it just won't work.
63. It will create more problems that it will solve.
64. I've heard that one before.
65. That's not your problem.
66. We should set up a committee to look into it.
67. It can't be done.
68. Here we go again.
69. Better wait till the boss comes back.
70. That's a subject for another meeting.
71. We'll lose our shirt.
72. Get back to me on that in a month or two.
73. (Laughter.)
74. (Silence.)
75. That's not your job.
76. Take a survey first.
77. It'll just cause more problems.
78. Oh—I thought you were going to come up with something else.
79. They won't let you do it.
80. Let's meet on it sometime.
81. That only solves half the problem.
82. That's very interesting, but . . .
83. It doesn't fit in with the way we do things here.
84. That's *really* off the wall.
85. Oh?
86. Why bother?
87. I have a better idea.
88. That's really fantastic, but . . .
89. It'll never sell.

90. What will people say?
91. That's a new one on me.
92. People will say we're silly.
93. Let me play devil's advocate here . . .
94. Just leave it all with me. I'll get right on it.
95. Do you really think *that* would work?
96. How about something a little more exciting?
97. Bring it up again next month.
98. Forget it.
99. It's too radical.
100. Remember that the client is pretty conservative.
101. Are you really proposing that?
102. People will say we're too reckless.
103. You obviously missed the point.
104. Have you really given it much thought?
105. It would step on too many toes.
106. There's no free lunch.
107. How in the world did you come up with that?
108. Stop fooling around.
109. It'll never fly.
110. It doesn't track.
111. They've been coming up with that one for years.

REFERENCES

[1]William Dudley Hunt, Jr., *Total Design: Architecture of Welton Becket and Associates,* McGraw-Hill Book Company, New York, 1972, p. 93.

[2]John Simonds, "Why Marketing Directors Fail," *SMPS News,* December 1981, p. 1. (Reprinted from Martin-Simonds Associates, *Report to Management.*)

INDEX

About the Author

GERRE JONES, president of Gerre Jones Associates and editor-publisher of *Professional Marketing Report*, the widely read newsletter on marketing for design professionals, has been active in marketing and communications for more than 25 years. He has written several books in this area, and, with McGraw-Hill and *Architectural Record*, has produced the first popular workshops on marketing design services.